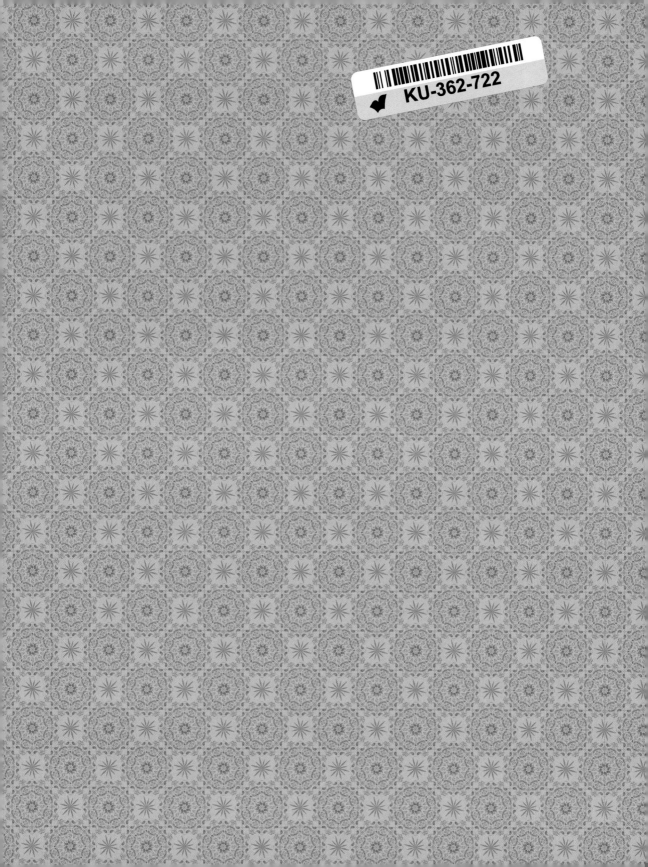

THE
COOKERY
COLLECTION

ORIGINAL AND DETAILED

500 RECIPES

Cook's Bible

Essential everyday recipes from soups and lunches
to cakes, biscuits and more

igloobooks

igloobooks

Published in 2018
by Igloo Books Ltd
Cottage Farm
Sywell
NN6 0BJ
www.igloobooks.com

LEO002 0218
2 4 6 8 10 9 7 5 3 1
ISBN 978-1-78810-192-9

All imagery: © iStock / Getty Images

Designed by Nicholas Gage
Edited by Richard Davis

Printed and manufactured in China

Contents

Lunches and brunches

Vegetable empanadas

PREPARATION TIME: **30–40 minutes**
COOKING TIME: **20 minutes**
MAKES: **8**

500 g pack puff pastry
1 egg, beaten

FOR THE FILLING
500 g / 1 lb / 2 cups floury potatoes,
peeled and cubed
2 carrots, peeled and diced
1 head broccoli, divided into florets
1 onion, peeled and finely chopped
1 tbsp olive oil
2 tbsp frozen peas
a pinch of cayenne pepper

FOR THE SIDE SALAD
2 red peppers
2 green peppers

- Preheat the oven to 200°C (180°C fan) / 400F / gas 6.
- Cook the potatoes in boiling salted water for 5 minutes with the carrots, then add the broccoli and cook for a further 2 minutes. Drain thoroughly.
- Tip into a bowl and lightly mash. Cook the onion in oil in a pan until translucent, then add to the crushed vegetables with the peas. Season and add the cayenne pepper.
- Roll the pastry out onto a lightly floured surface to about 1 cm (½ inch) thickness and cut out eight circles.
- Spread a small spoonful of the vegetable mixture into the centre of each circle, leaving a 1cm border around the edge. Brush the edges with a little beaten egg and fold the pastry over to enclose the filling.
- Using a fork, crimp the edges of the pastry together to seal the filling in and brush the parcels with beaten egg.
- Bake in the oven on a greased baking sheet for 10 minutes, then lower the oven temperature to 180°C and cook for another 10 minutes.
- For the side salad, simply deseed and dice the red and green pepper and serve in a ramekin.

Pork and paprika kebabs

PREPARATION TIME: **40 minutes**
COOKING TIME: **10 minutes**
SERVES: **4**

800 g / 1 ¾ lb / 3 ⅓ cups pork fillet, cubed
2 tbsp olive oil
1 clove garlic, finely sliced
½ lemon, grated zest
2 sprigs thyme
1 tsp paprika
1 tsp cayenne pepper
a pinch of smoked salt
black pepper
tomato salsa, to serve

- Tip the pork into a bowl and mix well with the oil, garlic, zest, thyme, paprika, cayenne pepper, smoked salt and pepper.
- Chill for 30 minutes.
- Thread the marinated pork onto pre-soaked skewers and cook on the barbecue or griddle for 8–10 minutes until cooked through.
- Serve with cold tomato salsa.

Pork and smoked paprika kebabs
Replace the paprika with the same amount of smoked paprika and follow the method as above. Serve with some tomato salsa or smoked mayonnaise.

Ratatouille pasta

PREPARATION TIME: **10 minutes**
COOKING TIME: **50 minutes**
SERVES: **4**

4–6 tbsp olive oil
2 onions, peeled and finely sliced
2 aubergines (eggplants), cut in half lengthways and finely sliced
3 courgettes (zucchinis), cut in half lengthways and finely sliced
2 cloves garlic, finely chopped
1 yellow pepper, deseeded and diced
6 cherry tomatoes, quartered
400 g can chopped tomatoes
1 tsp coriander seeds, crushed
500 g / 1 lb / 2 cups tubular pasta (such as macaroni)
a handful of rocket (arugula) leaves, to garnish
grated Parmesan, to sprinkle
a handful of fresh basil leaves

- Heat the oil in a pan and cook the onions until deep golden and sweet.
- Add the aubergines and cook for 2 minutes, then add the courgettes and garlic and cook for 2 minutes. Add the pepper and cook for a further 5 minutes.
- Add the tomatoes and coriander seeds and leave to simmer for at least 30 minutes over a very low heat, stirring occasionally, until the vegetables are very soft.
- Cook the pasta in boiling salted water, according to packet instructions, then drain.
- Divide the pasta between the 4 serving bowls and top with the ratatouille. Sprinkle over the rocket leaves, Parmesan and basil before serving.

Ratatouille pasta with sun-dried tomatoes
Add a handful of chopped sun-dried tomatoes to the ratatouille and a tablespoon of sun-dried tomato paste.

Healthy brown rice salad

PREPARATION TIME: **20 minutes**
COOKING TIME: **15 minutes**
SERVES: **4**

240 ml / 8 ½ oz / 1 cup long grain brown rice
480 ml / 1 pint / 2 cups vegetable stock
½ cucumber, diced
10 cherry tomatoes, quartered
2 bulbs cooked beetroot, diced
5 radishes, sliced
2 tbsp capers
2 tbsp white wine vinegar
1 lemon, juiced
4 tbsp olive oil
fresh parsley, chopped
fresh basil leaves, to garnish

- Measure the rice (in volume) into a saucepan and cover with the stock. Cover with a lid and cook for 10 minutes.
- Remove from the heat and leave to sit for 5 minutes with the lid on. Then remove the lid and leave to cool a little in a bowl while you prepare the remaining salad.
- Combine the cooked rice with the remaining vegetable ingredients and toss well.
- Add the warm rice to the bowl and stir through the vinegar, oil and fresh herbs. Season well and serve.

Feta and brown rice salad
Add 200 g diced feta to the rice with the rest of the vegetables before adding the dressing.

Chopped radish, sesame and alfalfa salad

PREPARATION TIME: **15 minutes**
SERVES: **4**

1 red cabbage, finely sliced
1 white cabbage, finely sliced
1 red pepper, deseeded and sliced
2 carrots, julienned
1 courgette (zucchini), julienned
4 radishes, finely sliced
1 handful alfalfa sprouts

FOR THE DRESSING
1–2 tbsp sherry vinegar
1 tsp Dijon mustard
6 tbsp extra virgin olive oil
1 tbsp sesame seeds

- Place all the salad ingredients in a large mixing bowl.
- Whisk together the ingredients for the dressing.
- Combine the salad with the dressing, coating thoroughly.
- Sprinkle over the sesame seeds and serve.

Chopped miso salad with seaweed
Add 4 tablespoons of dried and shredded nori to the salad and a teaspoon of white miso paste to the dressing. Mix well and enjoy.

Fennel and radish citrus salad

PREPARATION TIME: **10 minutes**
SERVES: **4**

1 fennel (finocchio) bulb, fronds removed
1 orange
½ bunch radishes
1 tbsp white wine vinegar
2 tbsp fresh orange juice
1 tbsp mixed dried herbs
4 tbsp extra virgin olive oil

- Halve and core the fennel bulb and remove the outer leaves. Slice very finely and tip into a bowl.
- Peel the orange and remove any pith. Holding it over the fennel bowl, cut out the orange segments and cut each one in half. Add to the fennel.
- Finely slice the radishes.
- Whisk together the vinegar, orange juice, herbs and oil with a little seasoning, toss thoroughly with the salad and serve.

Fennel and pomegranate citrus salad
Replace the radish with the seeds of 2 pomegranates. Simply combine the fennel, orange and pomegranate seeds and mix in the dressing. Season to taste.

Courgette and asparagus soup

PREPARATION TIME: 15 minutes
COOKING TIME: 30–40 minutes
SERVES: 4

2 tbsp olive oil
1 onion, peeled and finely chopped
2 cloves garlic, finely chopped
1 kg / 2 ¼ lb / 4 ¼ cups courgettes
(zucchinis), chopped
4 sprigs thyme
1 l / 2 ¼ pints / 4 ¼ cups chicken or vegetable stock
12 asparagus tips, ends removed
2 tbsp of lemon juice
60 ml / 2 oz / ¼ cup single cream

- Heat the oil in a large pan and sweat the onion until softened and translucent.
- Add the garlic, courgettes and thyme and cook very slowly over a low heat until the courgettes have darkened to a khaki colour and are very soft.
- Add the stock and simmer for 20 minutes.
- Meanwhile, set a pan to medium heat and lightly sauté the asparagus tips for 3–4 minutes with a little olive oil, half of the lemon juice and salt. Set to one side.
- Liquidize ⅔ of the soup, then return to the pan, reheat and season well. Add the rest of the lemon juice.
- Stir in the cream, heat gently and garnish with the asparagus tips. Season to taste and enjoy with some fresh bread.

Vegan courgette and asparagus soup
Use vegetable stock and replace the single cream with the same amount of dairy-free coconut yogurt for a delicious vegan variation.

Spinach and feta spanakopita

PREPARATION TIME: **25 minutes**
COOKING TIME: **15–20 minutes**
SERVES: **4–6**

FOR THE FILLING
2 tbsp olive oil, plus extra as required
1 onion, peeled and finely chopped
500 g / 1 lb / 8 cups spinach leaves, washed
2 tbsp pine nuts
4 tbsp Parmesan, grated
200 g / 7 oz / ¾ cup feta cheese, crumbled

FOR THE PASTRY
300 g / 10 oz / 1 ¼ cups self-raising flour
½ tsp salt
4 tbsp olive oil
2 tbsp white wine
100 ml / 3 ½ fl. oz / ½ cup water

- Preheat the oven to 200°C (180°C fan) / 400F / gas 6.
- Make the filling: Heat the olive oil in a pan and fry the onion until softened. Wilt the spinach in the same pan and season, then tip the whole lot into a food processor. Add the pine nuts, Parmesan and a little oil and blitz to make a rough paste, adding more oil if necessary.
- Make the pastry: Sieve the flour and salt into a bowl. Heat the olive oil, wine and water in a pan until hand hot. Pour the warm liquid into the flour and knead until soft and elastic. Shape into a ball.
- Turn out onto a floured surface and divide into 20 equal pieces.
- Roll each piece into a circle about 8cm (3 inches) in diameter.
- Place a teaspoon of spinach pesto onto one half of the pastry, place some crumbled feta cheese on top and fold over the other half to enclose it, pressing down around the edges to seal it in. Repeat to make 20 little turnovers.
- Place on an oiled baking sheet and make small slashes in the top of the pastry. Bake for 15–20 minutes until golden brown.
- Cut into squares and serve hot or cold.

Spinach and goat's cheese spanakopita
Replace the feta with the same amount of crumbled goat's cheese and follow the method as normal.

Mushroom, tofu and lentil salad

PREPARATION TIME: **10 minutes**
SERVES: **4**

200 g / 7 oz / ¾ cup rocket (arugula) leaves
250 g / 9 oz / 1 cup smoked tofu, diced
1 red pepper, deseeded and diced
200 g / 7 oz / ¾ cup button mushrooms, sliced
4 tbsp orange lentils, cooked
3 tbsp extra virgin olive oil
1 lemon, juiced and zested
1 tsp mustard seeds
1 tsp runny honey
1 tsp apple cider vinegar

- Combine the rocket, tofu, pepper, mushrooms and lentils.
- Mix the oil, lemon juice and zest, mustard seeds, honey and apple cider vinegar until emulsified.
- Drizzle the dressing over the salad and toss well to coat. Season to taste and serve.

Mushroom and lentil salad with chicken
Omit the tofu and serve the salad alongside a grilled chicken breast for a heartier meal.

Vegetable couscous with asparagus

PREPARATION TIME: 15 minutes
COOKING TIME: 12 minutes
SERVES: 4

250 g / 9 oz / 1 cup couscous
400 ml / 14 fl. oz / 2 cups vegetable stock
2 tbsp olive oil
1 clove garlic, crushed
1 red onion, diced
2 carrots, peeled and thickly sliced
1 red pepper, finely chopped
1 yellow pepper, finely chopped
10 asparagus spears, ends removed
1 lemon, juiced
½ bunch parsley, roughly chopped

- Place the couscous in a bowl, cover with ⅔ of the hot stock and cling film the bowl. Leave for 10 minutes or so until tender, then fork through the grains and add the lemon juice.
- Meanwhile heat the oil in a pan and sauté the garlic, onion, carrots and diced peppers, then toss to coat and cook for 3 minutes.
- Add the asparagus and cover with the remaining vegetable stock. Leave to simmer for 5–8 minutes until everything is tender.
- Tip the sautéed vegetables into the couscous.
- Season generously with the lemon juice and some salt and black pepper, then add the parsley and serve.

Arancini with basil

PREPARATION TIME: 20 minutes
COOKING TIME: 10 minutes
SERVES: 4

60 g / 2 oz / ½ cup leftover risotto rice, cooked
1 ball mozzarella, cut into small cubes
1 tbsp plain (all-purpose) flour
1 egg, beaten
40 g / 1 ½ oz panko breadcrumbs
vegetable oil, for deep frying
tomato sauce, to serve (optional)
½ bunch basil leaves

- Leave the leftover risotto to get completely cold – preferably refrigerated overnight.
- Shape the rice into equal balls, pushing a small cube of mozzarella into the centre of each one and shaping the rice around it.
- Lay out the flour, egg and breadcrumbs on separate plates.
- Dip the risotto balls into the flour, then the egg, then the breadcrumbs. Use one hand and keep the other clean for ease.
- Heat the oil to 180°C / 360 F or until a cube of bread sizzles when dunked in. Fry the risotto balls until golden and crisp all over. Drain on kitchen paper.
- Garnish with the basil leaves and serve hot or warm with some tomato sauce on the side.

Sun-dried tomato arancini
Finely chop 6 sun-dried tomatoes and combine with the risotto rice before adding the mozzarella and rolling into balls.

Crab and coriander cakes

PREPARATION TIME: **15 minutes**
COOKING TIME: **20 minutes**
SERVES: **4**

250 g / 9 oz / 1 cup white crabmeat, picked
3 tbsp breadcrumbs
1 egg, beaten
1 clove garlic, crushed
1 tbsp unsweetened desiccated coconut
½ red chilli, deseeded and finely chopped
1 tbsp coriander (cilantro), finely chopped
vegetable oil for deep-frying
baby gherkins, to serve (optional)
1 lemon, cut into wedges

- Mix together the crabmeat, breadcrumbs, egg, garlic, coconut, chilli and coriander. Season and combine thoroughly.

- Form into small patties of roughly equal size.

- Heat a 1 cm (½ inch) depth of oil in a pan and fry the crab cakes in batches until golden brown on both sides.

- Drain on kitchen paper and keep warm in a low oven while you cook the rest.

- Serve with the baby gherkins, some lemon wedges and a dip of choice.

Crab and Worcester cakes
Add a tablespoon of Worcester sauce to the crab cake mixture for a tangy flavour.

Mexican tacos

PREPARATION TIME: 25 minutes
COOKING TIME: 10 minutes
SERVES: 4

2 tbsp vegetable oil
1 onion, peeled and finely sliced
350 g / 12 oz / 1 ½ cups chicken, diced
1 clove garlic, finely chopped
½ green chilli (chili), finely chopped
1 tsp paprika
4 small flour tortillas, grilled
1 beefsteak tomato, diced
1 hass avocado, sliced
fresh coriander (cilantro), chopped
2 limes, cut into wedges

- Heat the oil in a pan and fry the onion until softened.
- Add the chicken and increase the heat. Fry quickly for 2 minutes, adding the garlic, chilli and paprika. Remove from the heat.
- Lay the tortillas out on a surface and spoon the chicken mixture down the middle and top with the tomato, avocado and coriander.
- Season well and serve with some lime wedges on the side.

Vegan tacos
Omit the chicken and replace it with some oven-baked sweet potato wedges for a yummy snack or meal.

Breaded chicken

PREPARATION TIME: 20 minutes
COOKING TIME: 8–10 minutes
SERVES: 4

4 chicken breasts, skinned and cut into strips
3 tbsp flour
2 eggs, beaten
200 g / 6 ½ oz / ¾ cup panko breadcrumbs
olive oil
lettuce leaves, to garnish

- Season each piece of chicken then dunk into the flour, egg and breadcrumbs.
- Heat the oil in a large pan and fry for 8–10 minutes or until golden and crisp and the chicken is cooked through.
- Serve the chicken strips with some lettuce leaves and a salad dressing.

Breaded cornflake chicken
Replace the breadcrumbs with the same amount of plain cornflakes. Simply crush the cornflakes in a sandwich bag and coat the chicken in the flour, egg and cornflakes. Follow the method as normal.

Ham, mushroom and pepper slice

PREPARATION TIME: **10 minutes**
COOKING TIME: **20–25 minutes**
SERVES: **4–6**

500 ml / 17 ½ fl. oz / 2 cups milk
35 g / 1 ¼ oz butter
2 tbsp plain (all-purpose) flour
100 g / 3 ½ oz button mushrooms, chopped
1 red pepper, deseeded and sliced
100 g / 3 ½ oz ham, cubed
450 g / 1 lb all-butter puff pastry
1 egg, beaten
tomato sauce, to serve

- Preheat the oven to 220°C (200°C fan) / 430F / gas 7.
- Heat the milk to simmering point and set aside.
- Heat the butter in a small saucepan and stir in the flour. Stirring constantly, slowly add the hot milk and cook until the sauce is thick and smooth.
- Stir in the mushrooms, peppers and ham and season with salt and pepper, then leave to cool completely
- Roll out the pastry and divide into 2 equal rectangles.
- Transfer one rectangle to a baking tray and spread over the filling, leaving a 2 cm border round the outside.
- Brush the edge of the pastry with beaten egg and lay the other pastry sheet on top. Squeeze the edges to seal and trim the pastry to neaten.
- Score a pattern on top with a sharp knife.
- Bake in the oven for 25–35 minutes or until the top is golden brown.
- Slice into portion sizes and serve with a side of tomato sauce.

Mushroom slice with sun-dried tomatoes
For veggies, omit the ham and replace with 6 roughly chopped sun-dried tomatoes. Stir the tomatoes into the mixture with the peppers and mushrooms.

Broccoli and leek soup

PREPARATION TIME: **10 minutes**
COOKING TIME: **40 minutes**
SERVES: **4**

60 g / 2 oz / ¼ cup butter
4 leeks, green ends discarded and finely sliced
2 floury potatoes, peeled and diced
1 head broccoli, stalks removed and chopped
1 tsp dried thyme
850 ml / 1 ½ pints / 3 ½ cups vegetable stock
250 ml / 9 fl. oz / 1 cup milk
croutons, to serve (optional)
sprig thyme, to garnish

- In a large pan, melt the butter and add the leeks when it begins to foam. Cook gently over a low heat until soft and slithery.
- Add the potatoes, broccoli and dried thyme and cook for a couple of minutes, then add the stock and milk. Bring to a simmer and cook gently for 20–25 minutes, until the potatoes are soft.
- Once cooked, whiz in a blender until smooth.
- Return to the heat and season carefully.
- Serve with the croutons and a sprig of thyme on top.

Tuna pasta with olives

PREPARATION TIME: **5 minutes**
COOKING TIME: **25 minutes**
SERVES: **4**

500 g / 1 lb / 2 cups multicoloured penne pasta
2 tbsp olive oil
handful pitted black olives, sliced
1 lemon, juiced
2 x 185 g cans tuna in olive oil, drained
½ bunch basil, stalks removed
1 lemon, cut into wedges

- Cook the pasta in boiling salted water according to packet instructions. Drain and tip into a bowl.
- Toss with the oil, olives and lemon juice and season to taste.
- Flake in the tuna and basil and season then serve with the lemon wedges.

Tuna pasta with capers
Replace the olives with 2 tablespoons of capers and garnish with some rocket leaves before serving.

Marinated lamb and veg kebabs

PREPARATION TIME: **35 minutes**
COOKING TIME: **10 minutes**
SERVES: **4**

500 g / 1 lb 2 oz lamb fillet or leg steak, cut into
2 cm (1 inch) cubes
2 cloves garlic, crushed
2 tbsp balsamic vinegar
1 tbsp rosemary leaves, chopped
olive oil
8 wooden skewers, soaked in water
8 cherry tomatoes, halved
1 aubergine (eggplant), thickly sliced
1 courgette (zucchini), thickly sliced
1 white onion, thickly sliced

- Toss the cubed lamb with the garlic, balsamic vinegar, rosemary, a little oil and salt and pepper and leave to marinate for up to 30 minutes.
- Thread the lamb onto skewers, alternating with the tomatoes, aubergine, courgette and onion. Sprinkle a little seasoning over the top.
- Cook over hot embers for 8–10 minutes until the lamb is rose pink inside and charred outside.

Marinated tofu and veg kebabs
For a vegan-friendly variation, replace the lamb with 400 g firm tofu, cut into cubes. Pat the tofu, removing any excess water. Toss with the marinade ingredients and follow the cooking method as above.

Spiral pasta with mixed vegetables

PREPARATION TIME: **5 minutes**
COOKING TIME: **12 minutes**
SERVES: **4**

500 g / 1 lb / 2 cups spirali pasta
2 tbsp olive oil
1 clove garlic, finely sliced
2 x 400 g cans of plum tomatoes
1 red pepper, deseeded and diced
1 courgette (zucchini), diced
5 button mushrooms, sliced
fresh parsley, roughly chopped
½ lemon, juiced
2 tbsp capers

- Cook the pasta in boiling salted water according to packet instructions.
- Meanwhile, heat the olive oil in a pan until quite hot, throw in the garlic and the whole tomatoes without the juice. Cover with a lid, as it will spit.
- Add the remaining vegetables and stir well.
- When the spitting dies down, remove the lid and break down the tomatoes. Stir in the parsley and lemon juice, season and remove from the heat.
- Drain the pasta and toss with the vegetable sauce.
- Stir in the capers and a little fresh parsley before serving.

Vegetable pasta with mozzarella
Stir some freshly torn mozzarella through the cooked pasta before serving.

Spring greens salad

PREPARATION TIME: **10 minutes**
COOKING TIME: **10–15 minutes**
SERVES: **4**

30 g / 1 oz butter
1 bunch spring onions (scallions), sliced
10 asparagus spears, heads removed
100 g / 3 ½ oz / ½ cup fresh garden peas
100 g / 3 ½ oz / ½ cup fresh broad beans
250 ml / 8 fl. oz vegetable stock
fresh coriander (cilantro), to garnish

- Heat the butter in a frying pan until foaming, then add the spring onions and cook until softened.
- Add the asparagus spears, peas and beans and move everything around, then just cover with vegetable stock. Season and cook for 5–10 minutes or until everything is tender.
- Serve with the fresh coriander.

Feta and spring greens salad
Add 200 g of crumbled feta and garnish with a handful of pumpkin seeds.

Potato and ham gratin

PREPARATION TIME: **20 minutes**
COOKING TIME: **1 ½–2 hours**
SERVES: **4–6**

50 g / 1 ¾ oz butter, softened
1 kg / 2 ¼ lb / 4 ¼ cups floury potatoes, peeled
4 slices cooked ham, finely diced
½ bunch thyme
freshly grated nutmeg
2 cloves garlic, crushed
2 cups double (heavy) cream
500 ml / 1 pint milk
grated Parmesan, to sprinkle

- Preheat oven to 160°C (140°C fan) / 300F / gas 2.
- Use the softened butter to generously grease a large baking dish.
- Slice the potatoes as thinly as possible – about as thin as a coin – using either a sharp knife or, preferably, a mandoline.
- Layer the potatoes and chopped ham in the baking dish, seasoning and sprinkling with thyme leaves, nutmeg and garlic as you go.
- Pour the cream over the potatoes – it should come just to the top of the potatoes. If you don't have enough, just add some milk.
- Push the potatoes down into the cream and sprinkle some Parmesan on top. Bake for 1 ½–2 hours, until the potatoes are completely tender all the way through and the gratin is golden and bubbling.
- Leave for 5 minutes to settle before serving.

Veggie potato gratin
Omit the ham and use vegetarian Parmesan or Cheddar cheese instead.

Creamed mushroom soup with croutons

PREPARATION TIME: **10 minutes**
COOKING TIME: **40 minutes**
SERVES: **4–6**

50 g / 1 ¾ oz / ¼ cup unsalted butter
1 onion, peeled and finely chopped
500 g / 1 lb / 2 cups flat or wild mushrooms, finely chopped
1 clove garlic, crushed
50 g / 1 ¾ oz / ¼ cup plain (all-purpose) flour
1 l / 2 ¼ pints / 4 ¼ cups chicken or vegetable stock
½ bunch parsley, chopped plus stalks
3 slices crusty white bread
100 ml / 3 ½ fl. oz / ½ cup double (heavy) cream

- Heat the butter in a large deep pan and sweat the onion without browning for 5–10 minutes or until softened.
- Add the mushrooms and garlic and cook for a further 5 minutes or until the mushrooms have softened.
- Stir in the flour and cook out for a few minutes or until the flour has turned a biscuit colour.
- Pour over the stock, add the parsley stalks and bring to the boil, stirring constantly.
- Reduce to a simmer and cook for 10–15 minutes. Remove from the heat and allow to cool a little.
- Toast the slices of bread and, once cooled, tear the slices into small crouton sizes.
- Liquidize the soup in batches then return to the pan. Add the seasoning and cream and reheat the soup gently without boiling.
- Divide the soup between the serving bowls. Garnish with the croutons and sprinkle with some cracked black pepper.

Prawn paella

PREPARATION TIME: **20 minutes**
COOKING TIME: **30 minutes**
SERVES: **4**

5 tbsp olive oil
1 onion, peeled and finely sliced
2 cloves garlic, finely chopped
1 red pepper, seeded and sliced
300 g / 10 oz / 1 ¼ cups paella rice
pinch saffron threads
1 tsp paprika
1 tsp ground or fresh turmeric
1 l / 2 ¼ pints / 4 ¼ cups vegetable stock
50 g / 1 ¾ oz / ¼ cup garden peas (fresh or frozen)
12 raw prawns (shrimp), shell on
1 lemon, cut into wedges
fresh parsley, to garnish

- Heat the olive oil in a large shallow pan and cook the onion and garlic.
- Add the pepper, cooking for a further 5 minutes, then stir in the paella rice and coat thoroughly in the oil.
- Stir the saffron and spices into the stock then pour it over the rice. Bring to a simmer and leave uncovered for 10 minutes.
- Add the peas and prawns and cook for a further 8–10 minutes until everything is cooked through.
- Season well and garnish with the lemon wedges and parsley.

Prawn and chicken paella
Lightly fry 2 chopped chicken fillets for 5–6 minutes once the onion and garlic is slightly browned. Follow the method as above, adding the rice, spices and stock. Ensure the chicken is cooked through before serving.

Cabbage with bacon and caraway seeds

PREPARATION TIME: **10 minutes**
COOKING TIME: **10 minutes**
SERVES: **4**

260 g / 2 oz / ¼ cup butter
1 clove garlic, finely sliced
4 rashers smoked streaky bacon, diced
1 savoy cabbage, outer leaves and core removed, leaves finely shredded
1 tbsp caraway seeds

- Heat the butter in a large pan with the garlic, then add the diced bacon. Cook until the fat starts to render.
- Add the shredded cabbage and a glass of water and cover with a lid. Shake the pan for 4–5 minutes, then check to see if the cabbage has wilted. Give it another 2 minutes if necessary.
- Mix in the caraway seeds and season to taste.

Cabbage with juniper berries
Add 2 tbsp spoons of juniper berries to the pan with the garlic for a spicy edge.

Broad bean and feta salad

PREPARATION TIME: **15 minutes**
COOKING TIME: **4 minutes**
SERVES: **4**

300 g / 10 oz / 1 ¼ cups broad beans (fava beans) in the pod
300 g / 10 oz / 1 ¼ cups garden peas
150 g / 5 oz rocket (arugula) leaves, washed
150 g / 5 oz feta cheese, crumbled
1 lemon, juiced
1 tbsp extra-virgin olive oil

- Remove the broad beans from their pods.
- Cook the broad beans and garden peas in boiling salted water for about 4 minutes until tender, then drain and plunge into iced water.
- Using the tips of your fingers, pinch the bright green beans from the grey casings.
- Tip into a pan and toss with the rocket, feta, lemon juice and olive oil. Season well and serve.

Broad bean and tofu salad
Replace the feta with 250 g / 9 oz firm herbed tofu. Simply crumble or dice the tofu and toss with the rest of the ingredients.

Marinated sardines on rye

PREPARATION TIME: **10 minutes**
COOKING TIME: **10 minutes**
SERVES: **4**

4 sardines, halved
2 tbsp extra virgin olive oil
½ lemon, juiced
1 loaf of rye bread, cut into slices
flat leaf parsley, chopped
fennel fronds, chopped
2 tbsp capers

- Place the sardines in a dish with a little oil and lemon juice. Season to taste.
- Heat a griddle pan until smoking, then cook the sardines for 4–5 minutes each side until cooked through.
- Toast the rye bread and add the parsley and fennel fronds.
- Lay two sardine halves on top of the herbs.
- Garnish with the capers and a squeeze of lemon. Season well and enjoy.

Sardines and cream cheese on rye
Add a generous layer of cream cheese on the slices of bread, before layering with the herbs, capers and sardines.

Pan-fried chilli prawns

PREPARATION TIME: **10 minutes**
COOKING TIME: **5 minutes**
SERVES: **6**

36 raw prawns (shrimp)
3 tbsp groundnut oil
2 cloves garlic, finely sliced
1 red chilli, deseeded and finely chopped
1 lemon, juiced
sprig fresh basil, to garnish (optional)
fresh ciabatta bread, to serve

- Peel the prawns, leaving the tail intact.
- Heat the oil in a pan, add the prawns and garlic and sauté over a high heat for two minutes.
- Add the chilli and cook for a further minute, then season and add lemon juice.
- Garnish with some fresh basil and serve with the ciabatta.

Pan-fried chilli and ginger prawns
Add 2 tablespoons of freshly grated ginger to the pan with the chilli flakes, garlic and lemon.

THE COOKERY COLLECTION

Broccoli, cod and basil quiche

PREPARATION TIME: 1 hour
COOKING TIME: 1 hour
SERVES: 4

400 g / 14 oz / 1 ½ cups cod fillet
1 head broccoli, separated into small florets
2 eggs, plus 1 egg yolk
275 ml / 10 fl. oz / 1 ¼ cups double (heavy) cream
1 tbsp Parmesan, grated
fresh basil leaves, to garnish

FOR THE QUICHE PASTRY
50 g 1 ¾ oz / ¼ cup cold, diced butter
110 g / 3 ½ oz / ½ cup plain (all-purpose) flour
a pinch of salt
cold water, to mix

- Preheat the oven to 200°C (180°C fan) / 400F / gas 6 and put in a baking sheet to warm.
- Rub the butter into the flour with the salt until you have coarse breadcrumbs. Add water a little at a time using a round-bladed knife to mix until the mixture just comes together. Form into a ball, cover with cling film and refrigerate for 20–30 minutes.
- Meanwhile, bake the cod in a dish in the oven with a little butter for about 15 minutes or until the fish just starts to flake apart. Leave to cool, then flake and remove any bones and skin. Steam the broccoli for two minutes.
- Roll out the pastry and press it into a greased flan tin. Prick all over with a fork and bake in the oven for 20 minutes until pale gold.
- Spread the broccoli and cod evenly over the pastry base. Whisk the eggs and the additional egg yolk, together with the cream, Parmesan and seasoning, then pour over the vegetables.
- Bake in the oven for 35 minutes. Leave to cool and garnish with the fresh basil leaves.

Broccoli, salmon and dill quiche
Replace the cod with the same amount of deboned salmon. Follow the method as above and garnish with some fresh dill.

Chicken, carrot and dill soup

PREPARATION TIME: **15 minutes**
COOKING TIME: **35 minutes**
SERVES: **4**

2 tbsp olive oil
1 onion, peeled and finely sliced
2 carrots, peeled and finely chopped
1 clove garlic, crushed
4 chicken thighs, halved
1 1/2 ¼ pints / 4 ¼ cups chicken stock
½ bunch dill, chopped

- Heat the oil in a large pan and cook the onion and carrot until softened.
- Add the garlic and cook for 3 minutes.
- Add the chicken, turning the heat up a little and cook until golden in patches.
- Pour over the stock and simmer gently for about 15 minutes.
- Season, stir in the dill and serve.

Chicken and butternut soup
Replace the carrot with butternut squash for a heartier version. Simply peel and dice a medium butternut squash; sauté with the onion and garlic before adding the stock and chicken.

Mac and cheese

PREPARATION TIME: 15 minutes
COOKING TIME: 25 minutes
SERVES: 4

2 tbsp butter
2 tbsp plain (all-purpose) flour
500 ml / 1 pint / 2 cups milk
1 bay leaf
1 tsp mustard powder
a pinch of cayenne pepper
grated nutmeg
150 g / 5 oz / ⅔ cup strong Cheddar cheese, grated
320 g / 11 oz / 1 ¼ cups macaroni pasta
4 tbsp white breadcrumbs, to garnish

- Preheat the oven to 180°C (160°C fan) / 350F / gas 4.
- Melt the butter in a pan, add the flour and stir to form a paste. Cook for a couple of minutes, then gradually whisk in the milk to form a smooth sauce.
- Stir in the seasonings and ⅔ of the cheese and simmer very gently for 10–15 minutes to cook out any traces of flour.
- Cook the pasta in boiling salted water according to packet instructions. Drain thoroughly, retaining a little of the cooking water.
- Tip the pasta into 4 individual ramekins and cover with the cheese sauce, adding a little of the cooking water to each to loosen.
- Scatter over the remaining cheese and breadcrumbs and bake for 20–25 minutes until bubbling and golden.

Apple, pecan and feta salad

PREPARATION TIME: **15 minutes**
SERVES: **4**

2 crisp green eating apples, cored and sliced
1 lemon, juiced
a handful of spinach
200 g / 7 oz / ¾ cup feta, crumbled
100 g / 3 ½ oz / ½ cup pecan nuts, halved
1 red onion, sliced
1 tbsp extra-virgin olive oil

• Halve the apples and core, then slice into thin half moons. Tip into a bowl and stir in the lemon juice to prevent browning.
• Add the spinach leaves, feta, pecans and red onion and toss until thoroughly combined.
• Dress the salad with a little extra virgin olive oil and season to taste.

Pear, walnut and spinach salad
Replace the apple with 2 peeled and sliced conference pears and swap the pecans for the same amount of walnut halves.

Waldorf salad with pecans

PREPARATION TIME: **15 minutes**
SERVES: **4**

225 g / 8 oz / 1 cup celery sticks, finely chopped
225 g / 8 oz / 1 cup pecans, toasted under a hot grill
2 eating apples, cored and diced
4 tbsp mayonnaise
½ lemon, juiced
a handful of lamb's lettuce and watercress, to serve
½ white French baguette, torn into pieces

• Place the celery, pecans and apple in a bowl.
• Mix together the mayonnaise, a little lemon juice and seasoning
• Stir into the salad ingredients and serve with the lettuce leaves and the torn bread.

THE COOKERY COLLECTION

Loaded potato skins

PREPARATION TIME: **10 minutes**
COOKING TIME: **25 minutes**
SERVES: **4**

4 medium baking potatoes
150 g / 5 ½ oz streaky bacon, chopped
1 tbsp olive oil
2 tbsp crème fraiche
2 tbsp chives, chopped
grated Cheddar cheese
1 spring onion, chopped
sour cream, to serve

- Preheat the oven to 220°C (200°C fan) / 430F / gas 7.
- Prick the potatoes and cook them in a microwave on high for 5 minutes.
- Meanwhile, fry the bacon in the oil for 4 minutes then stir in the crème fraiche and chives.
- Cut a slice off the top of the potatoes and scoop out the centres with a teaspoon.
- Mix 4 tablespoons of the scooped out potato with the bacon mixture, then stuff it back into the potato shells.
- Sprinkle each potato with some Cheddar cheese and spring onion then bake in the oven for 20 minutes or until golden brown.
- Serve with the sour cream.

Tomato and cheese potato skins
Replace the bacon with tomatoes. Deseed and dice 1 large beefsteak tomato and combine with the crème fraiche before stuffing the skins.

Country vegetable soup

PREPARATION TIME: 15 minutes
COOKING TIME: 20–25 minutes
SERVES: 4–6

3 tbsp olive oil
1 large onion, chopped
2 carrots, roughly chopped
2 sticks celery, chopped
2 large potatoes, peeled and chopped
1 clove garlic, finely chopped
2 bay leaves
2 x 400 g can chopped tomatoes
1.5 l / 3 pints / 6 ⅓ cups vegetable stock
crusty brown bread, to serve (optional)

- Heat the oil in a large pan and sweat the onion, carrot and celery until beginning to soften.
- Add the potatoes, garlic and bay leaves, cook for 3 minutes, then add the tomatoes and stock and bring to a simmer.
- Cook for 20 minutes or until the vegetables are tender.
- Season well and serve with some chunky bread.

Steamed salmon with asparagus

PREPARATION TIME: **5 minutes**
COOKING TIME: **12–16 minutes**
SERVES: **4**

4 thick salmon steaks
4 sprigs thyme or marjoram or chervil
20 asparagus stems, ends removed
extra virgin olive oil
½ lemon, juiced

- Set the salmon fillets (probably 2 at a time) on a plate in a steamer, tucking in the herbs and seasoning.
- Steam over a medium heat for 6–8 minutes, depending on thickness. The inside should be coral pink (not pale pink) all the way through, otherwise it will be dry.
- Keep the salmon warm while you steam the remaining salmon.
- Meanwhile, lay the asparagus on a griddle pan and drizzle with oil, salt and pepper and lemon juice.
- Sauté for 4–5 minutes and then serve the salmon on top with a squeeze of lemon.
- Season well before serving.

Steamed cod with asparagus
Replace the salmon with the same amount of boneless cod and follow the method as above. Garnish with some chilli flakes for a spicy kick.

Chicken and pepper fajitas

PREPARATION TIME: **35 minutes**
COOKING TIME: **10–15 minutes**
SERVES: **4**

2 chicken breasts, skinned and thinly sliced
2 tsp paprika
2 tsp ground cumin
2 tsp ground coriander
1 tsp dried chilli (chili) flakes
4 tbsp olive oil
1 red onion, peeled and finely sliced
1 red pepper, deseeded and finely sliced
1 yellow pepper, deseeded and finely sliced
8 tortilla wraps
sour cream, to serve
tomato salsa, to serve
1 lime, quartered
a bunch of fresh coriander (cilantro), chopped

- Coat the chicken in half the spices and leave to marinate for 30 minutes.
- Heat half the oil in a pan until nearly smoking, then cook the onion and peppers until golden and tender. Remove from the pan, keep warm and set aside until the chicken is ready.
- Add the remaining oil and reheat the vegetables, then add the meat and sprinkle over the remaining spices.
- Stir briskly for 2–3 minutes until the chicken is cooked through.
- Wipe out the pan and use to warm the tortillas through.
- Serve the vegetables with the meat, tortilla wraps and sauces.
- Garnish with the lime wedges and coriander.

Turkey and pepper fajitas
Replace the chicken with the same amount of turkey breast for a slightly leaner, healthier version.

Tomato and mozzarella salad

PREPARATION TIME: **20 minutes**
SERVES: **4**

500 g / 1 lb / 2 cups mixed heritage tomatoes (yellow and red)
½ clove garlic, crushed
1 tbsp red wine or balsamic vinegar
6 tbsp extra virgin olive oil
10 balls baby mozzarella
½ red onion, finely sliced
1 tsp dried mixed herbs
½ bunch basil

- Roughly chop the tomatoes and tip into a bowl.
- Sprinkle over a little salt and leave for 10 minutes.
- Whisk together the garlic, vinegar and oil until thickened.
- Add the mozzarella, onion and mixed herbs to the tomatoes, tip in the dressing and toss thoroughly to coat.
- Decorate with torn basil leaves and serve.

Chicken Caesar salad

PREPARATION TIME: 15 minutes
SERVES: 4

4 little gem lettuces
100 g / 3 ½ oz / ½ cup ready-made croutons
2 cooked chicken breasts, diced

FOR THE DRESSING
2 anchovy fillets
½ clove garlic, crushed
150 ml / 5 fl. oz / ⅔ cup crème fraiche
squeeze of lemon juice
2 tbsp Parmesan, grated
Parmesan shavings, to serve

- Tip the salad leaves into a large bowl and add the croutons and cooked chicken breasts.
- For the dressing, mash the anchovy fillets with the garlic to a pulp, then stir in the crème fraiche, lemon juice and grated Parmesan, then season carefully. Add more lemon juice if desired.
- Add 2 tablespoons of the dressing to the salad leaves and coat thoroughly.
- Place the salad in the serving bowls then spoon over the remaining dressing, scattering over the Parmesan shavings.

Caesar salad with radicchio
Replace the little gem lettuce with one head of radicchio. Simply remove the outer layers and wash the radicchio. Combine the leaves with the remaining ingredients and dressing.

Sweet potatoes with bacon

PREPARATION TIME: **2 minutes**
COOKING TIME: **30–40 minutes**
SERVES: **4**

4 large sweet potatoes, scrubbed and halved
2 tbsp olive oil
150 g / 5 ½ oz streaky bacon, chopped
fresh coriander (cilantro), chopped
½ lemon

- Preheat the oven to 200°C / 400F / gas 7.
- Rub the potatoes all over with oil, prick a few times with a fork, place on a baking sheet and bake in the oven for 30–40 minutes until completely soft.
- Meanwhile, fry the bacon in the oil for 4 minutes.
- Once the potatoes are ready, mash the flesh with olive oil, salt and pepper.
- Garnish with the bacon and coriander and a squeeze of lemon.

Sweet potatoes with coconut yogurt
Omit the bacon and garnish with a dollop of dairy-free coconut yogurt for a creamy variation.

Baked potatoes with feta

PREPARATION TIME: **10 minutes**
COOKING TIME: **10–15 minutes**
SERVES: **4**

4 baking potatoes, halved
2 tbsp olive oil
200 g / 7 oz / ¾ cup feta cheese, crumbled
fresh chives, chopped
fresh dill, chopped
4 cherry tomatoes, halved

- Preheat the oven to 200°C (180 fan) / 400F / gas 6.
- Transfer the potatoes onto a baking tray and drizzle with olive oil and season well.
- Bake in the oven for 35–40 minutes or until the potatoes are soft and crispy.
- Add the crumbled feta, chives, dill and tomatoes before serving.

Baked potatoes with goat's cheese
Replace the feta with the same amount of goat's cheese for a softer, creamier flavour. Try garnishing with a different herb, such as mint or tarragon.

Mushroom and Parmesan baked potatoes

PREPARATION TIME: **5 minutes**
COOKING TIME: **70–100 minutes**
SERVES: **4**

4 large baking potatoes, such as King Edward or Maris Piper, scrubbed and halved

2 tbsp olive oil

30 g / 1 oz butter

2 cloves garlic, crushed

5 button mushrooms, sliced

1 red chilli (chili), deseeded and chopped

150 g / 5 oz / ⅔ cup grated Parmesan

fresh parsley, chopped

- Preheat the oven to 200°C (180 fan) / 400F / gas 6.
- Rub the potatoes all over with olive oil, prick the skins a few times with a fork and sprinkle generously with salt. Bake in the oven for at least 1 hour until completely cooked.
- Once the potatoes are cooked, heat the butter in a pan and sauté the garlic, mushrooms and chilli.
- Spoon the topping over each potato half and garnish with a little cheese and parsley.
- Return to the oven until the topping is hot and the cheese melting.
- Serve immediately.

Smoky baked potatoes with bacon
Replace the mushrooms with sliced pieces of bacon and sprinkle with smoked paprika before returning to the oven for a rich, meaty flavour.

Moules marinière

PREPARATION TIME: **10 minutes**
COOKING TIME: **10 minutes**
SERVES: **2**

1kg / 2 lb / 4 ¼ cups mussels, scrubbed and
de-bearded
1 tbsp olive oil
1 onion, peeled and very finely chopped
4 cloves garlic, finely chopped
300 ml / 10 fl. oz / 1 ½ cups dry white wine
crusty brown bread, to serve (optional)
fresh parsley, roughly chopped

- Wash the mussels in a bowl of deep,
  cold water.
- Discard any that remain open when tapped.
- Heat the oil in a large pot and gently fry the
  onion and garlic until softened.
- Drain the shellfish and add to the pot, then
  toss in the white wine and bubble up.
- Cover with a lid, shake the pot a little and
  leave the shellfish to open for about
  8–10 minutes.
- When they are all just open, taste the sauce
  and adjust the seasoning if necessary.
- Serve in deep bowls with some bread on the
  side and garnish with the chopped parsley.

Spicy deep-fried mushrooms

PREPARATION TIME: **15 minutes**
COOKING TIME: **20 minutes**
SERVES: **4**

100 g / 3 ½ oz / ½ cup plain (all-purpose) flour, seasoned with salt and black pepper
2 eggs, beaten
100 g / 3 ½ oz / ½ cup plain cornflakes, crushed
1 tsp mustard powder
1 tsp chilli (chili) flakes
2 tbsp Parmesan, finely grated
100 g / 3 ½ oz / ½ cup button mushrooms, cleaned
vegetable oil, for deep frying
fresh coriander (cilantro), to garnish

- Lay the flour, eggs and cornflakes out in separate dishes, adding the mustard powder and chilli flakes to the flour and Parmesan to the cornflakes.
- Dip the mushrooms one by one into each dish, coating thoroughly.
- Heat the oil to 180°C / 35oF and deep-fry the mushrooms a few at a time until golden brown all over.
- Drain on kitchen paper and serve with the fresh coriander.

Herby fried chestnut mushrooms
For a flavour with less spice but great taste, use chestnut mushrooms and replace the mustard and chilli with dried mixed herbs and garlic salt.

Courgetti Greek salad

PREPARATION TIME: **40 minutes**
SERVES: **4**

150 g / 5 oz / ⅔ cup cherry tomatoes
6–8 tbsp extra virgin olive oil
4 medium-sized courgettes (zucchinis), spiralized
200 g/ 7 oz / ¾ cup feta cheese, cubed
2–3 tbsp red wine vinegar
1 tsp dried oregano or small handful fresh oregano leaves

- Halve the cherry tomatoes and place in a bowl with a little salt and a drizzle of olive oil. Leave for up to 3o minutes.
- Combine the tomatoes with the courgetti and feta cheese.
- In a separate bowl, whisk together the vinegar and a little seasoning and the oregano, then whisk in enough extra virgin olive oil to make a thickened emulsion.
- Drizzle the dressing over the courgetti and toss thoroughly before serving.

Courgetti Asian salad
Omit the feta and add 250 g firm herbed tofu. Simply cut into cubes and combine with the courgetti and tomatoes. Dress with a little soy sauce and a squeeze of lime.

Mexican quinoa salad

PREPARATION TIME: 20 minutes
SERVES: 4

400 g cooked quinoa
200 g / 7 oz / ¾ cup sweetcorn kernels
2 avocados, skins removed and diced
400 g can aduki beans, drained
1 red onion, diced
fresh coriander (cilantro), roughly chopped

FOR THE DRESSING
½ red chilli (chili), deseeded and finely chopped
1 shallot, finely chopped
1 lime, juiced
2 tbsp tomato juice
4 tbsp extra virgin olive oil

• Combine the quinoa, sweetcorn, avocado, beans, onion and coriander.
• Whisk together the ingredients for the dressing until emulsified, then carefully mix with the salad ingredients.
• Season to taste and serve.

Mexican feta salad
Add 200 g diced feta to the salad and sprinkle with some toasted sunflower seeds for a tasty crunch.

Mange tout and walnut salad

PREPARATION TIME: 5 minutes
COOKING TIME: 4 minutes
SERVES: 4

200 g / 7 oz / ¾ cup mange tout (snow peas)
50 g / 2 oz walnut halves
200 g / 7 oz feta, crumbled
1 red onion, sliced
1 lemon, juiced
2 tbsp extra virgin olive oil

• Cook the mange tout in boiling salted water until crisp-tender for about 4 minutes.
• Drain and plunge into iced water to keep the colour.
• Toss the mange tout with the walnuts, feta and red onion.
• Combine the lemon juice with the olive oil and season to taste.
• Drizzle over the salad and serve with some crusty bread.

Mange tout, feta and squash salad
Add 200 g cooked butternut squash for a delicious autumnal salad. Sprinkle with some pumpkin seeds before serving.

Quinoa with kaboucha squash

PREPARATION TIME: 5 minutes
COOKING TIME: 40 minutes
SERVES: 2

1 kaboucha squash, deseeded and sliced
3 tbsp olive oil
1 lemon, juiced
140 g / 5 oz white and red quinoa
280 ml / 9 ½ fl. oz / 1 cup water
a handful of spinach leaves
1–2 tbsp white wine vinegar
1 tsp runny honey

- Preheat the oven to 200°C / 400F / gas 6.
- Roast the squash, drizzled with oil, lemon juice and seasoning, for 30 minutes until completely tender and caramelised.
- Place the quinoa in the pan with the water and bring to the boil – do not add salt.
- Once boiling, turn the heat down and simmer for 10 minutes until the germ separates.
- Remove from the heat, cover with a lid and leave to absorb the remaining water.
- Add the squash to a bowl with the spinach leaves.
- Combine the remaining oil, vinegar, honey and seasoning in a small bowl.
- Once the quinoa is ready, stir into the squash mixture with the dressing.
- Adjust the seasoning if necessary.

Quinoa with butternut squash
Replace the kaboucha squash with a medium butternut squash. Remove the stalk and seeds and dice, leaving the skin on. Follow the method as above.

Bacon, leek and potato soup

PREPARATION TIME: **10 minutes**
COOKING TIME: **40 minutes**
SERVES: **4**

60 g / 2 oz / ¼ cup butter
4 leeks, green ends discarded and finely sliced
2 medium floury potatoes, peeled and diced
2 sprigs of thyme
850 ml / 1 ½ pints / 3 ½ cups chicken or vegetable stock
250 ml / 9 fl. oz / 1 cup milk
150 g / 5 ½ oz streaky bacon, chopped
2 tbsp olive oil
½ bunch chives, chopped
fresh bread, to serve

- In a large pan, melt the butter and add the leeks once it starts to foam.
- Cook gently over a low heat until soft.
- Add the potatoes and thyme, then cook for a couple of minutes. Add the stock and milk, bring to a simmer and cook gently for 20–25 minutes, until the potatoes are soft.
- Meanwhile, fry the bacon in the oil for 4 minutes and set to one side.
- Remove the thyme stalks and whiz the soup in a blender until smooth.
- Return to the heat and warm through, seasoning carefully before pouring into 4 serving bowls.
- Garnish with the bacon and chives sprinkled on top.
- Serve alongside some fresh crusty bread.

Leek, potato and rocket soup
Omit the bacon and garnish with some fresh rocket leaves and a squeeze of lemon.

Prawns with glass noodles

PREPARATION TIME: 10 minutes
COOKING TIME: 10 minutes
SERVES: 2

2 tbsp vegetable oil
½ onion, peeled and finely sliced
1 cm piece fresh ginger, finely sliced
1 clove garlic, finely sliced
1 head of broccoli, chopped
200 g / 7 oz / ¾ cup raw prawns (shrimp)
2 nests glass noodles
3–4 tbsp soy sauce
2 tbsp oyster sauce
1 tbsp chilli (chili) sauce
1 tbsp sesame oil
1 tsp dried chilli (chili) flakes
1 tsp sesame seeds

- Heat the oil in a wok until nearly smoking then stir fry the onion, ginger and garlic until golden.
- Add the broccoli and stir fry until just tender, then add the prawns and cook through.
- Meanwhile cook the noodles in boiling, salted water according to packet instructions, then drain.
- Add the sauces to the pan and bubble up, then add the noodles and sesame oil.
- Serve topped with the chilli flakes and sesame seeds.

Tofu with glass noodles
Replace the prawns with 250 g of marinated tofu. Simply stir-fry the cubed tofu with the onion, ginger and garlic. Omit the oyster sauce for a version suitable for vegans or those allergic to shellfish.

Spicy beef empanadas

PREPARATION TIME: **30 minutes**
COOKING TIME: **20 minutes**
MAKES: 8

1 tbsp olive oil
1 onion, peeled and finely chopped
1 clove garlic, finely chopped
500 g / 1 lb / 2 cups minced beef
400 g can kidney beans, drained
½ tsp cayenne pepper
½ tsp chilli (chili) flakes
1 tsp ground cumin
500 g / 1lb ready-made puff pastry
1 egg, beaten
tortilla chips, to serve (optional)
salsa, to serve (optional)

- Preheat the oven to 200°C (180°C fan) / 400F / gas 6.
- Heat the oil in a pan and cook the onion and garlic until translucent. Add the beef, increase the heat and cook until browned. Add the beans, spices and seasoning and cook for 5–10 minutes until cooked through.
- Roll the pastry out onto a lightly floured surface to about 1 cm (½ inch) thickness and cut out eight circles about 10 cm (4 inches) wide.
- Spread a small spoonful of the beef mixture into the centre of each circle, leaving a 1 cm border around the edge. Brush the edges with a little beaten egg and fold the pastry over to enclose the filling.
- Using a fork, crimp the edges of the pastry together to seal the filling in and brush the parcels with beaten egg.
- Bake in the oven on a greased baking sheet for about 10 minutes, then lower the oven temperature to 180°C / 350F / gas 4 and cook for another 10 minutes.
- Once cooked, transfer to a serving plate and enjoy with some tortilla chips and salsa.

Spicy tofu empanadas
Replace the beef with 250 g smoked tofu. Simply crumble or mash the tofu with the back of a fork and lightly fry with the onion and garlic, before filling the pastry.

Daikon and apple salad

PREPARATION TIME: **15 minutes**
SERVES: **4**

1 large daikon radish, peeled and julienned
2 eating apples, peeled and julienned

1 bunch coriander (cilantro), finely chopped
1 tbsp mayonnaise
½ lemon, juiced

- Combine the daikon, apples and coriander in a large mixing bowl.
- Whisk together the mayonnaise and lemon and season to taste. Whisk until thoroughly combined.
- Toss the salad in the dressing and leave for 10 minutes to soften slightly.
- Divide the salad between the 4 serving bowls.

Apple and cabbage salad
Replace the daikon radish with a white cabbage. Simply wash and roughly chop the cabbage and follow the method as above.

Tomato, feta and asparagus salad

PREPARATION TIME: **5 minutes**
SERVES: **4**

16 asparagus tips, ends removed
4 tbsp extra virgin olive oil
1 lemon, juiced
300 g / 10 oz / 1 ¼ cups cherry tomatoes, halved
100 g / 3 ½ oz / feta, cubed
fresh mint leaves, chopped
1 tbsp red wine vinegar or balsamic vinegar

- Heat a pan over medium heat and sauté the asparagus tips for 4–5 minutes with some olive oil and lemon juice.
- Place the tomatoes and feta in a large bowl. Add the asparagus and mint leaves.
- Drizzle over some balsamic or red wine vinegar, season to taste and then serve.

Tomato, asparagus and artichoke salad
For an even healthier version, replace the feta with 100 g of chopped chargrilled artichokes.

Potato and dill salad

PREPARATION TIME: **5 minutes**
COOKING TIME: **20 minutes**
SERVES: **4**

1 kg / 2 ¼ lb / 4 ¼ cups new or salad potatoes such as Anya or Charlotte
200 g / 7 oz / ¾ cup mayonnaise
½ bunch fresh dill, chopped
1 tsp mustard seeds

- Cook the potatoes whole in boiling, salted water covered with a lid, for about 20 minutes or until tender.
- Drain thoroughly.
- Leave to cool slightly then thickly slice.
- Mix the mayonnaise with the dill, mustard seeds and seasoning, then toss with the potatoes while still warm.

Lemony potato salad
Add the juice and zest of a lemon to the mayonnaise before tossing with the potatoes.

Minestrone with mimolette

PREPARATION TIME: **20 minutes**
COOKING TIME: **2 hours**
SERVES: **4**

2 tbsp olive oil
1 onion, peeled and finely chopped
2 celery stalks, finely chopped
2 carrots, peeled and finely chopped
2 cloves garlic, finely chopped
2 potatoes, peeled and finely chopped
1.5 l / 2 ½ pints / 5 cups vegetable stock
200 g / 6 ½ oz / ¾ cup cavolo nero, finely sliced
100 g / 3 ½ oz / ½ cup macaroni pasta
aged mimolette cheese, finely sliced
extra virgin olive oil

- Heat the oil in a large pan. Add the vegetables in the order given, giving each one a good 5 minutes to cook without colouring, stirring regularly, before adding the next one.
- Pour in the stock and bring to a gently simmer, then cook very gently for about an hour.
- Add the sliced cavolo nero and the pasta, then cook for a further 30 minutes. Adjust the seasoning.
- Serve sprinkled with aged mimolette and drizzled with olive oil.

Minestrone with Parmesan
Replace the aged mimolette with some grated Parmesan for a deliciously salty flavour.

Potato and parsley omelette

PREPARATION TIME: **15 minutes**
COOKING TIME: **5 minutes**
SERVES: **2**

250 g / 9 oz / 1 cup potatoes, peeled
2 eggs
1 tbsp butter
fresh parsley sprigs, to garnish

- Cut the potatoes into dice and cook in boiling, salted water until tender. Drain thoroughly and set aside.
- Meanwhile, crack the eggs into a bowl and beat lightly with the butter. Tip into a deep pan and swirl gently to cover the base of the pan and help it set.
- When the omelette is nearly set, sprinkle over the potatoes, parsley and seasoning and place under a hot grill to set it completely.
- Remove from the pan, flip and serve. Garnish with a sprig of parsley and season to taste.

Pea and potato omelette
Add a handful of fresh or frozen garden peas to the omelette along with the diced potatoes.

Cheddar and broccoli bake

PREPARATION TIME: **20 minutes**
COOKING TIME: **20 minutes**
SERVES: **4-6**

1 head of broccoli
100 g / 3 ½ oz / ½ cup butter
2 tbsp plain (all-purpose) flour
1 tsp mustard powder
500 ml / 1 pint / 2 cups milk
2 bay leaves
grated nutmeg, as desired
1 lemon, juiced
¼ tsp mace
275 g / 10 oz / 1 ¼ cups Cheddar, grated

- Cut the broccoli into florets and cook in boiling, salted water for 5 minutes. Drain and set aside.
- Preheat the oven to 200°C (180°C fan) / 400F / gas 6.
- Heat the butter in a pan and whisk in the flour and mustard powder to make a paste. Gradually whisk in the milk and stir until thick and smooth. Add the bay leaves, nutmeg, lemon juice and mace, then leave to simmer for 10 minutes.
- Stir in most of the cheese until melted.
- Tip the broccoli into a round baking dish and spoon over the sauce. Sprinkle with the remaining cheese and bake for 20 minutes.

Cheddar and cauliflower bake
Replace the broccoli with 1 head of cauliflower and follow the method as above.

Grilled citrusy sea bass

PREPARATION TIME: **10 minutes**
COOKING TIME: **16-18 minutes**
SERVES: **2**

1 sea bass, gutted and cleaned
2 tbsp extra virgin olive oil
1 lemon, juiced
2 tbsp freshly grated ginger
a handful of fennel fronds
1 spring onion, roughly chopped
1 lime, cut into wedges

- Rub the outsides of the sea bass with a little olive oil and grill for about 8 minutes per side, turning carefully until the fish is just cooked through and pulls away easily from the bone.
- Combine the olive oil with the lemon juice and ginger. Season to taste.
- Transfer the fish onto a serving plate and pour the lemon and ginger dressing over the top.
- Garnish with the fresh fennel fronds, spring onion and lime wedges. Serve at the table for everyone to help themselves.

Grilled citrusy salmon
Replace the sea bass with a whole salmon and follow the method as above. Garnish with fennel fronds or dill before spooning over the dressing.

Gnocchi in spicy tomato sauce

PREPARATION TIME: 1 hour
COOKING TIME: 5 minutes
SERVES: 4

700 g / 1 lb 8 oz floury potatoes, such as Maris Piper
250 g 9 oz / 2 cups plain (all-purpose) flour
1 egg, beaten
a pinch of nutmeg

FOR THE TOMATO SAUCE
2 tbsp olive oil
1 clove garlic, finely chopped
400 g can chopped tomatoes
1 tsp dried chilli (chili) flakes
1 tsp smoked paprika
1 lemon, juiced
½ bunch parsley, chopped

- Boil the potatoes whole and unpeeled in salted water for at least 25 minutes until completely tender.
- Drain and mash thoroughly.
- To make the tomato sauce, heat the oil in a pan and fry the garlic gently, then add the tomatoes, spices and lemon juice with a splash of water. Simmer for 10 minutes, then season and stir in half the parsley.
- Tip the cooled potatoes into a bowl and work in the flour, egg, a pinch of salt and nutmeg until you have a smooth dough. Cut the dough in half and roll out to make 2 fat sausages.
- Cut into pieces about 3 cm (1 inch) long and press down gently with the tines of a fork to make the traditional indentations. Place on a floured baking sheet to cook when ready.
- To cook the gnocchi, bring a large pan of salted water to the boil then add the gnocchi. When they float to the top, they are ready. Remove and drain and toss with the tomato sauce.
- Garnish with the remaining chopped parsley, season well, then serve.

Creamy tomato gnocchi
Stir in 4 tablespoons of crème fraiche to the gnocchi and tomato sauce for a creamier dish.

Quinoa, spinach and pepper salad

PREPARATION TIME: **15 minutes**
SERVES: **4**

400 g / 4 oz / 3 cups cooked quinoa
1 red pepper, deseeded and roughly chopped
200 g / 7 oz spinach leaves
2 avocados, skins removed and sliced

FOR THE DRESSING
1 tbsp Dijon mustard
2 tbsp red wine vinegar
6 tbsp extra virgin olive oil
1 lemon, juiced

- Combine the quinoa, pepper, spinach and avocado in a large mixing bowl.
- Whisk together the dressing ingredients until thickened.
- Coat the salad thoroughly in the dressing and mix well before serving.

Quinoa, avocado and pistachio salad
Replace the spinach with rocket leaves and follow the method as above. Sprinkle over some plain roasted pistachio nuts for added crunch.

Smoked salmon pâté

PREPARATION TIME: **15 minutes**
SERVES: **4-6**

250 g / 9 oz / 1 cup smoked salmon trimmings
100 g / 3 ½ oz / ½ cup cream cheese
2 tbsp crème fraiche
½ lemon, juiced
fresh loaf of bread, sliced
fresh dill, to garnish

- Place the salmon, cream cheese, crème fraiche and lemon in a food processor and pulse until roughly chopped.
- Season carefully.
- Spread a generous layer of the pâté on the slices of bread and garnish with the fresh dill.

Tuna pâté
Replace the smoked salmon with the same amount of tuna. Follow the method as above and garnish with some cracked black pepper and some wedges of lemon.

Chilli ratatouille

PREPARATION TIME: **10 minutes**
COOKING TIME: **50 minutes**
SERVES: **4**

4-6 tbsp olive oil
2 white onions, peeled and finely sliced
2 aubergines (eggplants), cut in half lengthways and finely sliced
3 courgettes (zucchinis), cut in half lengthways and finely sliced
2 cloves garlic, finely chopped
1 red pepper, seeded and cut into strips
1 green pepper, seeded and cut into strips
1 yellow pepper, seeded and cut into strips
400 g can chopped tomatoes
1 tsp dried chilli (chili) flakes
1 tsp coriander seeds, crushed
handful fresh thyme leaves
French baguette, to serve (optional)

- Heat the oil in a pan and cook the onions until deep gold and sweet.
- Add the aubergines and cook for 2 minutes.
- Add the courgettes and garlic and cook for 2 minutes, then add the peppers and cook for a further 5 minutes.
- Add the tomatoes, chilli flakes and coriander seeds, then leave to simmer for at least 30 minutes over a very low heat, stirring occasionally, until the vegetables are tender and very soft.
- Season and sprinkle over the thyme before serving with some baguette.

Butter bean ratatouille
Add 400 g butter beans, drained and washed, to the ratatouille with the tomatoes and spices.

Pizza margherita

PREPARATION TIME: **2 hours**
COOKING TIME: **8-10 minutes**
SERVES: **3-4**

FOR THE PIZZA DOUGH
400 g / 13 ½ oz / 1 ½ cups strong white bread flour
100 g / 3 ½ oz / ½ cup fine ground semolina flour
½ tbsp salt
7 g sachet dried yeast
½ tbsp caster (superfine) sugar
350 ml / ½ pint / ⅓ cup lukewarm water

FOR THE TOPPING (PER PIZZA)
6 tbsp passata
1 clove garlic, finely chopped
1 tsp dried oregano
½ ball mozzarella, sliced
extra virgin olive oil
black pepper
fresh basil leaves

- Pour the flours and salt into a bowl and make a well in the centre. Add the yeast and sugar to the water and mix with a fork. When froth forms, pour into the well. Using a fork in a circular movement, slowly bring in the flour from around the insides and mix into the water.

- When it starts to come together, use your hands and pat it into a ball.

- Knead the dough by pushing it away from you with the heel of your hand for around 10 minutes until the dough is smooth and elastic. Flour the dough, cover with cling film and leave to rest for 30 minutes.

- Roll the pizzas out about 30 minutes before you want to cook them. Preheat the oven to 250°C (230°C fan) / 500F / gas 9.

- Flour the work surface, tear off a piece of dough and roll into a rough circle about ½ cm (¼ inch) thick.

- Spread the base of each pizza with the passata, followed by the garlic and oregano, then lay over the mozzarella.

- Place either directly on the bars of the oven or on a preheated baking sheet for 8–10 minutes until golden and crisp. Drizzle with extra virgin olive oil, grind over some pepper and garnish with some basil leaves.

Marinara pizza
Omit the cheese and add a handful of sliced tomatoes and 2 crushed garlic cloves to the base. Garnish with some fresh oregano.

Mixed peppers with caperberries

PREPARATION TIME: **5 minutes**
COOKING TIME: **40-50 minutes**
SERVES: **4**

2 red peppers
2 yellow peppers
olive oil
a handful of purple stoneless olives
fresh parsley, chopped
6 caperberries

- Preheat the oven to 200°C (180°C fan) / 400F / gas 6.
- Halve and deseed the peppers and place in a roasting tin.
- Drizzle with the oil and season, then roast in the oven for at least 40 minutes until blackened and collapsed.
- Place the peppers in a freezer bag and leave to steam for 10 minutes before removing the skins.
- Mix the peppers with the olives, parsley and caperberries. Season to taste and serve.

Mixed pepper bruschetta
Serve the mixed peppers on some crusty toasted sourdough and drizzle with some extra-virgin olive oil.

Mixed bean salad with vinaigrette

PREPARATION TIME: **10 minutes**
COOKING TIME: **4 minutes**
SERVES: **4**

300 g / 10 oz / 1 ¼ cups green beans, chopped
1 shallot, finely chopped
2 tbsp extra virgin olive oil
½ lemon, juiced
1 tsp mustard seeds
1 tsp runny honey
1 tsp white wine vinegar
400 g can cannellini beans, drained
400 g can aduki beans, drained
1 spring onion, chopped

- Blanch the green beans in boiling salted water for 4 minutes, then drain and refresh in iced water to keep the colour.
- Whisk together the shallot, oil, lemon juice, mustard seeds, honey, vinegar and seasoning and toss with the cannellini, aduki and green beans.
- Stir well to ensure the beans are evenly coated with the dressing.
- Top with the spring onion and serve.

Mixed bean salad with mackerel
Roughly chop 2 fillets of pre-cooked peppered mackerel and combine with the rest of the ingredients and dressing.

Saffron and butternut risotto

PREPARATION TIME: **5 minutes**
COOKING TIME: **25 minutes**
SERVES: **4**

2 tbsp olive oil
80 g / 2 oz butter
1 onion, peeled and finely chopped
2 cloves garlic, finely chopped
½ butternut squash, peeled and diced
320 g / 11 oz / 1 ⅓ cups risotto rice
100 ml / 3 ½ fl. oz / ½ cup dry white wine
1 l / 2 ¼ pints / 4 ¼ cups chicken or vegetable stock
with a pinch of saffron threads soaking
120 g / 4 oz / ½ cup Parmesan, grated
a sprig of rosemary, to garnish

- Heat the oil and half of the butter in a large pan and add the onion, garlic and butternut squash. Cook until the onion is soft and translucent.
- Add the rice and stir to coat in the butter. Pour in the wine and stir the rice while the wine is absorbed.
- Once the wine has cooked in, reduce the heat a little and add the hot stock, a ladleful at a time, stirring fairly continuously. This will give the risotto its creamy texture.
- Keep stirring in the stock and tasting the rice. After about 15–20 minutes, the rice and squash should be soft but with a slight bite. If you've run out of stock before the rice is cooked, simply use water.
- Season and remove from the heat. Add the remaining butter and Parmesan, then leave to melt into the risotto.
- Garnish with the sprig of rosemary and serve immediately.

Vegan butternut risotto
Use vegetable stock and dairy-free butter and replace the Parmesan with vegan Parmesan or omit altogether.

Smoked cauliflower soup

PREPARATION TIME: **10 minutes**
COOKING TIME: **35 minutes**
SERVES: **4**

25 g / 1 oz butter
1 onion, peeled and finely chopped
2 heads cauliflower, roughly chopped
1 large potato, peeled and finely diced
2 cloves smoked garlic, chopped
500 ml /1 pint / 2 cups vegetable stock
150 ml / 5 fl. oz / ⅔ cup double (heavy) cream
1 tsp smoked paprika
pinch smoked salt
1 tbsp extra-virgin olive oil
1 spring onion, sliced

- Heat the butter in a pan and sweat the onion without colouring for about five minutes.
- Add the florets of 1 cauliflower, potato and garlic and cook for a further five minutes until softened.
- Add the stock, cream, paprika and salt and bring to the boil. Simmer for about 20 minutes until the cauliflower is completely tender.
- Meanwhile, preheat the oven to 200°C (180°C fan) / 400F / gas 6. Add the remaining cauliflower florets and coat in olive oil and season well.
- Roast the cauliflower for 20 minutes or until tender and golden brown.
- Liquidise the soup in a blender, then return to the pan. Season well and garnish with the spring onions, a drizzle of olive oil and some roasted cauliflower.

Creamy herb and cauliflower soup
Instead of 2 cloves of smoked garlic, use a clove of ordinary garlic. Leave out the paprika and salt and add a tablespoon of dried mixed herbs.

Asparagus and pea risotto

PREPARATION TIME: **10 minutes**
COOKING TIME: **25 minutes**
SERVES: **4**

2 tbsp olive oil
40 g / 1 oz butter
1 white onion, peeled and finely chopped
2 cloves garlic, chopped
1 bunch of asparagus, woody ends snapped off
320 g / 11 oz / 1 ⅓ cups risotto rice
100 ml / 3 ½ fl. oz / ⅓ cup dry white wine
1 l / 2 ¼ pints / 4 ¼ cups chicken or vegetable stock
50 g / 2 oz garden peas
1 lemon, juiced and grated zest
120 g / 4 oz / ½ cup Parmesan, grated

- Heat the oil and butter in a large pan and add the onion and garlic. Cook until soft and translucent.
- Chop the asparagus into short lengths and add to the pan. Cook for a few minutes.
- Add the rice and stir to coat in the butter. Pour in the wine and stir the rice while the wine is absorbed.
- Once the wine has cooked in, reduce the heat a little and add the hot stock, a ladleful at a time, stirring fairly continuously. This will give the risotto its creamy texture.
- Keep stirring in the stock and tasting the rice. After about 15–20 minutes, the rice should be soft but with a slight bite. If you've run out of stock before the rice is cooked, simply use water.
- Add the garden peas and lemon juice.
- Season and remove from the heat. Add the Parmesan and leave to melt into the risotto. Garnish with the lemon zest before serving.

Ham and pea risotto
Replace the aspargus with good quality, thick pre-cooked ham. As an option, consider using ham or pork stock instead of chicken or vegetable.

Pear, rocket and balsamic salad

PREPARATION TIME: **15 minutes**
SERVES: **4**

2 ripe pears, cored, peeled and diced
2 tbsp lemon juice
250 g / 9 oz / 1 cup rocket (arugula) leaves
2 tbsp capers
1 tsp flaxseeds
a handful of cashew nuts
3 tbsp extra virgin olive oil
1 tbsp balsamic vinegar

- Combine the pear with half the lemon juice to prevent browning.
- Add the rocket, capers, flaxseeds and cashew nuts and toss well.
- Whisk together the oil, remaining lemon juice, balsamic vinegar and seasoning and toss with the salad.
- Divide the salad between 4 serving plates.

Pear, rocket and goat's cheese salad
Add 100 g crumbled goat's cheese to the salad before adding the dressing. Replace the cashews with walnuts for a better flavour combination.

Creamy tomato soup

PREPARATION TIME: **5 minutes**
COOKING TIME: **35 minutes**
SERVES: **4**

500 g / 1 lb / 2 cups ripe tomatoes, halved
olive oil, for drizzling
2 sprigs of rosemary
4 cloves of garlic, whole
1 l / 2 ¼ pints / 4 ¼ cups vegetable stock
100 ml / 3 ½ fl. oz / ½ cup double cream
1 bunch fresh parsley, chopped

- Preheat the oven to 200°C (180°C fan) / 400F / gas 7. Tip the tomatoes into a roasting tin and drizzle with oil.
- Season and tuck the rosemary and garlic cloves in and around the tomatoes. Roast in the oven for about 25 minutes or until tender.
- Remove the rosemary sprigs and discard. Squeeze the garlic flesh from the skins into a blender and carefully tip in the tomatoes and their juices. Add the stock and blend.
- Return the soup to a pan and heat through with the cream. Heat without boiling and garnish with the fresh parsley.

Red pepper and tomato soup
Add 2 red peppers, deseeded and roughly chopped, to the roasting tin with the tomatoes. Follow the method as above.

Battered cod

PREPARATION TIME: **15 minutes**
COOKING TIME: **10 minutes**
SERVES: **4**

4 thick fillets cod, cut into large chunks
225 g / 8 oz / 1 cup self-raising (self-rising) flour
300 ml / 10 fl. oz / 1 ½ cups cold lager
vegetable oil, for deep frying
1 lemon, cut into wedges, to serve (optional)
tartar sauce, to serve (optional)

- Dust the cod chunks in a little seasoned flour to help the batter stick.
- Whisk the flour and lager together to make a batter to the consistency of double cream.
- Heat the oil to 180°C / 35oF.
- Dip the cod chunks in the batter, thoroughly coating both sides then cook 2 at a time for about 10 minutes until deep golden brown and crisp.
- Keep warm in a low oven while you cook the remaining fish.
- Serve with lemon wedges and tartar sauce.

Battered halloumi
Replace the cod with the a block of halloumi, cut into suitable chunks. Follow the method as above and serve with tomato or tartar sauce.

Aubergine pizzas

PREPARATION TIME: **20 minutes**
COOKING TIME: **45 minutes**
SERVES: **2**

2 aubergines (eggplants)
4 tbsp olive oil
1 onion, peeled and finely chopped
1 tsp dried oregano
2 tomatoes, finely sliced
2 cloves garlic
1 red pepper, finely sliced
4 tbsp Parmesan, grated
a handful of grated mozzarella
fresh basil leaves, to garnish

- Preheat the oven to 200°C / 400F / gas 6.
- Cut the aubergines in half lengthways, drizzle with half of the oil and bake in the oven for about 20 minutes until tender.
- Meanwhile, heat the remaining olive oil in the pan and cook the onion with the oregano, tomatoes, garlic and pepper until softened.
- Spoon the sautéed vegetables onto the aubergine halves.
- Sprinkle over the Parmesan and mozzarella and pop back into the oven for 10 minutes or until the cheese is bubbling.
- Garnish with the fresh basil, season to taste and serve immediately.

Ratatouille pizzas
Add courgetti or thinly sliced courgette (zucchini) to the sautéed vegetables. Leave out the cheeses unless desired and lightly toast in the oven.

Mexican stuffed red peppers

PREPARATION TIME: **30 minutes**
COOKING TIME: **30 minutes**
SERVES: **2**

1 onion, peeled and finely chopped
2 cloves garlic, finely chopped
1 tbsp olive oil
300 g / 10 oz / 1 ¼ cups minced beef
2 tbsp tomato purée
400 g can mixed beans, drained and rinsed
200 g / 7 oz / ¾ cup white rice, cooked
4 ripe red peppers, deseeded
2 tbsp Cheddar, grated
fresh coriander (cilantro), chopped

- Fry the onion and garlic in the oil until translucent.
- Add the beef and fry briskly, stirring, until the beef is cooked. Season well.
- Stir in the tomato purée, beans and a cup of water and leave to simmer until the water is absorbed.
- Stir in the rice and leave to cool a little.
- Preheat the oven to 200°C (180°C fan) / 400F / gas 6.
- Fill the peppers with the beef mixture and place in a roasting tin.
- Sprinkle with the cheese and coriander and bake in the oven for about 30 minutes or until they are soft but retaining their shape.

Mexican stuffed tomatoes
Replace the peppers with large tomatoes, such as beefsteak tomatoes, and follow the method as above. Add chilli flakes for an extra kick.

Creamy pea and chive soup

PREPARATION TIME: 5 minutes
COOKING TIME: 10 minutes
SERVES: 4

25 g / 1 oz butter
1 onion, peeled and finely chopped
1 garlic clove, finely chopped
250 g / 9 oz / 1 cup peas, fresh or frozen
1 large potato, peeled and chopped
500 ml / 1 pint / 2 cups vegetable stock
¼ bunch mint leaves, chopped
150 ml / 5 fl. oz / ⅔ cup single cream
4 tbsp crème fraiche
fresh chives, to garnish

- Heat the butter in a pan and sweat the onion and garlic for about five minutes without browning.
- Add the peas, potato, stock and half the mint and bring to the boil.
- Simmer for five to six minutes until the peas are tender.
- Remove and discard the herb stalks and liquidize the soup in a blender until completely smooth.
- Return to the heat, season and pour in the single cream. Do not allow to boil. Mix well.
- Serve in bowls, garnishing with a little crème fraiche, chives and black pepper.

Creamy pea and rocket soup
Garnish with a handful of rocket (arugula) and a little lemon juice before serving.

Carrot and lentil soup

PREPARATION TIME: **15 minutes**
COOKING TIME: **35-40 minutes**
SERVES: **4**

50 ml / 1 ½ fl. oz / ¼ cup olive oil
1 large onion, finely chopped
2 cloves garlic, minced
3.5 cm / 1 inch piece of ginger, minced
1 tbsp ground coriander
2 tsp ground cumin
1 tsp madras curry powder
½ tsp chilli (chili) powder
½ tsp turmeric
250 g / 9 oz / 1 cup split lentils
3 large carrots, peeled and diced
1.4 l / 2 ½ pints / 5 cups vegetable stock
chopped parsley, to garnish
crusty bread, to serve (optional)

- Heat the olive oil in a large saucepan set over a medium heat. Sweat the onion, garlic and ginger for 6–8 minutes until soft.
- Add the ground spices and some salt and pepper. Stir well and cook for a few minutes over a reduced heat.
- Add the lentils and carrots, stir well then cover with the stock. Bring to the boil, skimming any scum that comes to the surface.
- Boil for 5 minutes, then reduce to simmer and cook for 20–25 minutes until the lentils have absorbed about half of the stock.
- Adjust the seasoning to taste. Ladle into serving bowls and garnish with parsley before serving with some crusty bread.

Tomato and coconut lentil soup
Replace the carrot with 4 large tomatoes and the stock with 2 (400 g each) cans of coconut milk. Simply dice the tomatoes and add them to the spices with the lentils and coconut milk. Add a little water if necessary.

Pumpkin soup with coconut yogurt

PREPARATION TIME: **10 minutes**
COOKING TIME: **40 minutes**
SERVES: **4**

1 onion, peeled and sliced
2 garlic cloves, sliced
30 g / 1 oz butter
1 large pumpkin, peeled, halved, deseeded and cut into chunks
2 sprigs thyme
1 tbsp runny honey
1 litre chicken or vegetable stock
100 ml / 3 ½ fl. oz / ½ cup coconut yogurt

- Sweat the onion and garlic in the butter in a large pan until golden and soft.
- Add the pumpkin and cook for five minutes, then add half of the thyme, honey and stock.
- Simmer for about 20 minutes or until the squash is tender.
- Allow to cool a little, remove the thyme stems, then blitz in a food processor or with a hand-held blender until smooth.
- Season and stir in the coconut yogurt.
- Divide the soup between 4 serving bowls and garnish with the remaining thyme.

Spiced sweet potato soup
Replace the pumpkin with 4 medium-sized sweet potatoes. Simply peel and dice the flesh and follow the method as above. Add a teaspoon of ground ginger and a teaspoon of chilli (chili) flakes for a spicy kick.

Mackerel with bacon and sweet potato mash

PREPARATION TIME: 10 minutes
COOKING TIME: 40-45 minutes
SERVES: 4

1 head of broccoli, chopped
16 asparagus spears, ends removed
150 g / 5 ½ oz streaky bacon, chopped
1 kg / 2 ¼ lb / 4 ¼ cups sweet potato, peeled and cut into cubes
600 g / 1 lb / 2 ½ cups smoked mackerel, deboned
1 tbsp sesame seeds, to garnish

- Set a pan of water over medium heat and once simmering, add the broccoli.
- Boil for 5 minutes or to desired softness. Add the asparagus spears 3 minutes before the end of cooking time. Drain the liquid and leave in the pan with the lid on.
- Lightly fry the bacon over a medium heat for a few minutes on each side. Set to one side.
- Steam the sweet potato cubes until cooked through for about 10 minutes. Mash thoroughly.
- Preheat the oven to 180°C (160°C) / 350F / gas 5.
- Bake the mackerel for 15–20 minutes. Transfer the mackerel onto serving plates with the sweet potato mash, bacon, broccoli and asparagus spears.
- Garnish with some sesame seeds and season to taste.

Cod with bacon and sweet potato mash
Substitute the mackerel for cod and follow the recipe as above, for a milder taste.

Sesame scallops with asparagus

PREPARATION TIME: **2-3 minutes**
COOKING TIME: **5 minutes**
SERVES: **4**

20 asparagus spears, ends removed
4 tbsp olive oil
12 scallops, washed
1 tbsp sesame seeds
1 lemon, cut into wedges

- Steam the asparagus for 1 to 2 minutes until al dente. Remove from heat and set aside.
- Heat the oil in a wok or large frying pan. Stir fry the scallops with the sesame seeds for 3 minutes.
- Add the asparagus and stir-fry for 30 seconds.
- Season to taste, then serve the scallops with a wedge of lemon.

Sesame king prawns with asparagus
Replace the scallops with king prawns and cook for 5 minutes until the prawns are opaque.

Prawns with cracked pepper

PREPARATION TIME: **10 minutes**
SERVES: **4**

250 g / 9 oz / 1 cup North Atlantic prawns
(shrimp), cooked
1 tbsp olive oil
2 cloves garlic
1 lemon, juiced
black peppercorns, crushed
pinch of salt
fresh parsley, to garnish
tomato sauce, to serve (optional)

- Peel the prawns, leaving the tail intact.
- Heat the oil in a pan; add the prawns and
  garlic and sauté over a high heat for 2 minutes.
- Add the lemon juice, peppercorns and salt
  and cook for a further minute.
- Transfer the prawns onto a serving plate and
  season to taste.
- Garnish with the fresh parsley and serve
  alongside some tomato sauce (optional).

Prawns with chilli
Follow the method as above, adding a chopped
and deseeded red chilli and a pinch of chilli
flakes with the lemon juice.

Classic French onion soup

PREPARATION TIME: **15 minutes**
COOKING TIME: **1 hour, 35 minutes**
SERVES: **6**

60 g / 2 oz / ¼ cup butter
1 tbsp olive oil
700 g / 1 ½ lb / 3 cups onions, peeled and
thinly sliced
2 cloves garlic, crushed
1 tbsp plain (all-purpose) flour
200 ml / 7 fl. oz / ¾ cup dry white wine
1.5 l / 3 pints / 6 ⅓ cups beef stock
1 bay leaf
1 small glass Madeira or dry sherry

TO SERVE
6 slices French baguette
Gruyère cheese, grated
balsamic vinegar
fresh thyme, to garnish

- Heat the butter and oil until foaming, then add the onions and garlic. Cook very slowly over a low heat for at least 30 minutes until deep golden.
- Stir in the flour to make a paste, then pour in the wine. Stir until thickened, then add the stock and bay leaf.
- Simmer gently for 1 hour. Add the Madeira or sherry at the end of cooking.
- Meanwhile, heat a grill and toast the slices of baguette on both sides. Add the cheese and allow to crisp.
- Divide the soup among 6 serving bowls and top with the grilled bread and cheese.
- Drizzle with some balsamic vinegar and garnish with fresh thyme.

French onion and bacon soup
For a meaty flavour, fry bacon lardons with the onions and garlic, according to preference. Follow the method as above, optionally adding a rich red wine in place of the Madeira or sherry.

Sides, snacks
and treats

Ciabatta with rosemary

PREPARATION TIME: 9 hours, 50 minutes
COOKING TIME: 25 minutes
MAKES: 3 loaves

500 g / 18 oz / 2 cups 'oo' flour
380 ml / 13 fl. oz / 1 ½ cups water
25 g / 1 oz fresh yeast
1 tbsp olive oil
12 g / ½ oz salt
a sprig of fresh rosemary, stalks removed and leaves finely chopped
olives, to serve (optional)

- Mix half of the flour with half of the water in a large bowl and add 15 g of the yeast. Mix together well for a few minutes, then cover and leave to rise overnight.
- Next day, add the rest of the flour and yeast and mix well. Gradually add the rest of the water and the oil, mixing together in a food mixer for a few minutes. Then add the salt and rosemary and mix until you have a very sticky dough.
- Transfer the dough to a large oiled bowl and leave to rise, covered, for 1 hour.
- Move from the bowl and leave to rest on a floured work surface for 30 minutes.
- Preheat the oven to 240°C (220°C fan) / 465F / gas 8.
- Pull the dough into 3 approximate long flat slipper shapes. Place on a lined baking sheet, score a line lengthways on each loaf and leave to rest for 10 minutes.
- Bake in the oven for 25 minutes or until risen and golden brown. Transfer to a wire rack to cool.
- Serve alongside some olive oil with balsamic vinegar and a pot of olives.

Barbecued sweetcorn with chilli butter

PREPARATION TIME: **10 minutes**
COOKING TIME: **30 minutes**
SERVES: **4**

1 red chilli (chili), deseeded and finely chopped
1 tsp paprika
½ bunch coriander (cilantro), chopped
60 g / 2 oz / ¼ cup butter, softened
4 sweetcorn in their husks
1 lime, cut into wedges

- Mash together the chilli, paprika, coriander and butter into a fragrant paste, then refrigerate.
- Peel the husks back off the corn, then lay them back again and twist the top together to seal in.
- Wrap the corn in foil and barbecue for about 30 minutes until the kernels are tender.
- Slather with the flavoured butter, season generously and serve with the wedges of lime.

Sweetcorn with smoked paprika
Replace the paprika for the same amount of smoked paprika and add a pinch of smoked salt to the butter. Follow the method as above.

Garlic parsley ciabatta

PREPARATION TIME: **10 minutes**
COOKING TIME: **25 minutes**
SERVES: **4**

1 large ciabatta
250 g / 9 oz / 1 cup butter, softened
3–4 cloves garlic, crushed
a bunch of parsley, chopped
squeeze of lemon juice

- Preheat the oven to 180°C (160°C fan) / 350F / gas 4.
- Make deep slashes along the length of the ciabatta about 2–3 cm (1 inch) apart.
- Mix the softened butter with the rest of the ingredients, stirring well to combine.
- Liberally spread the inside of the slashes with the garlic butter.
- Wrap in foil and bake for about 20 minutes. Open the foil and bake for a further 5 minutes to crisp the top of the baguette.

Garlic, chilli and coriander ciabatta
Add a teaspoon of chilli (chili) flakes to the butter and mix well. Replace the parsley with chopped coriander (cilantro) and follow the method as normal.

Cheesy bread rolls

PREPARATION TIME: 2 hours
COOKING TIME: 10 minutes
MAKES: 12

450 g / 1 lb / 2 cups strong white bread flour
2 tbsp butter
1 tsp sugar
1 tsp salt
1 ¼ tsp fast action dried yeast
275 ml / 9 ½ fl. oz / 1 cup warm water
1 egg yolk, beaten
5 tbsp Parmesan cheese

- Place the flour in a bowl and rub in the butter using your fingertips until the mixture resembles breadcrumbs.
- Stir in the sugar, salt and yeast and enough water to make a soft, smooth dough.
- Turn out onto a floured surface and knead for 5 minutes until smooth and elastic. Return to the bowl, cover with cling film and leave in a warm place to rise for 1 hour or until doubled in size.
- Tip the dough back out onto the surface and knead, then cut into 12 equal pieces. Shape into smooth balls with any seams tucked underneath and place on greased baking sheets, cover loosely and leave to rise for 30 minutes.
- Preheat the oven to 200°C (180°C fan) / 400F / gas 6.
- Brush with beaten egg and some grated Parmesan. Spray the tray lightly with water and bake for 10 minutes until golden and they sound hollow when tapped. Transfer to a wire rack to cool.

Two-cheese bread rolls
Mix some grated Cheddar with the Parmesan before sprinkling over the buns and baking.

Egg and tomato tartlets

PREPARATION TIME: 50 minutes
COOKING TIME: 35 minutes
MAKES: 10

320 g / 11 oz shortcrust pastry
1 tbsp butter
1 onion, peeled and finely sliced
3 eggs
100 ml / 3 ½ fl. oz / ½ cup double cream
2 tbsp Parmesan cheese, finely grated
20 cherry tomatoes
fresh thyme, to garnish

- Preheat the oven to 200°C (180°C fan) / 400F / gas 6.
- Roll out the rested pastry to about 5mm thick. Using individual tartlet cases as a guide, cut out circles large enough to line the cases, then proceed to do so.
- Prick the bases of the pastry cases and bake for 10–15 minutes until pale gold and cooked.
- Meanwhile, cook the onion slowly in butter until golden and sweet. Whisk the eggs in a bowl with the cream, seasoning and cheese, then add the onion.
- Pour the mixture into the baked, cooled tartlet cases, then add the tomatoes on top.
- Bake for about 20 minutes, until just set. Cool on a wire rack before releasing from the tartlet moulds.
- Garnish with some fresh thyme and enjoy hot or cold.

Egg and pesto tartlets
Add 2 tablespoons of green pesto to the egg filling ingredients and mix well. Follow the method as above.

Potato crisps with truffle salt

PREPARATION TIME: **10 minutes**
COOKING TIME: **10 minutes**
SERVES: **6-8**

450 g / 1 lb / 2 cups floury potatoes, peeled
1 l / 2 ¼ pints / 4 ¼ cups vegetable oil
truffle salt
sprigs of rosemary, to garnish

- Slice the potatoes into very thin slices, either using a mandolin or a very sharp knife – as thin as you can.
- Wash in cold water to get rid of the starch.
- Heat the oil until a cube of bread sizzles immediately when dropped in, then fry the crisps in batches until golden.
- Remove to kitchen paper to drain and sprinkle liberally with the truffle salt and garnish with some rosemary sprigs.

Potato crisps with smoked salt
Replace the truffle salt with smoked salt and garnish with some black peppercorns.

Potatoes with paprika and fennel seeds

PREPARATION TIME: **10 minutes**
COOKING TIME: **15 minutes**
SERVES: **4**

2 tbsp groundnut oil
500 g / 1 lb / 2 cups potatoes, peeled and diced
½ tbsp paprika
½ tbsp fennel seeds
250 ml / 9 fl. oz / 1 cup vegetable stock
½ lemon, juiced

- Heat the oil in a large pan, then tip in the potatoes, paprika, fennel seeds and the stock.
- Cover with a lid and cook gently for 10–15 minutes until the potatoes are tender. Stir every now and then to prevent sticking.
- To serve, season well and add the lemon juice.

Potatoes with garlic and mustard seeds
Replace the paprika and fennel spices with 2 cloves of crushed garlic and a tablespoon of mustard seeds. Add to the pan with the potatoes and cook as above.

Potatoes with aioli

PREPARATION TIME: **5 minutes**
COOKING TIME: **30 minutes**
SERVES: **4**

750 g / 1 ⅓ lb / 3 cups new potatoes, scrubbed
2 tbsp butter, softened
2 egg yolks
4 cloves garlic, crushed
1 tsp mustard powder
130 ml / 4 ½ fl oz / ½ cup groundnut oil
130 ml / 4 ½ fl oz / ½ cup olive oil
1 tsp white wine vinegar
chives, finely chopped

- Cook the potatoes in boiling salted water, lid on, for 20 minutes or until tender to the point of a knife.
- Drain thoroughly, then return to the pan. Add the butter and seasoning and swirl to coat the potatoes.
- Place the egg yolks in a bowl with the garlic, mustard powder and a little salt and pepper. Whisk well.
- Using an electric whisk or hand whisk, pour in the oils one drop at a time, whisking each one in thoroughly.
- Once the mixture begins to thicken, add the oil a little faster, whisking well.
- After half the oil has been added, stir in a teaspoon of vinegar.
- Add the remaining oil in a thin trickle, constantly whisking. Season and garnish with the chives. Serve hot with the aioli.

Potatoes with spicy aioli
Add a pinch of chilli powder and some chilli flakes with the mustard powder. Adjust the amounts to taste, depending on your personal preference. You could also garnish with a red chilli, deseeded and chopped, instead of the chives.

Spicy lamb koftas

PREPARATION TIME: **10 minutes
(plus marinating time)**
COOKING TIME: **5-6 minutes**
SERVES: **4**

500 g / 1 lb / 2 cups lamb, cut into long chunks

FOR THE MARINADE
2 tbsp tomato paste
½ onion, peeled and chopped
2–3 green chillies (chilis), deseeded if preferred and chopped
3 cloves garlic, peeled
2 tsp fresh ginger, chopped
1 tsp ground cumin
1 tsp ground coriander

TO SERVE
1 tbsp fresh coriander (cilantro)
4 tbsp plain yogurt
8 wholemeal pittas

- Pat the chunks of lamb dry with kitchen paper.
- Place the ingredients for the marinade in a food processor with a little water, then blend until smooth.
- Toss the lamb in the paste and leave to marinate in the refrigerator for at least 1 hour or overnight.
- Thread the lamb onto skewers and cook either on a barbecue or very hot griddle pan until charred on the outside and pink in the centre – about 5–6 minutes.
- Once cooked, garnish with some coriander leaves and serve alongside the yogurt and pitta breads.

Fish fingers with a mustard crust

PREPARATION TIME: 10 minutes
COOKING TIME: 20 minutes
SERVES: 3

400 g / 14 oz / 1 ½ cups skinless firm white fish
100 g / 3 ½ oz / ½ cup breadcrumbs
1 tsp dried oregano
a pinch of cayenne pepper
½ lemon, grated zest
1 tsp mustard
1 egg, beaten
olive oil
1 lemon, cut into wedges
tomato sauce, to serve

- Preheat the oven to 200°C (180°C fan) / 400F / gas 7.
- Cut the fish into 12 equal sized pieces.
- Mix together the breadcrumbs with oregano, cayenne, lemon zest, mustard and seasoning.
- Dip the fish pieces first into the egg, then thoroughly coat in the breadcrumb mix.
- Brush a baking sheet generously with oil and lay the fish fingers on it.
- Bake in the oven for about 20 minutes, turning once, until golden brown.
- Serve with some lemon wedges and a side of tomato sauce.

Mango chilli chutney

PREPARATION TIME: 10 minutes
COOKING TIME: 2-3 hours
MAKES: 250 g

8 cardamom pods, seeds removed and finely ground
1 tsp cumin seeds
1 tsp fenugreek seeds
1 tsp mustard seeds
10 black peppercorns
8 cloves
1 onion, peeled and finely sliced
4 slightly under-ripe mangoes, peeled and cut into chunks
4 cloves garlic, crushed
1 red chilli (chili), finely chopped
2 tbsp fresh ginger, grated
350 g / 12 oz soft light brown sugar
2 tsp salt
400 ml / 4 fl. oz white wine vinegar

- Use a pestle and mortar to finely ground the cardamom seeds.
- Heat a heavy-based frying pan and dry-fry the whole spices for 2 minutes until the aroma fills the kitchen.
- Add to a preserving pan along with all the other ingredients.
- Bring gently to a simmer, then cook for 2–3 hours until the liquid has almost evaporated and is thick and syrupy.
- Allow to cool then ladle into sterilized jars and seal.
- Add a label with the date the chutney was made when the jars are completely cold.
- Leave for 8 weeks to mature before serving

Pineapple chilli chutney
Replace the mango with the flesh of 2 peeled and cored pineapples. Cut into chunks and follow the method as normal.

Pretzels with rock salt

PREPARATION TIME: **2 hours**
COOKING TIME: **10 minutes**
MAKES: **16**

325 g / 11 oz / 1 ½ cups strong white bread flour
75 g / 2 ½ oz / ⅓ cup rye flour
2 tsp soft light brown sugar
4 tsp salt
1 tsp fast action dried yeast
1 tbsp rock salt, to garnish

- Place the flours in a bowl, then stir in the sugar, a teaspoon of salt and yeast. Gradually mix in enough water to make a dough.

- Knead on a floured surface for 5 minutes until smooth and elastic, then return to the bowl. Cover loosely and leave in a warm place to rise for 1 hour.

- Tip the dough out on to a floured surface and knead well. Divide into 16 equal pieces.

- Roll each piece into a thin sausage about 30 cm (12 in) long. Shape to form a rainbow, then twist the ends of the rainbow together in the centre and press the ends to seal.

- Transfer to a greased baking sheet and cover loosely. Leave to rise for 30 minutes or until half as big again.

- Preheat the oven to 200°C (180°C fan) / 400F / gas 6. Bake the pretzels for 10 minutes or until browned.

- Meanwhile, warm the rest of the plain salt and a little water in a small pan. Stir until dissolved.

- Brush the salt water over the baked pretzels and sprinkle over the rock salt.

Pretzels with sugar crystals
Replace the rock salt with the same amount of sugar crystals for a sweeter treat.

Sweet potato mash with oregano

PREPARATION TIME: **5 minutes**
COOKING TIME: **15 minutes**
SERVES: **4**

4 large sweet potatoes, peeled
50 g / 1 ¾ oz butter
1 lemon, juiced
sprig fresh oregano

- Cut the potatoes into large chunks and cook in boiling salted water until tender, for about 10–12 minutes.
- Drain thoroughly, then set the pan over a low heat and shake the pan to drive off any excess moisture.
- Mash thoroughly with the butter and lemon juice until smooth, then season generously.
- Garnish with the fresh oregano and serve.

Deep-fried herbed squid

PREPARATION TIME: **30 minutes**
COOKING TIME: **10 minutes**
SERVES: **4-6**

1 egg
200 ml / 7 fl. oz / ¾ cup ice cold water
225 g / 8 oz / 1 cup plain (all-purpose) flour
1 tbsp dried mixed herbs
1 kg / 2 ¼ lb squid, cleaned and cut into rings
1 tbsp salt
vegetable oil, for deep frying
tomato sauce, to serve
1 lemon, cut into wedges
fresh chopped parsley, to garnish

- Stir the egg into the cold water, then whisk in the flour to form a lumpy tempura-style batter. Add the dried herbs. Dip the squid rings in and coat thoroughly.
- Heat the oil to 180°C / 350F and cook the squid in batches, removing to drain on kitchen paper when golden brown.
- Serve with some tomato sauce and some lemon wedges on the side. Garnish with some chopped parsley and enjoy hot or cold.

Deep-fried herbed prawns
Replace the squid with the same amount of prawns and follow the method as above. Serve with some béarnaise sauce on the side.

Spicy cod fritters

PREPARATION TIME: 2 hours, 20 minutes
COOKING TIME: 10 minutes
MAKES: 20-24

1 tsp yeast
50 ml / 1 ¾ fl. oz / ¼ cup water
½ tsp sugar
250 g / 9 oz / 1 cup plain (all-purpose) flour
1 tsp baking powder
1 tsp black pepper
½ tsp allspice
100 ml / 3 ½ fl. oz / ½ cup milk
250 g / 9 oz / 1 cup deboned cod, cooked
2 red chillies (chilis), finely chopped
½ Scotch bonnet (Habanero) pepper, finely chopped
2 tsp mixed dried herbs
1 egg, beaten
200 g / 7 oz / ¾ panko breadcrumbs
vegetable oil for deep-frying

- Add the yeast to the water with the sugar, stir well and set aside for 10 minutes until it starts to foam.
- Whisk the flour, baking powder, pepper and allspice together, then stir in the yeast mixture and milk and make a smooth batter.
- Flake in the cod and stir to coat, then stir in the remaining flavourings. Leave to rest for 2 hours.
- Roll each fish ball in the panko breadcrumbs until evenly coated.
- Heat the oil to 180°C / 350°F and drop in the batter using a tablespoon. Fry on all sides until golden brown, then drain on kitchen paper.
- Serve hot.

Spicy haddock fritters
Replace the cod for the same amount of deboned haddock and season with plenty of freshly ground black pepper.

Veggie quiche

PREPARATION TIME: **50 minutes**
COOKING TIME: **1 hour**
SERVES: **4**

FOR THE QUICHE PASTRY
50 g / 1 ¾ oz / ¼ cup cold, diced butter
110 g / 3 ½ oz / ½ cup plain (all-purpose) flour
a pinch of salt

FOR THE FILLING
100 g / 3 ½ oz / ½ cup Gruyére cheese, grated
1 white onion, peeled and diced
2 eggs, plus 1 egg yolk
300 ml / 10 fl. oz / 1 ¼ cups double (heavy) cream
1 tbsp mixed dried herbs
a sprig of basil, to garnish

- Preheat the oven to 200°C (180°C fan) / 400F / gas 6 and put in a baking sheet to warm.
- Rub the butter into the flour with the salt until you have coarse breadcrumbs. Add cold water, a little at a time, until the mixture just comes together.
- Form into a ball, cover with cling film and refrigerate.
- Roll out the pastry and press it gently into a lightly greased flan tin. Prick all over with a fork and bake in the oven on the baking sheet for 20 minutes.
- Place the cheese and onion evenly over the pastry base. Whisk together the eggs and cream and season, then pour in, adding a little pepper but careful on the salt.
- Sprinkle the dried herbs over the top.
- Bake in the oven for 25–30 minutes until just set. Leave to cool before serving.
- Garnish with raw onion rings and a sprig of basil.

Quiche Lorraine
Add 8 rashers of diced streaky bacon. Grill the bacon and then cut into small pieces. Add to the egg mixture before pouring into the pastry case.

Homemade skinny fries

PREPARATION TIME: **10 minutes**
COOKING TIME: **10-15 minutes**
SERVES: **4**

4 large baking potatoes, peeled and cut into thin batons
vegetable oil, for deep frying
pinch rock salt
tomato ketchup, to serve

- To make the chips, soak well in cold water to remove the starch then dry thoroughly.
- Bring a pan a third full of oil to 140°C / 275F and plunge in the chips, in batches if necessary and cook for 10 minutes until pale but starting to look 'cooked'.
- Remove and drain on kitchen paper.
- Heat the oil to 180°C / 350F and plunge the chips back in until golden and crisp. Remove to kitchen paper, season well and serve hot.
- Sprinkle over the rock salt and enjoy with tomato ketchup.

Sweet potato skin-on fries
Replace the baking potatoes with 4 large sweet potatoes. Scrub the skin well before cutting into thin batons. Follow the method as above.

Coleslaw with mustard seeds

PREPARATION TIME: **40 minutes**
SERVES: **4-6**

1 white cabbage, finely shredded
2 carrots, peeled and grated
1 apple, peeled and cut into fine matchsticks

FOR THE DRESSING
6 tbsp mayonnaise
2 tbsp grain mustard
1 tbsp lemon juice
1 tsp mustard seeds
cracked black pepper

- Salt the shredded cabbage in a bowl and set aside for 30 minutes.
- Drain off any excess liquid, then tip into a large bowl.
- Add the carrots and apple.
- Mix together the ingredients for the dressing with a pinch of salt and toss the salad thoroughly in it.
- Serve within 2 hours.

Coleslaw with celery
Add a stick finely sliced celery to the mixture before adding mixing together with the dressing.

Lamb shanks with rosemary

PREPARATION TIME: **15 minutes**
COOKING TIME: **3 hours**
SERVES: **4**

4 tbsp olive oil
4 lamb shanks
300 ml / 10 fl. oz / 1 ½ cups red wine
500 ml / 1 pint / 2 cups chicken stock
1 tbsp black and pink peppercorns
1 bay leaf
4 sprigs rosemary
2 tbsp runny honey

- Preheat the oven to 150°C (130°fan) / 300F / gas 2.
- Heat the oil in a casserole and brown the shanks on all sides.
- Pour over the wine, stock, peppercorns, bay leaf, rosemary and honey and bubble up.
- Season, cover with a lid and cook for 3 hours in the oven or until the lamb is very tender.
- Serve alongside the sprigs of rosemary and some peppercorns for decoration.

Prawn and scallop skewers

PREPARATION TIME: **15 minutes**
COOKING TIME: **15 minutes**
SERVES: **8 (2 kebabs per serving)**

4 tbsp extra-virgin olive oil
2 cloves crushed garlic
1 tbsp mixed dried herbs
1 tsp dried chilli (chili) flakes
2 lemons, juiced
1 bunch dill, chopped
800 g / 1 ¾ lb / 3 ⅓ cups scallops
800 g / 1 ¾ lb / 3 ⅓ cups prawns (shrimp)

- Mix the oil, garlic, herbs, chilli flakes, lemon juice and dill in a large mixing bowl. Season to taste.
- Add the scallops and prawns and thoroughly coat with the dressing.
- Heat the oil in a pan to 180°C / 350°F and cook the scallops and prawns in batches (reserving the dressing) until golden brown all over. Drain on kitchen paper.
- Once cooled slightly, thread the prawns and scallops along the wooden skewers.
- Place the kebabs under a grill to warm through. Drizzle over any remaining dressing and serve with the wedges of lemon.

Tofu skewers
Replace the fish with 400 g of firm plain or herbed tofu. Cut the tofu into large cubes and transfer to the mixing bowl with the dressing. Follow the method as above.

Rosemary roasted new potatoes

PREPARATION TIME: **10 minutes**
COOKING TIME: **20-30 minutes**
SERVES: **4**

750 g / 1 ⅓ lb / 3 cups new potatoes, scrubbed
4 tbsp olive oil
1 lemon, juiced
2 cloves garlic, crushed
a sprig of fresh rosemary, stalks removed and chopped

- Preheat the oven to 200°C / 400F / gas 7.
- Parboil the potatoes in salted water for 6 minutes, until starting to soften.
- Drain thoroughly, then set back over a low heat to drive off any excess moisture.
- Tip into a roasting tin and coat with oil, lemon juice, garlic, rosemary and seasoning.
- Roast in the oven for 20–30 minutes until golden and crisp, tossing once.

Roast potatoes with nigella seeds
Add a tablespoon of nigella seeds to the roasting tin with the other ingredients and follow the method as above.

Hawaiian prawn skewers

PREPARATION TIME: **15 minutes**
COOKING TIME: **8-10 minutes**
SERVES: **4-6**

2 tbsp sweet chilli (chili) sauce
½ red chilli, deseeded and very finely diced
1 lime, juiced
1 kg / 2 ¼ lb prawns (shrimp)
12 wooden skewers, soaked in water

- Combine the sweet chilli sauce with the fresh chilli and lime juice. Season to taste.
- Coat the prawns in the marinade and thread onto the skewers.
- Heat the barbecue until the coals are glowing and there are no flames.
- Cook the skewers on the grill for about 8 minutes, or until the prawns are cooked through.
- Enjoy alongside some broccoli and grilled pineapple.

Prawn and pineapple skewers
Skin and core a pineapple and cut it into chunks. Combine the pineapple and prawns and coat in the sweet chilli sauce. Thread along the skewers and grill as described above.

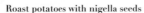

Chicken nuggets with ketchup

PREPARATION TIME: **2 hours**
COOKING TIME: **10 minutes**
SERVES: **4**

4 chicken breasts, skinned
300 ml / 10 fl. oz / 1 ¼ cups buttermilk
100 g / 3 ½ oz / ½ cup plain (all-purpose) flour
2 eggs, beaten
200 g / 7 oz / ¾ cup breadcrumbs
1 tsp mustard powder
a pinch of cayenne pepper
1 tsp dried oregano
vegetable oil

FOR THE KETCHUP
8 tbsp tomato paste
1 tbsp mayonnaise
1 tsp coriander seeds
1 tsp cumin seeds
pinch chilli (chili) flakes
pinch sugar
pinch salt
freshly ground black pepper

- Bash the chicken breasts between 2 pieces cling film with a rolling pin until about 2 cm (1 inch) thick.
- Cut each piece into chunks and place in a bowl with the buttermilk. Refrigerate for at least 2 hours or even overnight.
- The next day, dip them one at a time into the flour, egg, then breadcrumbs mixed with the flavourings and lay on a rack to dry slightly.
- Heat 1 cm (½ inch) depth oil in a pan and fry the chicken in batches until golden on both sides and cooked through.
- To make the ketchup, simply whisk the ingredients together and add a little water if necessary.
- Serve with some fresh basil leaves and the ketchup.

Herby fish cakes

PREPARATION TIME: 40 minutes
COOKING TIME: 10 minutes
SERVES: 3-4

225 g / 8 oz / 1 cup cod cut into small cubes
225 g / 8 oz / 1 cup mashed potato
2 tbsp parsley, chopped
1 tbsp chervil, chopped
3 tsp capers, chopped (optional)
squeeze of lemon juice
1 egg, beaten
3 tbsp breadcrumbs
vegetable oil
baby gherkins, to serve
hollandaise sauce, to serve

- Combine the fish, potatoes, herbs, capers and a little lemon juice in a bowl and season well.
- Chill for 30 minutes.
- Form into equal-sized patties, then dip into the egg, then the breadcrumbs.
- Heat 1 cm (½ inch) depth of oil in a pan and gently fry the fish cakes on both sides until golden and crisp.
- Drain on kitchen paper and serve with the baby gherkins and hollandaise sauce.

Spicy tuna fish cakes
Replace the cod with the same amount of tuna and add a tablespoon of dried chilli (chili) flakes to the mixture. Cook as described above and serve with some tomato ketchup.

Homemade steak burgers

PREPARATION TIME: **10 minutes**
COOKING TIME: **25 minutes**
SERVES: **4**

4 sirloin steaks, minced until coarsely ground (ask your butcher)
1 tbsp grain mustard (optional)
olive oil
4 tbsp tomato ketchup
4 slices Jarlsberg cheese
1 white onion, thinly sliced
1 large tomato, thickly sliced
8 leaves of lamb's lettuce
4 sesame burger buns

- Season the meat, mix well with the mustard if using and form into patties around 2 cm (1 inch) thick. Refrigerate until needed.
- Heat a griddle to very hot, then brush the burgers on each side with a little oil. Cook for 3–4 minutes each side, then leave to rest for 5–8 minutes wrapped in foil, the slices of cheese melting on top.
- Add the white onions to the pan and turn down the heat a little. Add some more oil if necessary. Cook until the onions are translucent.
- Serve in buns topped with tomatoes, onion, salad and sauces.

Sticky spare ribs

PREPARATION TIME: **20 minutes**
COOKING TIME: **3 hours, 30 minutes**
SERVES: **4-6**

2 racks pork spare ribs

FOR THE RUB
2 tbsp salt
1 tbsp freshly ground black pepper
4 tbsp soft dark brown sugar
2 tbsp smoked paprika
1-2 tbsp crushed dried chilli (chili) flakes
1 tbsp mixed dried herbs

FOR THE STICKY SAUCE
10 tbsp tomato ketchup
4 tbsp cider vinegar
3-4 tbsp runny honey
4 tbsp orange or apple juice
2 tbsp grain mustard

TO SERVE
fresh mixed herbs (parsley, rosemary, dill), chopped
tomato ketchup (optional)

- Preheat the oven to 100°C / 200F / gas ¼
- Combine all of the rub ingredients together in a bowl.
- Lay out the racks in a roasting tin then pat the rub into the meat, coating thoroughly on both sides. If you are preparing this ahead of time, you can leave them in the refrigerator for up to 24 hours at this stage.
- To make the sticky sauce: combine the ingredients in a bowl, tasting as you go to get a balance of sweet and savoury.
- Coat the ribs in the sauce and roast in the oven, covered with foil, for about three hours or until the meat pulls easily away from the bone, basting with the sauce every hour and turning them over.
- Serve the ribs with the fresh herbs and tomato ketchup.

Spicy spare ribs
Add a teaspoon of cayenne pepper and garnish with a chopped red chilli (chili), seeds removed, for a spicy kick.

Egg, sautéed potatoes and wilted spinach

PREPARATION TIME: **10 minutes**
COOKING TIME: **10-15 minutes**
SERVES: **4**

750 g / 1 ⅓ lb / 3 cups new potatoes such as Charlotte or Anya, quartered
5 tbsp olive oil
½ bunch thyme leaves
1 white onion, peeled and sliced
2 cloves garlic
4 eggs
200 g / 7 oz baby spinach leaves, washed

- Parboil the potatoes in salted water for 6 minutes or so, until they begin to soften.
- Drain thoroughly, set back over a low heat to drive off any excess moisture.
- Use the end of a rolling pin to lightly crack or crush the potatoes to create crisp edges in the pan.
- Heat the oil in a pan large enough to hold them in one layer, then add the potatoes.
- Season well, toss in the thyme, onion and garlic, then sauté until golden and crisp for approximately 10–15 minutes.
- In a separate pan, add a little olive oil and fry the eggs, one at a time. Season well, before transferring to a plate.
- Add the spinach to the potatoes 3 minutes before the end of cooking time and stir well.
- Divide the potatoes, spinach and fried eggs between the 4 serving plates or serve in a small frying pan for effect.

Egg, potato and Parmesan fry-up
Add some freshly grated Parmesan to the fry-up before serving for extra decadence.

Spicy potato wedges

PREPARATION TIME: **15 minutes**
COOKING TIME: **30 minutes**
SERVES: **4**

4 large floury potatoes, scrubbed
5 tbsp olive oil
½ lemon, juiced
1 tsp smoked paprika
1 tsp cayenne pepper
½ tsp dried chilli (chili) flakes
½ tsp smoked salt
1 tsp dried oregano

- Preheat the oven to 220°C / 450F / gas 7.
- Cut the potatoes into wedges lengthways, about 6–8 per potato. Parboil in salted water for 3–4 minutes.
- Drain thoroughly, then set back over a low heat to drive off any excess moisture.
- Place on a baking sheet and toss with the oil, lemon juice and seasonings until thoroughly coated.
- Bake in the oven for about 30 minutes until deep gold and crisp.
- Drain briefly on kitchen paper and serve hot or cold.

Spicy sweet potato wedges
Replace the potatoes with the same amount of sweet potatoes, skins left on. Follow the method as above and garnish with some fresh sprigs of rosemary.

Mashed potato with chives

PREPARATION TIME: **2 minutes**
COOKING TIME: **40 minutes**
SERVES: **4**

1 kg / 2 ¼ lb / 4 ¼ cups floury potatoes such as King Edward or Desiree
100 g / 3 ½ oz / ½ cup butter
fresh chives, chopped
75–100 ml / 2 ½–3 ½ oz / ⅓–½ cup milk, warmed
2 tbsp olive oil

- Cook the potatoes whole in their skins in boiling salted water until tender all the way through – about 30 minutes, but keep checking.
- Drain thoroughly and leave to cool for 5 minutes, then peel off the skins while still hot.
- Return the flesh to the pan, mash finely and stir in the butter, half the chives and enough milk with a wooden spoon to make a light, creamy, smooth mash.
- Season generously and garnish with some olive oil, the remaining chives and some freshly ground black pepper.

Rosemary and olive focaccia

PREPARATION TIME: 40 minutes (plus 2 hours proving time)
COOKING TIME: 20 minutes
MAKES: 2

750 g / 1 ¼ lb / 3 cups '00' flour
½ tsp salt
150 ml / 5 fl. oz / ⅔ cup extra virgin olive oil
2 tsp fast-action dried yeast
1 tbsp dried mixed herbs
a handful of black pitted olives, roughly chopped
450 ml / 1 pint / 2 cups lukewarm water
1 bunch rosemary leaves
coarse sea salt, to serve

- Sift the flour and salt into a bowl and make a well in the centre. Pour 50 ml of the oil into the flour, add the yeast, dried herbs and olives and rub together with your fingers until the mixture resembles breadcrumbs. Pour in about 400ml of the water and mix until the dough comes together. Add a little more water if necessary.

- Tip the dough onto a floured surface and knead for about 10 minutes until smooth and elastic, pushing the dough away from you with the heel of your hand. The dough will be very soft.

- Place in a lightly oiled bowl, cover with cling film and leave to rise in a warm, draught-free place until doubled in size – about 1 ½ hours.

- Take the dough out of the bowl, punch out the air and divide in to two balls. Roll into two 25 cm (10 inch) circles and place in 2 lightly oiled cake tins or pizza pans. Cover with cling film again and leave to rise for 30 minutes. Preheat the oven to 200°C (180°C fan) / 400F / gas 6.

- Uncover the dough and push your fingertips in at regular intervals to make deep dimples. Drizzle generously with oil so that the dimples almost fill up. Top with sprigs of rosemary and sprinkle with a generous amount of salt. Spray with a little water and bake for about 20 minutes or until risen and golden.

Olive and lemon focaccia
Finely zest 3 lemons and add to the dry ingredients along with the olives before mixing and kneading.

Sesame and poppy seed breadsticks

PREPARATION TIME: **2 hours**
COOKING TIME: **15-20 minutes**
MAKES: **20-24**

450 g / 1 lb / 2 cups strong white bread flour
7 g sachet dried yeast
1 ½ tsp salt
250 ml / 9 fl. oz / 1 cup lukewarm water
olive oil
2 tbsp sesame seeds
2 tbsp poppy seeds

- Place the flour, yeast and salt in a bowl, then add the water a little at a time to form a dough.
- Bring the dough together with your hands and knead well for 10 minutes until smooth and elastic.
- Divide the mixture into about 20 equal portions then roll into stick shapes. You can leave them like this or twist them at the ends.
- Place well-spaced on floured baking sheets, cover with a damp tea towel and leave in a warm place for 30 minutes.
- Preheat the oven to 200°C (180°C fan) / 400F / gas 7. Brush with the olive oil and sprinkle with sesame and poppy seeds, then bake for about 15-20 minutes or until cooked.

Cheddar and Parmesan cheese sticks
Replace the seeds with some grated Cheddar and Parmesan cheese for the ultimate cheesy snack.

New potatoes with white truffle salt

PREPARATION TIME: **5 minutes**
COOKING TIME: **25 minutes**
SERVES: **4**

750 g / 1 ⅓ lb / 3 cups new potatoes, scrubbed
50g / 1 ¾ oz butter
freshly cracked black pepper
1 tsp white truffle salt
1 tbsp parsley, chopped
1 tbsp mixed dried herbs

- Cook the potatoes in boiling salted water, lid on, for 20 minutes or until tender to the point of a knife.
- Drain thoroughly, then transfer to a frying pan.
- Add the butter, seasoning, salt and herbs, then swirl to coat the potatoes.
- Sauté on a medium heat for 5–6 minutes or until lightly browned.
- Serve hot.

Garlicky potatoes with white truffle salt
Add 2 crushed cloves of garlic to the pan and sauté with the rest of the ingredients. Add a squeeze of lemon before serving.

Naan pizza

PREPARATION TIME: 2 hours
COOKING TIME: 2 minutes
SERVES: 6-8

8 plain naan breads

TOPPINGS
250 g / 9 oz feta cheese, crumbled
1 beefsteak tomatoes, sliced
1 clove garlic, crushed
extra virgin olive oil
freshly ground black pepper
a handful of rocket (arugula)
fresh basil leaves

- Preheat the oven to 200°C (180°C fan) / 400F / gas 6.
- Top the naan bread with a combination of the ingredients listed (excluding any salad leaves or fresh herbs) as desired.
- Transfer the pizzas onto a baking tray and cook for 8–10 minutes.
- Add the salad leaves and fresh herbs and season to taste before serving.

> **Garlic and truffle oil pizza**
> Add a tablespoon of truffle oil and an extra clove of crushed garlic to the naan bread and cook as above. Garnish with some fresh oregano before serving.

Fried potato wedges with paprika

PREPARATION TIME: 15 minutes
COOKING TIME: 10-15 minutes
SERVES: 4

4 large floury potatoes, scrubbed
5 tbsp olive oil
1 tsp paprika
a sprig of fresh thyme
sun-dried tomato tapenade, to serve (optional)

- Cut the potatoes into wedges lengthways, about 6–8 per potato.
- Parboil in boiling water for 3–4 minutes.
- Drain thoroughly, then set back over a low heat to drive off any excess moisture.
- Heat the oil in a large pan, then add the potatoes and season well.
- Sauté on all sides until golden and crisp.
- Season with paprika, salt and the sprigs of thyme and serve with the sun-dried tomato tapenade.

Almond and raspberry tarts

PREPARATION TIME: **30-40 minutes**
COOKING TIME: **1 hour, 5 minutes**
MAKES: **16**

125 g / 4 oz / ½ cup plain (all-purpose) flour
75 g / 2 ½ oz / ⅔ cup butter
1 tbsp caster (superfine) sugar
2 tbsp ground almonds
1 egg yolk

FOR THE FILLING
2 heaped tbsp raspberry jam
150 g / 5 oz / ⅔ cup butter
150 g / 5 oz / ⅔ cup caster (superfine) sugar
3 eggs, beaten
1 egg yolk
150 g / 5 oz / ⅔ cup ground almonds
zest of 1 orange

FOR THE TOPPING
1 tbsp flaked almonds, toasted
175 g / 6 oz / ¾ cup icing (confectioners') sugar

- Tip the flour, butter, almonds and sugar into
  a food processor with a pinch of salt and whiz
  to form breadcrumbs. Add the egg yolk with a
  tablespoon of cold water and pulse. Flatten to
  a disc, cover with cling film and chill for 1 hour.
- Roll the pastry out on a floured surface to
  about 3 mm thick. Cut out 32 small discs using
  a cookie cutter.
- Preheat the oven to 180°C / 350F / Gas 4.
- Butter or oil 2 or 3 cupcake baking tins and
  gently press half of the discs (16 in total) into the
  individual tins.
- Spread the jam onto the bottom of each base.
- Cream the butter and sugar for the filling
  together. Add the beaten eggs and yolk,
  beating well after each addition. Fold in the
  almonds and zest.
- Spoon onto the jam, spread evenly and sprinkle
  with the flaked almonds and icing sugar.
- Bake for 20 minutes.

Sweet potato and chilli fritters

PREPARATION TIME: **15 minutes**
COOKING TIME: **15-20 minutes**
SERVES: **4**

2 large sweet potatoes, peeled
1 onion, peeled and very finely chopped
1 tsp dried chilli (chili) flakes
2 eggs, cracked and whisked
3 tbsp olive oil
2 limes, cut into wedges
mayonnaise, to serve

* Grate the sweet potatoes then tip into a tea towel and squeeze out any excess moisture.
* Tip into a bowl and mix with the onion, chilli flakes, whisked egg and seasoning to form a thick, sticky consistency.
* Form the mixture into equally shaped thin patties.
* Heat the oil in a pan and fry the patties for 8 minutes or until golden. Turn over and cook the other side. Drain on kitchen paper and serve with the lime wedges and mayonnaise.

Sweet potato and sweetcorn fritter
Add 100 g cooked or raw sweetcorn kernels to the dry ingredients and then mix with the egg to form a sticky, thick consistency. Follow the method as normal.

Marinated olives with rosemary and thyme

PREPARATION TIME: **10 minutes**
MAKES: **500 g / 1 lb**

250 g / 9 oz / 1 cup green pitted olives
250 g / 9 oz / 1 cup kalamata olives
185 g / 6 oz grilled red peppers, sliced
3 cloves garlic, peeled
a few of sprigs of thyme
a few of sprigs of rosemary
extra virgin olive oil

* Toss the olives and peppers with the garlic and herbs, then tip into a large jar or bowl.
* Cover with olive oil, seal and leave for 2 days to marinate before serving.

Marinated olives with caperberries
Add 4 tablespoons of caperberries to the jar or bowl with the remaining ingredients and omit the peppers.

Sausage and herb rolls

PREPARATION TIME: 30 minutes
COOKING TIME: 25 minutes
SERVES: 6

375 g ready-rolled puff pastry
6 Cumberland or traditional sausages
1 tbsp mixed dried herbs
1 egg, beaten

- Preheat the oven to 200°C (180°C fan) / 400F / gas 6.
- Roll the pastry out on a floured surface to the thickness of a coin.
- Remove the casing from the sausages and mash in a bowl with the back of a fork. Add the herbs and some freshly cracked black pepper.
- Spoon a little sausage meat in the top corner of the pastry rectangle.
- Score a line down the pastry the width of the sausage piece. Roll the pastry around the sausage, cutting it when you have encased the sausage. Place on a lined baking sheet. Repeat until all the sausages are used up.
- Make 2 small slashes in the top of each sausage roll and brush with beaten egg.
- Bake in the oven for 25 minutes or until golden brown. Leave to cool on a wire rack before eating.

Sausage rolls with nutmeg
Add some grated nutmeg to the sausage mix with the dried herbs, before mixing well and spooning onto the rolled pastry.

Chicken kebabs with chilli and lime

PREPARATION TIME: **4 hours**
COOKING TIME: **10 minutes**
SERVES: **4 (2 kebabs per serving)**

8 chicken thighs, boned and skinned and cut in half
8 wooden skewers, soaked in cold water
2 limes, cut into wedges, to garnish
fresh coriander (cilantro), to garnish

FOR THE MARINADE
2 shallots, peeled and finely chopped
½ red chilli (chili), finely chopped
2 cloves garlic, finely chopped
1 cm (½ inch) piece fresh ginger, grated
2 tbsp soy sauce
100 ml / 3 ½ fl. oz / ½ cup coconut milk
1 tsp palm or dark brown sugar
1 lime, juiced

- Mix together the marinade ingredients and pour over the chicken pieces.
- Leave to marinate for at least 4 hours or overnight.
- Skewer the chicken pieces and griddle over a high heat until blackened in patches and cooked through, around 6–8 minutes.
- Serve with the lime wedges and fresh coriander.

Satay chicken kebabs
Add a tablespoon of smooth peanut butter and a teaspoon of fish sauce to the marinade and stir well before coating the chicken.

Potato cakes with spiced beans

PREPARATION TIME: **20 minutes**
COOKING TIME: **15-20 minutes**
SERVES: **4**

1 kg / 2 ¼ lb / 4 ¼ cups cooked potatoes
3 tbsp butter
½ bunch fresh oregano
fresh chives, chopped
groundnut oil
2 tbsp plain (all-purpose) flour, seasoned
400 g cannellini beans, drained and washed
400 g can chopped tomatoes
1 tsp dried chilli (chili) flakes
1 tsp paprika

- Mash the potatoes thoroughly with the butter and salt and pepper until completely smooth. Mix with the herbs and shape into large patties.
- Dust both sides with seasoned flour. Heat a thin film of oil in a pan and cook the potato cakes 2 at a time until golden and crisp on both sides.
- For the beans, combine the beans and chopped tomatoes in a saucepan on medium heat. Add the chilli flakes, paprika, salt and pepper.
- Transfer the potato cakes onto a serving plate and spoon the beans on top. Garnish with the oregano and chives before serving.

Potato and sweetcorn cakes
Add 50 g of fresh or tinned sweetcorn to the mashed potato before adding the butter and herbs.

Sesame seed and Parmesan rolls

PREPARATION TIME: **2 hours**
COOKING TIME: **10 minutes**
MAKES: **12**

450 g / 1 lb / 2 cups strong white bread flour
2 tbsp butter
4 tbsp Parmesan
1 tsp sugar
1 tsp salt
1 ¼ tsp fast action dried yeast
275 ml / 9 ½ fl. oz / 1 cup warm water
1 egg yolk, beaten
3 tbsp white sesame seeds

- Place the flour in a bowl and rub in the butter using the pads of your fingertips until the mixture resembles breadcrumbs. Stir in the Parmesan, sugar, salt and enough water to make a soft, smooth dough.
- Turn out onto a floured surface and knead for 5 minutes until smooth and elastic. Return to the bowl, cover with cling film and leave in a warm place to rise for 1 hour or until doubled in size.
- Tip the dough back out onto the surface and knead well, then cut into 12 equal pieces. Shape into smooth balls with any seams tucked underneath and place on greased baking sheets, cover loosely and leave to rise for 30 minutes.
- Preheat the oven to 200°C (180°C fan) / 400F / gas 6. Brush with beaten egg, sprinkle over the sesame seeds, spray the tray lightly with water and bake for 10 minutes.

Wholemeal bread

PREPARATION TIME: **2 hours**
COOKING TIME: **25 minutes**
SERVES: **10**

300 g / 10 oz / 1 ¼ cups granary flour
1 tbsp butter
2 tsp soft brown sugar
½ tsp salt
1 tsp fast action dried yeast
175 ml / 6 fl. oz / ¾ cup warm water

- Tip the flour in a bowl, add the butter and rub in using your fingertips until it resembles breadcrumbs. Stir in the sugar, salt and yeast.
- Gradually add enough water to make a soft dough.
- Knead on a floured surface for 5 minutes until smooth and elastic. Place in a large bowl, cover loosely and leave in a warm place for 30 minutes or until the top of the dough reaches the top of the tin.
- Preheat the oven to 200°C (180°C fan) / 400F / gas 6.
- Remove the covering and bake the bread for 25 minutes or until browned and the loaf sounds hollow when tapped.
- Remove from the tin and transfer to a wire rack to cool. Serve with some butter and jam.

Seeded wholemeal bread
Sprinkle a tablespoon of flaxseeds and a tablespoon of sesame seeds on top of the loaf before baking.

Sesame bagels

PREPARATION TIME: **3 hours**
COOKING TIME: **12-15 minutes**
MAKES: **10**

500 g / 1 lb / 2 cups strong white bread flour
2 tbsp caster (superfine) sugar
1 tsp salt
1 ¼ tsp fast action dried yeast
300 ml / 10 fl. oz / 1 ¼ cups warm water
1 egg yolk, beaten
5 tbsp sesame seeds

- Mix the flour, half the sugar, salt and yeast in a large bowl, with enough water to make a dough. Knead on a floured surface for 5 minutes, then return to the bowl. Cover and leave for 1 hour.
- Tip the dough onto a floured surface again and knead. Cut into 10 equal pieces and roll into balls, then make a hole in the centre.
- Transfer to lined baking sheets, cover loosely and leave to rise for 30 minutes or until half as big again.
- Preheat the oven to 200°C (180°C fan) / 400F / gas 6. Bring 2 litres / 3 ½ pints of water to the boil in a pan with the remaining sugar. Lower the bagels into the water one at a time and cook for 2–3 minutes until they float. Remove with a slotted spoon and drain on kitchen paper.
- Transfer back to the baking sheets, brush with egg and sprinkle the seeds over the top.
- Bake for 12–15 minutes until golden brown.

Patatas bravas with tomato sauce

PREPARATION TIME: 25 minutes
COOKING TIME: 20 minutes
SERVES: 4

750 g / 1 ⅓ lb / 3 cups floury potatoes,
cut into small cubes

10 tbsp olive oil

3 cloves garlic, finely sliced

1 white onion, peeled and sliced

3 large tomatoes, skinned, deseeded and
finely chopped

4 tbsp passata

1 red chilli (chili), deseeded and chopped

1 tbsp paprika

fresh flat-leaf parsley, chopped

- Sprinkle the potatoes with salt and leave in a sieve for 10 minutes. Do not rinse afterwards.
- Add the potatoes to hot oil in a deep-sided frying pan and fry gently until soft but not coloured.
- Remove the potatoes from the pan, bring the oil back up to hot, then fry the potatoes again until crisp and golden brown. Drain on kitchen paper.
- Pour most of the oil out of the pan, then add the garlic and onion and fry for 1 minute. Add the tomatoes, passata, chilli and paprika and cook down until reduced and sticky.
- Adjust the seasoning and serve alongside the hot potatoes. Garnish with the chopped parsley.

Patatas bravas with green beans
Boil 200 g of green peas over a medium heat for 10 minutes, then and add the beans to the pan with the tomato sauce.

Steak and bean burritos

PREPARATION TIME: **25 minutes**
COOKING TIME: **10 minutes**
SERVES: **4**

2 tbsp vegetable oil
1 onion, peeled and finely sliced
350 g / 12 oz / 1 ½ cups rump steak, finely sliced
1 clove garlic, finely chopped
½ green chilli, finely chopped
1 tsp paprika
2 beefsteak tomatoes, diced
fresh coriander (cilantro)
4 flour tortillas, warmed briefly
400 g / 14 oz / 1 ½ cups refried beans, heated through
200 g / 7 oz cooked white or brown rice

- Heat the oil in a pan and fry the onion until softened. Add the steak, increase the heat and fry quickly for 2 minutes, adding the garlic, chilli, paprika, tomatoes and coriander. Remove from the heat.
- Lay the tortillas out on a surface and spoon the steak mixture down the middle and top with a line of refried beans and some rice.
- Wrap the tortilla around the filling and transfer onto serving plates.

Veggie burritos
Omit the steak and add some slices of grilled avocado and portobello mushrooms for a meaty texture.

Super seed flapjacks

PREPARATION TIME: **30 minutes**
COOKING TIME: **30 minutes**
MAKES: **5**

2 ripe bananas
100 ml / 3 ½ fl. oz / ⅓ cup raw honey
100 g / 3 ½ oz / ½ cup butter
450 g / 1 lb / 4 ½ cups rolled porridge oats
200 g / 7 oz / 1 ⅓ cups raisins
5 tbsp pumpkin seeds
5 tbsp sesame seeds
5 tbsp pumpkin seeds

- Preheat the oven to 190°C (170°C fan) / 375F / gas 5 and grease and line a 20 cm x 28 cm (8 in x 11 in) tray bake tin with greaseproof paper.
- Put the bananas in a blender with the honey and butter and blend until smooth. Stir in the oats, raisins and seeds, then spoon into a greased baking tin and level the surface.
- Bake for 30 minutes or until golden brown and cooked through.
- Cut into bars while still warm, but leave to cool completely before removing from the tin.

Nutty flapjacks
Replace the seeds with some mixed chopped nuts (such as pecans, almonds and walnuts) and follow the method as above.

Gluten-free shortbread biscuits

PREPARATION TIME: **35 minutes**
COOKING TIME: **20 minutes**
MAKES: **24**

120 g / 4 oz / ½ cup butter, softened
60 g / 2 oz / ¼ cup caster (superfine) sugar
180 g / 6 oz / ¾ cup ground almonds
1 tsp vanilla extract (optional)
icing (confectioners') sugar, for dusting

- Preheat the oven to 190°C (170°C fan) / 375F / gas 5.
- Cream the butter and sugar until pale and creamy.
- Whisk in the ground almonds a little at a time until thoroughly incorporated, adding the vanilla extract if desired. Turn the dough out onto a floured surface and roll out to 1 cm (½ inch) thickness.
- Cut out equal sized rounds or fingers and place on a baking tray. Refrigerate for 20 minutes.
- Bake in the oven for about 20 minutes or until pale gold. Set aside to cool on a wire rack, then dust with sugar.

Gluten-free lemon and poppy seed biscuits
Add the juice and zest of 2 lemons and a tablespoon of poppy seeds to the ground almonds before adding to the butter and sugar.

Chocolate hazelnut spread

PREPARATION TIME: **15 minutes**
COOKING TIME: **5 minutes**
MAKES: **1 jar**

100 g / 3 ½ oz / ½ cup dark chocolate, chopped
200 g / 7 oz / ¾ cup hazelnuts (cobnuts)
1 tbsp demerara sugar
50 ml / 1 ¾ fl. oz / ¼ cup coconut oil

- Place the chocolate in a bowl over a pan of simmering water and stir occasionally until melted. Set aside to cool.
- Toast the hazelnuts under a hot grill for a few seconds, watching them closely.
- Crush the nuts finely in a food processor, then add the sugar and a pinch of salt and combine well, scraping down the bowl as necessary.
- Add the melted chocolate until combined, then the oil in a steady stream until completely incorporated. Transfer to a sterilised jar and seal. Store in the refrigerator for at least 4 hours.

Healthy chocolate spread
For a healthier version, replace the demerara sugar with 2 tablespoons of coconut palm sugar, agave nectar or maple syrup.

White farmhouse loaf

PREPARATION TIME: **1 hour**
COOKING TIME: **25 minutes**
SERVES: **10**

300 g / 10 oz / 1 ¼ cups strong white bread flour
1 tbsp butter
1 tsp sugar
½ tsp salt
1 tbsp mixed dried herbs
1 tsp fast action dried yeast
175 ml / 6 fl. oz / ¾ cup warm water
a sprig of fresh rosemary, to garnish (optional)

- Tip the flour in a bowl, add the butter and rub in using the pads of your fingertips until it resembles breadcrumbs. Stir in the sugar, salt, mixed herbs and yeast.
- Gradually add enough water to make a soft dough.
- Knead on a floured surface for 5 minutes until smooth and elastic. Place in a greased 500 g / 1 lb loaf tin, cover loosely and leave in a warm place for 30 minutes or until the top of the dough reaches the top of the tin.
- Preheat the oven to 200°C (180°C fan) / 400F / gas 6.
- Remove the covering and bake for 25 minutes or until browned and sounds hollow when tapped.
- Remove from the tin and transfer to a wire rack to cool.
- Garnish with the rosemary and enjoy warm or cold.

Seeded farmhouse loaf
Cover the top of the loaf with 2 tablespoons of mixed seeds (such as flaxseeds, pumpkin seeds and sunflower seeds) before baking.

Lemon meringue cupcakes

PREPARATION TIME: 30 minutes
COOKING TIME: 30 minutes
MAKES: 12

120 g / 4 oz / ½ cup self-raising flour
120 g / 4 oz / ½ cup caster (superfine) sugar
120 g / 4 oz / ½ cup butter, softened
2 eggs, beaten
1 lemon, grated zest
1 tsp lemon extract
2 tbsp milk

FOR THE TOPPING
2 egg whites
120 g / 4 oz / ½ cup caster (superfine) sugar
blowtorch (optional)

- Preheat the oven to 200°C (180°C fan) / 400F / gas 6.
- Line a 12-hole muffin tin with cases.
- Place all the cupcake ingredients except the milk in a food processor and blitz until smooth and combined.
- Add the milk a little at a time to make a dropping consistency.
- Divide the mixture evenly between the cases and bake for 20 minutes or until risen and golden.
- Whisk the egg whites until stiff, then beat in a little sugar at a time until thick and glossy.
- For the best effect, use a piping bag to decorate the cupcakes, piling it up to make it look decorative.
- Go over the meringues with a blowtorch to colour. Alternatively, put under a preheated grill, checking regularly as this may only take a minute.

Honey and sultana scones

PREPARATION TIME: **20 minutes**
COOKING TIME: **15 minutes**
MAKES: **10-12**

225 g / 8 oz / 1 cup self-raising flour
60 g / 2 oz / ¼ cup butter, chilled and cubed
1 tbsp clear honey
1 lemon, zested
1 tbsp caster (superfine) sugar
1 tbsp sultanas
150 ml / 5 fl. oz / ⅔ cup milk

- Preheat the oven to 220°C (200°C fan) / 425F / gas 2. Lightly grease a baking sheet.
- Mix the flour with a pinch of salt in a bowl, then rub in the cubed butter using the pads of your fingertips until the mixture resembles breadcrumbs.
- Stir in the honey, lemon zest, sugar and sultanas, then the milk for a soft dough.
- Turn on to a floured surface and knead briefly, but do not overwork. Pat out to about 2 cm (1 inch) thick then use a cutter to cut out rounds. Place on a baking sheet. Keep gathering up the leftover dough to use up and stamp out more rounds.
- Brush with a little extra milk and bake for about 15 minutes or until golden and well risen.
- Cool on a wire rack before serving as desired.

Honey and cranberry scones
Replace the sultanas with the same amount of cranberries and follow the method as normal.

Ginger, toffee and chocolate shortbread

PREPARATION TIME: **30 minutes**
COOKING TIME: **35-40 minutes**
MAKES: **24**

225 g / 8 oz / 1 cup plain (all-purpose) flour
100 g / 3 ½ oz / ½ cup caster (superfine) sugar
1 tsp ground ginger
225 g / 8 oz / 1 cup butter, softened

FOR THE TOPPING
175 g / 6 oz / ¾ cup butter
175 g / 6 oz / ¾ cup caster (superfine) sugar
1 tsp ground ginger
4-5 tbsp golden syrup
400 g / 14 oz / 1 ½ cups condensed milk
200 g / 7 oz / ¾ cup dark chocolate

- Preheat the oven to 160°C (140°C fan) / 310F / gas 2. Lightly grease a rectangular tin.
- Whizz the flour, sugar, ginger and butter in a food processor until they form a smooth dough.
- Gather into a smooth ball and pat out flat with your hands. Press into the base of the tin and prick the base with a fork all over. Bake for 35–40 minutes until golden. Set aside to cool.
- Place the butter, sugar, ginger, syrup and condensed milk in a pan and stir over a low heat until the butter has melted.
- Bring the mixture gently to a bubble, then stir constantly until the mixture thickens and starts to look like fudge. Pour over the shortbread.
- Melt the chocolate in a bowl set over a pan of simmering water. Leave to cool enough so that it is still spreadable, then pour the chocolate over the fudge mixture and leave to set.
- Cut into 24 equal squares and serve.

Cardamom, toffee and chocolate shortbread
Replace the ground ginger with ground cardamom and follow the method as above.

Rich chocolate mint truffles

PREPARATION TIME: **20 minutes**
(plus chilling time)
SERVES: **4**

300 ml / 10 fl. oz / 1 ¼ cups double cream
2 tbsp butter
300 g / 10 oz / 1 ¼ cups dark chocolate, chopped
1 tsp peppermint extract
cocoa powder, for dusting

- Heat the cream and butter in a pan until simmering.
- Tip the chocolate into a bowl, then pour in the cream mixture and stir until the chocolate has melted and is fully incorporated.
- Add the peppermint extract, then chill in the fridge for about 4 hours.
- Roll the mixture into walnut-sized balls. Set on a baking sheet and dust with cocoa powder. Refrigerate until needed.

Chocolate and orange oil truffles
Replace the peppermint extract with the same amount of orange oil for a deliciously citrusy undertone.

Chocolate chip cookies

PREPARATION TIME: **20-30 minutes**
COOKING TIME: **20 minutes**
MAKES: **12-16**

150 g / 5 oz / ⅔ cup plain (all-purpose) flour
1 tsp bicarbonate of soda
120 g / 4 oz / ½ cup butter, softened
120 g / 4 oz / ½ cup caster (superfine) sugar
1 egg
1 tsp vanilla powder
350 g / 12 oz / 1 ½ cups chocolate chips, white or dark

- Preheat the oven to 170°C (150°C fan) / 325F / gas 3.
- Tip the flour and bicarbonate into a bowl and stir in a pinch of salt.
- Cream the butter and sugar in a bowl until pale and creamy.
- Whisk in the egg, then the dry ingredients together with the vanilla powder, then the chocolate chips.
- Roll the dough into even amounts and transfer to a lined baking sheet about 6 cm (2 ½ inches) apart. Cook for 20 minutes.
- Leave to cool, then transfer to a wire rack. Best eaten warm and soft.

Chocolate and ginger cookies
Add a teaspoon of ground ginger to the cookie dough with the dry ingredients and follow the method as normal.

Blueberry and almond muffins

PREPARATION TIME: **15 minutes**
COOKING TIME: **25 minutes**
MAKES: **12**

250 g / 9 oz / 1 cup caster (superfine) sugar
80 ml / 2 ½ fl. oz / ⅓ cup vegetable oil
1 egg
250 ml / 9 fl. oz / 1 cup buttermilk
200 g / 7 oz / ⅔ cup blueberries
150 g / 5 oz / ¾ cup plain (all-purpose) flour
150 g / 5 oz / ¾ cup ground almonds
2 tsp baking powder
1 tsp bicarbonate of soda

- Preheat the oven to 200°C (180°C fan) / 400F / gas 6.
- Line a 12-hole muffin tin.
- In a bowl, whisk together the sugar, oil, egg and buttermilk.
- Stir through the blueberries, reserving a few to garnish. Then sieve in the flour and ground almonds with the baking powder and bicarbonate of soda. Fold until lightly blended, but still a little lumpy. This will help keep the muffins light.
- Spoon evenly into the muffin cases or parchment paper then bake for about 25 minutes or until golden and risen.
- Garnish with some fresh blueberries before enjoying.

Vegan blueberry muffins
Replace the egg with a mashed banana and the buttermilk with the same amount of non-dairy milk (such as soya or almond).

Mixed fruit scones

PREPARATION TIME: **20 minutes**
COOKING TIME: **15 minutes**
MAKES: **10-12**

225 g / 8 oz / 1 cup self-raising flour
60 g / 2 oz / ¼ cup butter, chilled and cubed
1 tbsp sultanas
1 tbsp raisins
1 tbsp chopped dried figs
1 tbsp caster (superfine) sugar
150 ml / 5 fl. oz / ⅔ cup milk

• Preheat the oven to 220°C (200°C fan) / 425F / gas
  2. Lightly grease a baking sheet.
• Mix the flour and a pinch of salt in a bowl,
  then rub in the cubed butter using the pads
  of your fingertips until the mixture resembles
  breadcrumbs.
• Stir in the dried fruit and sugar, then the milk
  for a soft dough. Turn on to a floured surface and
  knead briefly, but do not overwork. Pat out to
  about 2 cm (1 inch) thick and divide into square
  or triangular scones. Place on a baking sheet.
• Keep gathering up the leftover dough to use up
  and shape. Brush with a little extra milk and
  bake for about 15 minutes or until golden and
  well risen. Cool on a wire rack before splitting
  in half and serve with some plain yogurt and
  dried fruit.

Cinnamon and raisin scones
Omit the figs and add a teaspoon of ground
cinnamon to the dried ingredients before adding
the milk and mixing to a dough.

Strawberry and raspberry jam

PREPARATION TIME: **24 hours**
COOKING TIME: **30 minutes**
MAKES: **1.5 kg / 3 lbs**

½ kg / 1 lb / 2 cups strawberries, not too ripe and soft
½ kg / 1 lb / 2 cups raspberries
850 g / 1 ½ lb / 3 ½ cups sugar
2 lemons, juiced

• Hull the strawberries and wipe clean, then layer
  them in a preserving pan or large saucepan with
  the raspberries, sprinkling with sugar.
• Leave overnight to macerate.
• Place the pan over a low heat to melt the sugar
  and allow the berries to pulp slightly. Try not to
  stir as this will break the berries up – just shake
  the pan a little.
• When the sugar has completely dissolved, add
  the lemon juice, increase the heat and when
  bubbling, cook for 8 minutes before removing
  from the heat.
• Spoon a little onto a plate. If it wrinkles when
  you push it with your finger, it's set. If not, cook
  for 3 minutes, then repeat the test. Continue
  until the jam is set.
• Allow the jam to settle off the heat for 15
  minutes before pouring into sterilised jars. Seal
  immediately with waxed lids.

Raspberry and blackberry jam
Replace the strawberries with the same amount
of blackberries and follow the method as above.

Cinnamon
iced buns

PREPARATION TIME: **2 hours**
COOKING TIME: **30 minutes**
MAKES: **24**

75 ml / 3 fl. oz / ⅓ cup lukewarm water
½ tsp dried yeast
50 ml / 1 ¾ fl. oz / ¼ cup maple syrup
50 ml / 1 ¾ fl. oz / ¼ cup butter, melted
1 egg, beaten
500 g / 1lb 1 oz / 2 cups plain (all-purpose) flour

FOR THE FILLING
40g / 1 ½ oz / butter, melted
1 tbsp ground cinnamon
¼ tsp grated nutmeg
2 tbsp soft dark brown sugar
2 tbsp maple syrup
3 tbsp pecans, chopped
2 tbsp sultanas

FOR THE ICING
500 g / 1 lb 1 oz icing sugar

- Tip the water, yeast and half the maple syrup into a bowl and leave for 15 minutes until it starts to bubble.
- Add the rest of the syrup, melted butter, egg and a little salt and mix.
- Tip the flour into a bowl and make a well in the centre. Pour in the yeast mixture and bring the flour into the liquid working until everything is combined.
- Tip out of the bowl onto a floured surface and knead for 8–10 minutes. Place back into the bowl, cover and leave to rise for 1 hour.
- Preheat the oven to 170°C (150°C fan) / 325F / gas 4.
- Knock the dough back and roll on a floured surface to make 38 x 25 cm (15 x 10 inch) rectangle. Brush with melted butter, then sprinkle over the rest of the filling ingredients. Roll the dough up like a fat sausage. Gently stretch it out with your hands to about 60 cm (24 inch) in length.
- Cut the roll into 5–6 cm (2 inch) lengths and place in greased muffin tins.
- Bake in the oven for 30 minutes. Remove to a wire rack to cool.
- Mix the icing ingredients together in a bowl and add enough water until it reaches a thick but runny consistency.
- Drizzle the icing over the buns in a zigzag pattern. Leave to cool at room temperature.

Honey gingerbread loaf

PREPARATION TIME: 20 minutes
COOKING TIME: 45 minutes
SERVES: 6

250 g / 9 oz / 1 cup self-raising flour
1 tsp baking powder
½ tsp bicarbonate of soda
½ tsp ground ginger
½ tsp ground cinnamon
½ tsp mixed spice
200 ml / 7 fl. oz / ¾ cup milk
1 egg
75 g / 2 ½ oz / ⅓ cup honey
75 g / 2 ½ oz / ⅓ cup unsalted butter, melted
2–3 tbsp stem ginger, finely chopped
a handful of raisins
a handful of flaked almonds, to sprinkle
1 tbsp sugar crystals, to sprinkle (optional)

- Preheat the oven to 200°C (180°C fan) / 400F / gas 6. Grease and line a loaf tin.
- In one bowl, combine the dry ingredients.
- Pour the milk in to a measuring jug and crack in the egg and whisk with a fork to combine.
- Pour the liquid ingredients into the dry ingredients, stirring with a wooden spoon. The batter should remain somewhat lumpy – do not whisk until smooth. Add the stem ginger and raisins to the batter and stir in.
- Pour into the loaf tin and sprinkle with the flaked almonds and sugar crystals.
- Bake in the oven for about 45 minutes or until an inserted skewer comes out clean.
- Remove to a wire rack and allow to cool.

Maple and lemon loaf
Replace the honey with the same amount of maple syrup for a deeper flavour. Add the zest of a lemon to the dry ingredients for a citrusy twist.

Chocolate buttercream cupcakes

PREPARATION TIME: **25 minutes**
COOKING TIME: **20 minutes**
MAKES: **12**

120 g / 4 oz / ½ cup self-raising flour
120 g / 4 oz / ½ cup caster (superfine) sugar
120 g / 4 oz / ½ cup butter, softened
2 eggs, beaten
1 tbsp cocoa powder
1 tsp vanilla essence
2 tbsp milk

FOR THE TOPPING
90 g / 3 ½ oz / milk chocolate, chopped
350 g / 12 oz / / 1 ½ cups butter, softened
300 g / 10 ½ oz / 1 ¼ cups icing (confectioners') sugar
120 ml / 4 fl. oz / ½ cup double cream
chocolate sprinkles, for decorating

- Preheat the oven to 200°C (180°C fan) / 400F / gas 6.
- Line a 12-hole muffin tin with cases.
- Place all the cupcake ingredients except the milk in a food processor and blitz until smooth and combined. Add the milk a little at a time to make a dropping consistency.
- Divide the mixture evenly between the cases and bake for 20 minutes or until risen and golden.
- Meanwhile place the chocolate in a bowl set over a pan of simmering water and stir until melted.
- Set aside to cool slightly.
- Whisk the butter and icing sugar until pale, then whisk in the melted chocolate. Whisk in the cream until smooth and lightened.
- Remove the cakes from the tin to a wire rack to cool, then use a piping bag to add the icing. Decorate with the chocolate sprinkles.

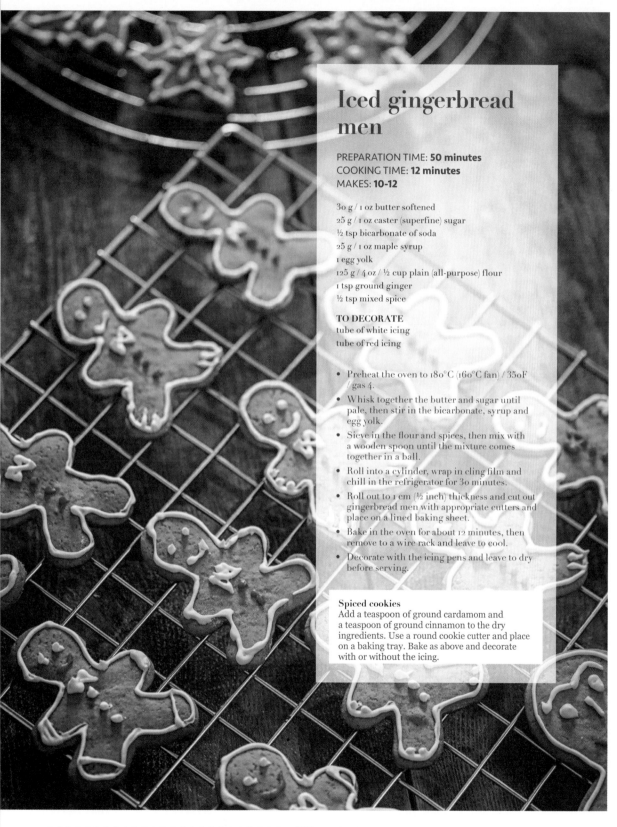

Iced gingerbread men

PREPARATION TIME: 50 minutes
COOKING TIME: 12 minutes
MAKES: 10-12

30 g / 1 oz butter softened
25 g / 1 oz caster (superfine) sugar
½ tsp bicarbonate of soda
25 g / 1 oz maple syrup
1 egg yolk
125 g / 4 oz / ½ cup plain (all-purpose) flour
1 tsp ground ginger
½ tsp mixed spice

TO DECORATE
tube of white icing
tube of red icing

- Preheat the oven to 180°C (160°C fan) / 350F / gas 4.
- Whisk together the butter and sugar until pale, then stir in the bicarbonate, syrup and egg yolk.
- Sieve in the flour and spices, then mix with a wooden spoon until the mixture comes together in a ball.
- Roll into a cylinder, wrap in cling film and chill in the refrigerator for 30 minutes.
- Roll out to 1 cm (½ inch) thickness and cut out gingerbread men with appropriate cutters and place on a lined baking sheet.
- Bake in the oven for about 12 minutes, then remove to a wire rack and leave to cool.
- Decorate with the icing pens and leave to dry before serving.

Spiced cookies
Add a teaspoon of ground cardamom and a teaspoon of ground cinnamon to the dry ingredients. Use a round cookie cutter and place on a baking tray. Bake as above and decorate with or without the icing.

Vanilla cupcakes with buttercream

PREPARATION TIME: **20 minutes**
COOKING TIME: **20 minutes**
MAKES: **12**

120 g / 4 oz / ½ cup self-raising flour
120 g / 4 oz / ½ cup caster (superfine) sugar
120 g / 4 oz / ½ cup butter, softened
2 eggs, beaten
1 tsp vanilla extract
2 tbsp milk

FOR THE BUTTERCREAM
350 g / 12 oz / / 1 ½ cups butter, softened
300 g / 10 ½ oz / 1 ¼ cups icing (confectioners') sugar
120 ml / 4 fl. oz / ½ cup double (heavy) cream

- Preheat the oven to 200°C (180°C fan) / 400F / gas 6.
- Line a 12-hole muffin tin with cases.
- Place all the ingredients except the milk in a food processor and blitz until smooth and combined.
- Add the milk a little at a time to make a dropping consistency.
- Divide the mixture evenly between the cases and bake for 20 minutes or until risen and golden.
- Remove the cakes from the tin to a wire rack to cool.
- For the buttercream, whisk the butter and icing sugar until pale. Whisk in the cream until smooth and lightened.
- Remove the cakes from the tin to a wire rack to cool then use a piping bag to add the icing.

White chocolate chip cookies

PREPARATION TIME: **1 hour, 20 minutes**
COOKING TIME: **15 minutes**
MAKES: **30-40**

370 g / 13 oz / 1 ½ cups plain (all-purpose) flour
250 g / 9 oz / 1 cup butter, softened
120 g / 4 oz / ½ cup caster (superfine) sugar
1 egg yolk
100 g / 3 oz white chocolate chips
1 tsp vanilla extract

- Sieve the flour and a pinch of salt into a bowl. Set aside.
- Cream the butter and sugar until pale and creamy. Whisk in the egg yolk, chocolate chips and vanilla extract, then work in the flour a little at a time.
- Bring the dough together into a ball, wrap in cling film and refrigerate for 1 hour.
- Preheat the oven to 180°C (160°C fan) / 350F / gas 4. Roll the dough out on a floured surface to about 3 mm thickness. Cut out with your preferred cookie cutter shapes, or simply stamp out circles and place on lined baking sheets.
- Bake for about 15 minutes until pale gold. Transfer to a wire rack to cool.

Milk chocolate and chilli cookies
Replace the white chocolate chips with the same amount of plain chocolate chips. For a spicy kick, add a teaspoon chilli (chili) flakes or ground ginger.

Orange and cardamom mince pies

PREPARATION TIME: 45 minutes
COOKING TIME: 15 minutes
MAKES: 36-40

250 g / 9 oz / 1 cup plain (all-purpose) flour
60 g / 2 oz butter, chilled
60 g / 2 oz vegetable shortening or baking
block, chilled
juice and zest of 1 orange
1 tsp orange essence
1 tsp ground cardamom
250 g / 9 oz / 1 cup mincemeat
icing (confectioners') sugar, to dust

- Whizz the flour, butter and shortening in a food processor until the mixture resembles breadcrumbs. Pour in the orange juice and a pinch of salt until the mixture starts to come together.

- Remove from the bowl and form into 3 balls. Press into a disc, cover with cling film and refrigerate for 20 minutes.

- Preheat the oven to 220°C (200°C fan) / 425F / gas 7.

- Roll out the discs as thinly as possible and use to line 4.5 cm (2 inch) tart tins – you may need to make these in batches if you don't have enough tart tins.

- Combine the orange essence, ground cardamom and mincemeat. Stir well.

- Place a spoonful of mincemeat in the base.

- Reroll any leftover pastry and use to cut out star shapes. Press lightly on top of the mincemeat.

- Bake for 15 minutes or until pale gold. Remove from the oven and cool on a wire rack.

- Dust with some icing sugar, before serving.

Lemon and cardamom mince pies
Replace the orange essence with lemon essence and the orange with the juice and zest of 2 lemons. Follow the method as above.

Bakewell and chocolate tart

PREPARATION TIME: **2 hours**
COOKING TIME: **45 minutes**
SERVES: **8**

FOR THE DOUGH
200 g / 7 oz plain flour
40 g / 1 ½ oz / ½ cup icing (confectioners') sugar
100 g / 4 oz / 1 stick butter, diced
1 small egg, beaten

FOR THE FILLING
200 g / 7 oz / 1 cup of whole almonds
130 g / 4 ½ oz of soft butter, unsalted
120 g / 4 ½ oz of sugar
3 eggs
5 glacé cherries, chopped
300 g / 11 oz of raspberry jam (jelly)
100 g milk chocolate, melted

- Butter and flour the pan. To prepare the dough, sift together the flour and icing sugar.
- Add the cold butter into cubes and work with fingertips. Add a pinch of salt and the beaten egg, working by hand until forming a ball. Wrap in cling film and refrigerate for 30 minutes.
- Chop the unblanched whole almonds finely. Meanwhile, whisk the butter and sugar until the mixture becomes creamy. Add the eggs, cherries and the almonds and whisk together.
- Spread the dough on a floured surface and line the mould with it. Refrigerate for 1 hour.
- Blind bake the pastry covered in foil and weighted down with rice or beans for 10 minutes in a preheated oven at 180°C / 350°F / gas 6.
- Let cool a few minutes then pour over the raspberry jam and smooth over. Spread the almond mix on top.
- Bake for 35 minutes then remove from the oven to cool for 30 minutes.
- Drizzle over the milk chocolate before serving.

Blueberry and vanilla cupcakes

PREPARATION TIME: **30 minutes**
COOKING TIME: **20 minutes**
MAKES: **12**

120 g / 4 oz / ½ cup self-raising flour
120 g / 4 oz / ½ cup caster (superfine) sugar
240 g / 8 oz / 1 cup butter, softened
2 eggs, beaten
2 tsp vanilla extract
2 tbsp milk
200 g / 7 oz / ⅔ cup blueberries
250 g / 9 oz / 1 cup icing (confectioners') sugar

- Preheat the oven to 200°C (180°C fan) / 400F / gas 6. Line a 12-hole muffin tin with cases.
- Place the flour, sugar, half of the butter, egg and half of the vanilla extract in a food processor and blitz until smooth and combined.
- Add the milk, a little at a time, to make a dropping consistency, then stir in the blueberries, reserving a few for decoration.
- Divide the mixture evenly between the cases and bake for 20 minutes or until risen and golden.
- Meanwhile, cream the remaining butter with the icing sugar until pale and creamy, then stir in the rest of the vanilla extract. Remove the cakes from the tin to a wire rack to cool. Pipe the icing over the top and decorate with the remaining fresh blueberries.

Sticky orange muffins

PREPARATION TIME: **20 minutes**
COOKING TIME: **20 minutes**
MAKES: **12**

120 g / 4 oz / ½ cup self-raising flour
120 g / 4 oz / ½ cup caster (superfine) sugar
120 g / 4 oz / ½ cup butter, softened
2 eggs, beaten
2 tbsp milk
1 tsp orange extract
1 large orange, grated zest and juiced
4 tbsp maple syrup

- Preheat the oven to 200°C (180°C fan) / 400F / gas 6. Line a 12-hole muffin tin with cases.
- Place all the flour, sugar, butter and eggs in a food processor and blitz until smooth and combined. Add the milk, a little at a time, to make a dropping consistency.
- Divide the mixture evenly between the cases and bake for 20 minutes or until risen and golden.
- Meanwhile combine the remaining ingredients and stir well to make an orange syrup.
- Remove the cakes from the tin to a wire rack to cool, then drizzle the orange syrup on top before serving.

Sticky lemon muffins
Replace the orange essence for lemon extract and for the syrup, use two medium lemons instead of the orange (juiced and zested).

Vanilla and almond fudge

PREPARATION TIME: **45 minutes**
(plus setting time)
MAKES: **36**

300 ml / 10 fl. oz / 1 ¼ cups milk
350 g / 12 oz / 1 ½ cups caster (superfine) sugar
100 g / 3 ½ oz / ½ cup butter
1 tsp vanilla extract
36 whole almonds

- Lightly grease an 18 cm (7 in) tin.
- Place the ingredients, except the vanilla and almonds in a saucepan and heat slowly, stirring constantly, until the sugar has dissolved and the butter has melted.
- Bring to the boil and boil for 15–20 minutes, stirring constantly, until the mixture reaches 'soft ball' stage (115°C) or until a small amount of mixture dropped into a glass of cold water will form a soft ball that you can pick up on the end of a teaspoon. Remove from the heat, stir in the vanilla and leave to cool for 5 minutes.
- Using a wooden spoon, beat the mixture until it thickens and the shine disappears and it starts to look more opaque.
- Pour into the tin and set at room temperature. Once set, cut into squares and press an almond firmly into the top of each square.

Vanilla and pecan fudge
Replace the almond with a pecan half and press into each piece of fudge.

Croissants with jam centre

PREPARATION TIME: 2 hours, plus overnight
COOKING TIME: 15 minutes
MAKES: 20

625 g / 1 lb 5 oz / 2 ¾ cups strong white (bread) flour
12 g / ½ oz salt
75 g / 3 oz / ⅓ cup sugar
20 g / ¾ oz dried yeast
500 g / 1 lb / 2 cups butter, cold, cubed
1 egg, beaten
20 tsp strawberry jam

- Place the flour, salt, sugar and yeast in a bowl and stir in enough water to make a pliable dough.
- Tip onto a floured surface, bring together and knead for 5–8 minutes. Refrigerate for 1 hour.
- Remove from the fridge, roll out on a floured surface into a 60 x 30 cm (24 x 12 inch) rectangle.
- Roll out the butter in the middle of the dough rectangle into a 40 x 30 cm (16 x 12 inch) rectangle so it covers two thirds of the dough. Fold the remaining dough third over the butter layer, then fold over the buttered half so the dough now has 3 layers with two layers of butter sandwiched in between. Wrap in cling film and refrigerate for another hour.
- Flour the work surface and roll the dough out again to 60 x 30 cm and repeat the folding process, then refrigerate again for another hour.
- Repeat twice more, wrap in film and rest overnight.
- The next day, roll out the dough to around 3 mm thickness and cut into 20 x 20 cm (8 x 8 inch) squares.
- Cut each square in half diagonally to make 2 triangles and place on a lightly floured surface.
- Spoon a teaspoon of jam into the centre of each triangle.
- Roll each dough triangle up without pressing down too hard and curl round to make the traditional crescent shape. Place on lined baking trays and leave to rise for 1 hour in warm place. Preheat the oven to 200°C (180°C fan) / 400F / gas 6.
- Lightly brush with beaten egg and bake for about 15 minutes or until golden brown and crisp.

Croissants with chocolate centre
Replace the jam with the same amount of chocolate spread (1 teaspoon per croissant) for a decadent treat.

Chocolate chip and orange muffins

PREPARATION TIME: **15 minutes**
COOKING TIME: **25 minutes**
MAKES: **12**

250 g / 9 oz / 1 cup caster (superfine) sugar
80 ml / 2 ½ fl. oz / ⅓ cup vegetable oil
1 egg
2 tbsp cocoa powder
1 tsp orange essence
250 ml / 9 fl. oz / 1 cup buttermilk
200 g / 7 oz / ⅔ cup dark chocolate chips
300 g / 10 oz / 1 ¼ cups plain (all-purpose) flour
2 tsp baking powder
1 tsp bicarbonate of soda

- Preheat the oven to 200°C (180°C fan) / 400F / gas 6. Line a 12-hole muffin tin.
- In a bowl, whisk together the sugar, oil, egg, cocoa powder, orange essence and buttermilk.
- Stir through the chocolate chips, then sieve in the flour with the baking powder and bicarbonate. Fold until lightly blended, but still a little lumpy. This will help keep the muffins light.
- Spoon evenly into the muffin cases then bake for about 25 minutes or until golden and risen.

Chocolate chip and vanilla muffins
Replace the orange essence with the same amount of vanilla essence and a teaspoon of vanilla powder for a sweet and creamy treat.

Pain au chocolat

PREPARATION TIME: **2 hours - make the day before**
COOKING TIME: **15 minutes**
MAKES: **12**

625 g / 1 lb 5 oz / 2 ¾ cups strong white (bread) flour
12 g / ½ oz salt
75 g / 3 oz / ⅓ cup sugar
20 g / ¾ oz dried yeast
500 g / 1 lb / 2 cups butter, cold, cubed
1 egg, beaten
250 g / 9 oz / 1 cup dark chocolate, 70%, cut into thick batons
icing (confectioners') sugar, to dust (optional)

- Place the flour, salt, sugar and yeast in a bowl and stir in enough water to make a pliable dough.
- Tip onto a floured surface, bring together and knead for 5–8 minutes. Refrigerate for 1 hour.
- Remove from the fridge, roll out on a floured surface into a 60 x 30 cm (24 x 12 inch) rectangle.
- Roll the dough out to about 6mm thick and cut into 12 x 12 cm (4 ½ x 4 ½ inch) squares.
- Place a chocolate baton at the top and base of each dough square and fold the pastry over repeatedly until it meets in the middle.
- Brush with beaten egg and place on a lined baking sheet to rest for 1 hour in a warm place.
- Preheat the oven to 200°C (180°C fan) / 400F / gas 6.
- Bake the pastries for about 15 minutes or until risen and golden.
- Cool on a wire rack for 5 minutes and dust with a little icing sugar.

Chocolate and vanilla whoopie pies

PREPARATION TIME: **30 minutes**
COOKING TIME: **8-12 minutes**
MAKES: **16-20**

150 g / 5 oz / ⅔ cup dark chocolate
1 tbsp butter
225 g / 8 oz / 1 cup caster (superfine) sugar
3 eggs
1 tsp vanilla extract
250 g / 9 oz / 1 cup plain (all-purpose) flour
1 tbsp cocoa powder
½ tsp baking powder
16-20 vanilla marshmallows

- Preheat the oven to 180°C (160°C fan) / 350F / gas 4. Line a baking tray.
- Melt the chocolate and butter in a bowl over a pan of simmering water. Set aside to cool a little.
- Whisk the sugar, eggs and vanilla together, then fold in the chocolate and cinnamon.
- Sieve the flour, cocoa and baking powder into a bowl, then fold into the chocolate mixture.
- Spoon tablespoons of the mixture (an even number) on to the baking tray, and bake for 8 minutes.
- Remove from the oven and place half the biscuits on a wire rack. Turn the remaining biscuits flat side up and top with a marshmallow. Return to the oven for 3 minutes. Press the cooled biscuits on top of the marshmallow.

Lemon curd

PREPARATION TIME: **5 minutes**
COOKING TIME: **20 minutes**
MAKES: **200g**

1 large lemon, grated zest plus juice
1 tsp lemon extract
75 g / 2 ½ oz / ⅓ cup caster (superfine) sugar
2 eggs
50 g / 1 ¾ oz butter

- Place the zest and sugar in one bowl. Place the juice and eggs
- in another and whisk together, then pour over the sugar.
- Add the butter, cubed up, and set over a pan of simmering water.
- Add the lemon extract and stir constantly until the mixture thickens and starts to look glossy. Approximately 18–20 minutes.
- Remove from the heat and cool. Spoon into a sterilised jar before storing.

Orange curd
Replace the lemon zest, juice and extract with the same approximate quantities of orange for a sweeter, less sour flavour.

Classic hot cross buns

PREPARATION TIME: 2 hours
COOKING TIME: 15 minutes
MAKES: 12

500 g / 1 lb / 2 cups strong white bread flour
75 g / 2 ½ oz / ⅓ cup butter
3 tbsp caster (superfine) sugar
1 tsp salt
1 tsp ground cinnamon
½ tsp ground mixed spice
¼ tsp grated nutmeg
1 ½ tsp fast action dried yeast
1 egg, beaten
275 ml / 9 ½ fl. oz / 1 scant cup milk
120 g / 4 oz / ½ cup golden sultanas
120 g / 4 oz / ½ cup sultanas (normal)

TO DECORATE
120 g / 4 oz / ½ cup plain (all-purpose) flour
8 tbsp water
4 tbsp milk
2 tbsp sugar

- Place the flour in a large bowl and rub in the butter using the pads of your fingertips until the mixture resembles breadcrumbs.
- Stir in the sugar, salt, spices and yeast, whisk in the egg and then gradually add the milk.
- Knead on a floured surface for 5 minutes until the dough is smooth and elastic. Work in the sultanas, then return to the bowl, cover with cling film and leave in a warm place to rise for 1 hour or until doubled in size.
- Tip the dough out onto the surface and knead well for 5 minutes. Cut into 12 equal pieces, then shape each one into a smooth ball, tucking any joins or seams underneath. Place, spaced well apart, on a greased baking sheet. Cover again with oiled cling film and leave in a warm place for 30 minutes.
- Preheat the oven to 200°C / 400F / gas 6.
- To make the crosses, sieve the flour into a small bowl and mix in the water to make a smooth paste. Pipe crosses onto the buns.
- Bake in the oven for about 15 minutes.
- Meanwhile place the milk and sugar in a pan and heat until the sugar has dissolved and the liquid is syrupy. Brush over the baked buns, transfer to a wire rack and cool.

Main meals

Poppy seed steak and kidney pie

PREPARATION TIME: 2 hours, 30 minutes
COOKING TIME: 45 minutes
SERVES: 4

FOR THE FILLING

2 tbsp vegetable oil or beef dripping
750 g / 1 ⅓ lb / 3 cups stewing beef
200 g / 7 oz / ¾ cup ox kidney, chopped
2 onions, peeled and chopped
1 tbsp tomato purée
1 ½ tbsp plain (all-purpose) flour
2 bay leaves
2 tbsp Worcestershire sauce
450 ml / 15 fl. oz / 1 ¾ cups beef stock
225 g / 8 oz / 1 cup mushrooms, sliced
4 pastry cases
8 florets of tenderstem broccoli, ends removed
1 tsp poppy seeds

- To make the filling, heat the fat in a pan and brown the meat on all sides. Remove with a slotted spoon and add the onions. Cook until softened and golden.

- Stir in the tomato purée, cook out for a few seconds, then tip the meat back into the pan with all its juices. Stir in the flour to make a paste, then the bay leaves, Worcestershire sauce and stock. Season and simmer very gently for 1 ½–2 hours until the meat is tender.

- Tip the filling into the pie dishes to come level with the top of the pastry – reserve any excess liquid for gravy. Use a couple of upturned egg cups in the filling to support the lid of the pastry, then carefully place the larger half of pastry onto the pie. Seal the edges by crimping. Brush the pastry with beaten egg then sprinkle the poppy seeds on top. Make a little hole in the top for the steam to escape

- Bake in the oven for about 40–45 minutes until the pastry is golden brown.

- Meanwhile, bring a pan to boil and add the tenderstem broccoli. Cook for 4–5 minutes.

- Serve the pies alongside the broccoli.

Lamb, potato and carrot hotpot

PREPARATION TIME: 25 minutes
COOKING TIME: 2 hours, 15 minutes
SERVES: 2-4

2 tbsp vegetable oil or dripping

1 kg / 2 ½ lb / 4 ½ cups neck of lamb, cut into large chunks

4 lamb's kidneys, cored and chopped small

4 large Maris Piper potatoes, peeled and quartered

1 tbsp butter

1 tbsp flour

4 white onions, peeled and chopped

500 ml / 1 pint / 2 cups lamb stock or water

1 tbsp Worcestershire sauce

2 bay leaves

4 carrots, peeled and chopped

fresh flat-leaf parsley, to garnish

- Preheat the oven to 170C / 325F / gas 3.
- Heat the fat in a large casserole and dry the meat in batches until browned. Add the kidney and cook alongside. Remove with a slotted spoon and set aside.
- Adding a little butter, cook the onions until translucent, then stir in the flour to make a paste.
- Whisk in the stock and Worcestershire sauce to make a smooth sauce and bring to a simmer. Return the meat and kidneys to the sauce.
- Add the vegetables and herbs and season to taste.
- Cover with a lid and cook for 1 ½ hours, then remove the lid and add a little water if the contents are sticking. Cook for a further 45 minutes.

Beef, potato and carrot hotpot
Replace the lamb with the same amount of beef and follow the method as above.

Sausage, cheese and potato gratin

PREPARATION TIME: **15 minutes**
COOKING TIME: **30 minutes**
SERVES: **2**

2 large floury potatoes, peeled and sliced
2 tbsp butter
2 tbsp vegetable oil
1 onion, thickly sliced
2 carrots, peeled and thickly sliced
4 Cumberland sausages, cut into chunks
200 ml / 7 fl oz / ¾ cup chicken stock
grated mozzarella, to sprinkle
1 sprig thyme
grated Cheddar, to sprinkle

- Cook the potatoes in boiling salted water until tender. Drain then set to one side.
- Heat the butter and oil in a pan and cook the onion until soft and sweet. Add the carrots and cook for a further 10 minutes until soft.
- Add the sausages and cook for another 10 minutes, then pour over the stock and thyme and bubble up.
- Spoon into a gratin dish and season. Top with the sliced potato, then top with the cheese.
- Grill until golden and bubbling.

Cheese, bean and potato gratin
Replace the sausage with two 400 g tins of cooked mixed beans for a vegetarian version. Add some garden peas (optional) and follow the method as above.

Penne with spicy chorizo

PREPARATION TIME: **5 minutes**
COOKING TIME: **10 minutes**
SERVES: **2**

200 g / 7 oz penne pasta
1 tbsp olive oil
100 g / 3 ½ oz / ½ cup chorizo sausage, sliced
400 g chopped tomatoes
1 tsp dried chilli (chili) flakes
flat-leaf parsley, chopped

- Cook the pasta according to packet instructions.
- Drain and set aside.
- Meanwhile heat the oil in a pan and fry the chorizo until the fat runs and the onion is soft.
- Add the chopped tomatoes and cook for a further 5 minutes.
- Toss in the pasta then add the chilli flakes. Serve topped with the parsley.

Penne with smoked paprika and Parmesan
Add 1 tsp of smoked paprika to the chopped tomatoes and chorizo. Cook as above and then garnish with some freshly grated Parmesan before serving.

Curried new potatoes with nigella seeds

PREPARATION TIME: **5 minutes**
COOKING TIME: **15-20 minutes**
SERVES: **4**

500 g / 1 lb / 2 cups new potatoes, peeled and cut into chunks
3 tbsp groundnut oil
1 tsp nigella seeds
½ tbsp ground cumin
½ tbsp ground coriander
1 tsp turmeric
fresh parsley, to garnish

- Cook the potatoes in boiling salted water for 5 minutes.
- Drain thoroughly.
- Heat the oil in a large lidded pan and cook the nigella seeds for 30 seconds.
- Add the potatoes, coat in the spices, add a glass of water and cook with the lid on, turning regularly, for 10 minutes or until golden and starting to crisp.
- Add a little more water if the pan looks too dry, put the lid back on and cook for a few more minutes.
- Season and serve hot with the parsley.

Curried potatoes with shallots
Peel and slice 5 shallots and to the pan with the potatoes. Cook as above and serve with a wedge of lemon on the side.

BBQ chicken with spring onions

PREPARATION TIME: **1 hour**
COOKING TIME: **10 minutes**
SERVES: **4**

8 chicken thighs, boned and skinned
2 tsp Chinese 5 spice
2 tbsp runny honey
1 tbsp soy sauce
1 tbsp groundnut oil
4 spring onions (scallions), finely sliced
1 clove garlic, crushed

- Cut the chicken into bite size pieces.
- Marinate the chicken for at least 1 hour in the 5 spice, honey and soy sauce.
- Heat the oil in a wok until nearly smoking, then add some of the spring onions and garlic and stir-fry for a few seconds.
- Add the chicken, shaking off any marinade, and stir-fry over a high heat until just cooked through.
- Add the reserved marinade and bubble up until thickened and coats the chicken.
- Serve scattered with some more spring onions.

BBQ chicken with cashews and sesame seeds
Add a handful of chopped cashews and 1 tsp sesame seeds to the chicken once it's cooked.

Spicy braised pork with onions

PREPARATION TIME: **40 minutes**
COOKING TIME: **3 hours, 30 minutes**
SERVES: **4**

1 piece pork, about 2 kg / 4 ½ lb, cut into large chunks

250ml / 9 fl oz / 1 cup dry sherry or Shaoxing rice wine

1 l / 2 ¼ pints / 4 ¼ cups chicken stock

8 tbsp soy sauce

100g / 3 ½ oz / ½ cup sugar

3 cm piece fresh ginger, sliced

4 cloves garlic, sliced

1 white onion, peeled and sliced

1 tbsp Chinese 5 spice

2 star anise

1 stick cinnamon

1 red chilli (chili), pricked with a knife

flat-leaf parsley, chopped

- Add the pork to a pan of boiling water, reduce the heat and simmer gently, skimming, for 30 minutes to remove excess fat. Drain well.
- Combine the rest of the ingredients in a large stockpot and bring to a simmer.
- Add the blanched pork, return to a gentle simmer and cook for 3 hours, covered with a lid, skimming occasionally until the pork is very tender.
- Skim as much fat as possible from the braising liquid and reduce over a high heat by half.
- Serve the pork in small bowls with the braising liquid poured over. Serve with a side of rice (optional) and garnish with some parsley.

Braised chicken with shallots
Replace the pork with the same amount of chicken breast. Peel and roughly chop 5 shallots to replace the onion.

Mushroom tart

PREPARATION TIME: **25 minutes**
COOKING TIME: **30 minutes**
SERVES: **8**

60 g / 2 oz / ¼ cup butter
1kg / 2 ¼ lb / 4 ¼ cups mixed mushrooms, sliced
1 sprig thyme
2 sprigs tarragon
2 cloves garlic, finely sliced
1 tbsp plain (all-purpose) flour
50 ml / 1 ¾ oz / ¼ cup red wine
300 ml / 10 fl. oz / 1 ¼ cups vegetable stock
2 tbsp double (heavy) cream
500 g / 1 lb ready-made puff pastry
fresh basil leaves, to serve

- Preheat 200°C (180°C fan) / 400F / gas 6.
- Heat the butter in a large frying pan and cook the mushrooms with the herbs and garlic gently until all the excess liquid has evaporated.
- Add the flour and cook out for 2 minutes, then add the wine and the stock gradually, stirring as you go until smooth. Leave to simmer for 10 minutes until smooth and thick.
- Cut the pastry into one large circle slightly larger than a 20 cm (8 in) pie dish and roll out on a floured surface to about 5mm thickness.
- Line the pie dish with the pastry, then spoon the mushroom filling in, reserving any excess sauce.
- Bake on a preheated baking tray for 30 minutes.
- Garnish with the basil leaves and enjoy hot or cold.

Parmesan and mushroom tart
Sprinkle some grated Parmesan over the top of the tart before baking.

Beef Wellington

PREPARATION TIME: **15 minutes**
COOKING TIME: **20 minutes**
SERVES: **6**

1 beef fillet, weighing 1 kg / 2 ¼ lb
3 tbsp olive oil
250 g / 9 oz / 1 cup mushrooms
1 shallot, finely chopped
3 tbsp butter
2 sprigs thyme leaves
1 tbsp dried rosemary
75 ml / 2 ½ oz / ⅓ cup dry white wine
1 sheet ready rolled puff pastry
1 tbsp flour
2 egg yolks, beaten
fresh sprigs rosemary, to garnish

- Preheat oven to 220°C (200°C fan) / 450F / gas 7.
- Place the beef in a roasting tin, drizzle with oil and roast for 15 minutes.
- Meanwhile, place the mushrooms in a food processor with the shallot and process as finely as possible.
- Heat the butter in a pan and dry the mushroom mixture with thyme leaves and dried rosemary and a little seasoning until softened. Add the wine and cook until the wine has been absorbed. Set aside to cool.
- Roll the pastry out a little more on a floured surface. Spoon the cooled mushrooms over the pastry, leaving a small margin around the edges.
- Place the beef in the centre and roll the pastry up like sausage, fully encasing the beef. Seal the edges with egg yolk, then brush the pastry with the remaining egg.
- Reduce the oven to 200°C (180°C fan) / 400F / gas 6 and roast for 20 minutes until puffed and golden.
- Serve with Brussels sprouts and garnish with some rosemary sprigs before serving.

Beef Wellington with potatoes
Replace the Brussels sprouts with the same amount of roasted baby potatoes. Roast with 2 cloves crushed garlic and the juice of 1 lemon.

Beef lasagne

PREPARATION TIME: 2 hours
COOKING TIME: 40 minutes
SERVES: 6

12 sheets of lasagne
4 tbsp Parmesan cheese
150 g fresh mozzarella, torn into pieces
fresh basil leaves, to garnish

FOR THE BOLOGNESE SAUCE
1 tbsp butter
olive oil
1 onion, peeled and finely chopped
2 celery stalks, finely chopped
2 cloves garlic, finely chopped
2 carrots, finely chopped
120 g / 4 oz / ½ cup pancetta, cubed
500 g / 1 lb minced beef
120ml / 4 fl oz / ½ cup white wine
2 x 400 g can chopped tomatoes
450 ml / 1 pint / 2 cups beef stock

- To make the Bolognese sauce, heat the butter with a little oil in a pan and add the finely chopped vegetables, the carrots and pancetta and cook for about 10 minutes.

- Add the beef, breaking it up with a wooden spoon until cooked through. Season well.

- Add the wine and stir for about 5 minutes until it has been absorbed. Add the tomatoes and half the stock and then lower the heat. Partially cover the pan and leave to simmer for about 1 ½ - 2 hours, adding more stock as it absorbs. Don't let it get too thick.

- Preheat the oven to 190°C / 375F / gas 5. Spread a third of the Bolognese sauce in the bottom of a baking dish then 4 sheets of lasagne.

- Repeat twice more, then cover the top layer of lasagne with the Parmesan and mozzarella cheese.

- Bake in the oven for about 40 minutes, then garnish with the basil leaves.

Veggie lasagne
For a vegetarian version, replace the minced beef for the same amount of vegetarian mince and swap the beef stock for vegetable stock.

Roast shoulder of lamb with veggies

PREPARATION TIME: **10 minutes**
COOKING TIME: **2-3 hours**
SERVES: **4**

1 lamb shoulder weighing 1 ½ kg / 3 lb
5 small carrots, washed
1 red chilli (chili)
3 scallions
1 bunch rosemary
1 tbsp oregano
4 tbsp olive oil
2 tbsp runny honey
water or red wine

- Preheat the oven to 180C / 350F / gas 5.
- Place the shoulder in a tin and rub in the whole vegetables, herbs, oil, honey and seasoning, massaging them into the meat.
- Pour a glass of water or wine into the bottom of the tin, cover tightly with foil and bake for about 2–3 hours until the lamb is meltingly tender and falls from the bone.
- Allow to rest for a few minutes before carving. Serve alongside the vegetables and season well.

Lamb with potatoes
Add 300 g baby new potatoes. Simply wash and halve the potatoes and season well. Add the juice of 1 lemon and cook with the shoulder of lamb.

Sesame noodles with smoked salmon

PREPARATION TIME: **10 minutes**
COOKING TIME: **10 minutes**
SERVES: **4**

4 nests dried egg noodles
1 tbsp sesame oil
4 spring onions (scallions), finely chopped
1 cm piece ginger, finely sliced
2 pieces smoked salmon, cut into strips
2 tbsp soy sauce
2 tbsp chilli (chili) sauce
1 red chilli (chili), seeds removed and sliced
1 tbsp sesame seeds, to garnish

- Cook the noodles in boiling salted water according to packet instructions.
- After 1 minute add the sliced chilli.
- Drain well.
- Meanwhile heat the oil in a wok and add the spring onions and ginger. Sauté for a few minutes.
- Add the noodles and vegetables and pour in the sauces.
- Toss well to coat, then serve drizzled with sesame oil, sesame seeds and the smoked salmon.

Sesame noodles with smoked tofu
For a vegan version, replace the smoked salmon for 250 g sliced cooked smoked tofu. Either sauté with the noodles or enjoy cold on top of the noodles.

Meatballs in tomato sauce with mozzarella

PREPARATION TIME: 20 minutes
CHILLING TIME: 30 minutes
COOKING TIME: 30 minutes
SERVES: 4-6

400 g / 14 oz / 1 ½ cups minced beef
1 egg
1 clove garlic, crushed
½ lemon, grated zest
2 tbsp parsley, chopped
1 thick slice of white bread, crusts removed
and soaked in 2 tbsp milk
3 tbsp olive oil
1 x 400 g can chopped tomatoes
400 ml / 14 fl oz / 1 ½ cups beef stock
1 tsp sugar
150 g / 5 oz mozzarella, grated
fresh flat-leaf parsley, chopped
crusty bread, sliced and toasted

- Preheat the oven to 140°C / 275°F / gas 1.
- Place the meat in a large bowl with the egg, garlic, lemon zest and 1 tbsp parsley and season well.
- Mulch the bread in your fingers and crumble into the mix. Mix everything together with your hands to become smooth and sticky.
- Roll into small walnut-sized balls with cold wet hands, place on a tray and chill for 30 minutes.
- Heat the oil in a pan and fry the meatballs in batches until brown.
- Add the tomatoes and stock, then add the sugar and season and bring to the boil. Lower the heat and simmer for about 20 minutes.
- Transfer the meatballs and sauce to a deep saucepan or casserole dish and sprinkle the mozzarella on top.
- Bake in the oven for 10 minutes or until the cheese has melted.
- Season to taste and garnish with some parsley before serving. Enjoy with some crusty bread (optional).

Meatballs in tomato sauce with Parmesan
Replace the mozzarella with grated Parmesan and garnish with some fresh basil leaves for a delicious variation.

Griddled steak with peppercorns

PREPARATION TIME: **5 minutes**
COOKING TIME: **15 minutes**
SERVES: **2**

olive oil
2 courgettes (zucchinis), sliced
5 button mushrooms, sliced
1 clove garlic
2 rump steaks
1 tbsp butter
1 tbsp heather honey
1 bay leaf
1 tsp black and pink peppercorns
½ bunch parsley, chopped

- Heat the oil in a large griddle pan and add the courgette and mushroom slices and garlic. Season and cook over a low heat until golden.
- Season the steaks and rub with oil. Heat a frying pan and sear the steaks on each side for 2 minutes.
- Add the butter to the pan and then the honey and bay leaf. Baste the steaks as they cook for 2 minutes more, then remove from the pan and rest for 5 minutes.
- Serve the steak with the courgette, mushrooms, tomatoes and mustard (optional).
- Garnish with the peppercorns, chilli and herbs.

Peking duck with rice noodles

PREPARATION TIME: **35 minutes**
COOKING TIME: **30 minutes**
SERVES: **4**

4 duck breasts
4 nests dried rice noodles
2 tbsp runny honey
2 tbsp rice vinegar
1 ½ tbsp soy sauce
1 tbsp Chinese 5 spice
1 tbsp soft dark brown sugar
2 spring onions, ends chopped
100 g / 3 oz alfalfa sprouts, to garnish
1 sheet nori seaweed, cut into strips
2 tbsp gomasio (optional)

- Place the duck on a wire rack skin side up and dry thoroughly with kitchen paper. Score the skins with a sharp knife.
- Mix together the ingredients and brush the skin and leave to marinate for about 30 minutes.
- Preheat the oven to 190C (170 fan) / 375F / gas 5.
- Brush the duck all over with the sauce and transfer the wire rack to a roasting tin. Pour a cup of water into the bottom of the tin and roast/steam for 30 minutes until the duck is cooked through and the skin is crisp.
- You can quickly grill the skin if it hasn't crisped up.
- In the meantime, cook the rice noodles according to the packet instructions.
- Divide the noodles between the 4 serving bowls. Slice the duck and lay on top of the noodles.
- Garnish with the nori seaweed, sprouts, spring onions and a little gomasio.

Avocado noodle bowl
Replace the duck with sliced avocado. Simply slice 2 large hass avocados and place on top of the noodles. Add a little water to the sauce to thin, before drizzling over the top. Garnish with the remaining ingredients.

Mushroom-filled pastries with Parmesan

PREPARATION TIME: 20 minutes
CHILLING TIME: 30 minutes
COOKING TIME: 30-35 minutes
SERVES: 6

350 g / 12 oz / 1 ½ cups ready-made puff pastry

1 egg, beaten

3 tbsp butter

500 g / 1 lb / 2 cups mixed wild mushrooms, chopped

2 sprigs thyme leaves

2 tbsp plain (all-purpose) flour

300 ml / 10 fl. oz / 1 ¼ cups milk

1 tsp grain-free mustard

2 tbsp Parmesan, grated

- Roll the pastry out on a floured surface to 2.5cm (¼ in) thick.
- Cut out six 7 cm (3 inch) circles with a pastry cutter and score a smaller circle just inside the rim.
- Place on a baking sheet and chill for 30 minutes. Preheat the oven to 200°C (180°C fan) / 400F / gas 6.
- Brush the pastry cases with a little egg and bake for 20 minutes, or until risen and golden. Leave to cool, then carefully remove the lids and scoop out the centres.
- Melt the butter in a pan and cook the mushrooms with thyme and seasoning until any excess liquid has evaporated.
- Stir in the flour and cook out for 2 minutes, then whisk in the milk and simmer for 5–10 minutes until thickened and smooth. Whisk in the Parmesan and mustard.
- Spoon into the pastry cases, replace the lids and cook for 10–15 minutes until the filling is bubbling.
- Top with any leftover mushrooms and garnish with the fresh watercress.

Mushroom-filled pastries with mimolette
Replace the Parmesan with the same amount of aged mimolette for a slightly more intense flavour.

Lamb curry with yogurt

PREPARATION TIME: **15 minutes**
COOKING TIME: **30 minutes**
SERVES: **4**

1 kg / 2 ¼ lbs / 4 ¼ cups lamb shoulder, deboned
3 tbsp oil
2 cloves garlic, peeled and chopped
2 onions, peeled and chopped
3 tsp curry powder
400 g chopped tomatoes
100 g / 3 oz plain yogurt
fresh coriander (cilantro), chopped

- Cut the lamb shoulder into cubes.
- Heat the oil in a pan and add the meat. Cook briskly until golden-brown all over, then remove to a plate with a slotted spoon.
- Add the chopped garlic and onions and cook for two minutes. Return the meat to the pan, add the curry powder, chopped tomatoes and the yogurt and stir well. Cover and cook gently for about 30 minutes, stirring regularly.
- Season to taste then sprinkle with fresh coriander and swirl in a little more yogurt.
- Serve with a side of naan bread and rice.

Lamb and spinach curry
Add a handful of washed baby spinach leaves 10 minutes before the end of cooking time before serving.

Lemony salmon steaks

PREPARATION TIME: **10 minutes**
COOKING TIME: **16-18 minutes**
SERVES: **4**

4 salmon steaks, weighing about 200 g / 7 oz each
250 ml / 9 fl. oz / 1 cup dry white wine
8 black peppercorns
1 lemon, halved and sliced
500 ml / 1 pint / 2 cups fish stock or water
1 green chilli (chili), sliced, to serve (optional)

- Place all the ingredients, except the salmon, in a roasting tin you can set over heat and gently heat until simmering.
- Add the salmon steaks skin side down, cover the tin with foil and poach gently for about 10 minutes until just coral inside – not pale pink as they will be dry.
- Pour the poaching liquor over the top of the steaks and place the lemon slices on top. Serve with the green chillies (optional).

Fiery salmon steaks with ginger
For a spicy kick, add 1 tsp dried chilli (chili) flakes and 1 tbsp grated ginger to the roasting tin with the rest of the ingredients.

Lobster linguine

PREPARATION TIME: 20 minutes
COOKING TIME: 30 minutes
SERVES: 2

1 lobster, cooked, tail and claws removed and set aside, body halved lengthways

250 g / 9 oz linguine, cooked according to packet instructions, drained

FOR THE SAUCE
3 tbsp olive oil

lobster body

1 onion, peeled and chopped

3 cloves garlic, chopped

2 tbsp tomato purée

300 ml / 10 fl. oz / 1 ¼ cups dry white wine

2 jars roasted piquillo peppers, drained

1 tsp smoked paprika

1 Ibarra chilli (chili), drained and chopped or any preserved chilli pepper

4 ripe tomatoes, chopped

fresh parsley, to garnish

1 tsp dried chilli (chili) flakes

- Heat the oil in a pan and cook the lobster halves for a few minutes.
- Add the onion, garlic and cook until the onion softens.
- Stir in the tomato purée and white wine and bubble up, then tip in the peppers, paprika, chilli and tomatoes. Season, bring to a simmer and cook until thickened and reduced.
- Adjust the seasoning then serve the hot sauce with the lobster over the cooked linguine.
- Garnish with the fresh parsley and chilli flakes before serving

Lobster linguine with garden peas
Add some fresh garden peas to the sauce ingredients 10 minutes before the end of cooking time. Garnish with the parsley and a wedge of lemon.

Thai green chicken curry

PREPARATION TIME: **15 minutes**
COOKING TIME: **25-30 minutes**
SERVES: **4**

3 tbsp vegetable oil
1 onion, peeled and finely sliced
2 cloves garlic, finely chopped
2 tbsp green Thai curry paste
3–4 chicken breasts, skinned and cubed
2 tsp tamarind paste
2 tbsp fish sauce
4 lime leaves
400 ml / 14 fl. oz / 1 ½ cups coconut milk
200 ml / 7 fl. oz / ½ cup chicken stock
1 red chilli (chili), chopped
1–2 limes, juiced
boiled rice to serve (optional)

- Heat the oil in a wok or large pan and fry the onion until golden brown and sweet.
- Add the garlic and curry paste and cook out for 2 minutes.
- Add the cubed chicken and allow to colour on all sides.
- Stir in the tamarind paste, lime leaves, chilli and fish sauce, then pour over the coconut milk and chicken stock.
- Lower the heat and leave to simmer for 15–20 minutes until the chicken is cooked through.
- Adjust the seasoning and stir in the lime juice just before serving with the rice (optional).

Red Thai curry
Replace the green Thai curry paste with the same amount of red Thai curry paste for a delicious alternative.

Turkey and runner beans wrapped in bacon

PREPARATION TIME: **10 minutes**
COOKING TIME: **45 minutes**
SERVES: **4**

4 turkey breast steaks
4 tbsp crème fraiche
12 runner beans, ends removed and washed
8 slices streaky bacon
olive oil
fresh basil leaves

- Preheat the oven to 200°C (180°C fan) / 400F / gas 6. Place the turkey steak on the surface and cut in half down one side, opening it out like a book.
- Spread the crème fraiche into the cavity and add the runner beans.
- Roll the turkey back up into a sausage shape and wrap around with the bacon and secure with a cocktail stick.
- Place in a roasting tin, drizzle with oil, season and roast for 45 minutes, until cooked through and the juices run clear. Leave to rest for 10 minutes before serving. Garnish with basil.

Turkey with mozzarella
Add 100 g torn mozzarella in the cavities with the runner beans. Omit the crème fraiche for less cheese.

Lamb chops with thyme, chilli and lemon

PREPARATION TIME: **40 minutes**
COOKING TIME: **10 minutes**
SERVES: **4**

2 red chillies (chilis), deseeded and chopped
1 bunch thyme
½ lemon, juiced
1 clove garlic, peeled
olive oil
8 lamb chops

- Whiz the chilli, thyme, lemon juice, garlic and a little oil in a blender until a rough paste.
- Coat the lamb chops in the paste and set aside for at least 30 minutes.
- Cook on a hot griddle for 4 minutes per side or until rosy pink in the middle.

Lamb chops with smoked paprika
Omit the thyme and add 1 tsp smoked paprika and a pinch of smoked salt to the blender before blending.

Sweet and sour pork with chilli

PREPARATION TIME: **15 minutes**
COOKING TIME: **20 minutes**
SERVES: **4**

500 g / 1 lb pork loin, cubed
1 egg white
2 tsp cornflour
1 tsp sesame oil
1 tbsp vegetable oil
1 red chilli (chili), deseeded and finely sliced
50 g / 1 ¾ oz / ¼ cup pineapple chunks
2 tbsp fresh coriander (cilantro), chopped
400 g / 14 oz cooked white rice

FOR THE SAUCE
125ml / 4 fl oz / ½ cup pineapple juice
splash dry sherry or rice wine
2 tbsp tomato ketchup
2 tbsp soy sauce
2 tbsp Chinese vinegar or red wine vinegar

- Bring a saucepan to boil and cook the rice according to the packet instructions, set to one side.
- Slice the pork into strips. Combine the egg white, cornflour, a pinch of salt and sesame oil in a bowl then thoroughly coat the chicken strips in the mixture.
- Heat the vegetable oil in a wok until smoking, then add the coated pork and stir fry over a high heat until the chicken turns white.
- Remove the pork from the pan and set aside. Discard the oil.
- Heat the oil in the wok again and stir fry the vegetables over a high heat for 4 minutes.
- Mix together the sauce ingredients. Add the pork back to the pan with the sauce and bubble up.
- Garnish with the chopped coriander before serving with the white rice.

Beef kebabs with rosemary and lime

PREPARATION TIME: **10 minutes**
COOKING TIME: **6 minutes**
SERVES: **4**

800 g / 1 ¾ lb rump steak cubed
1 tsp paprika
½ tsp cayenne
olive oil
1 lime, cut into wedges
8 sprigs rosemary
8 wooden skewers, soaked in water

- Rub the cubes of beef with paprika and Cayenne and a little oil and season with salt.
- Thread onto the skewers with the rosemary sprigs going through the beef. Season well.
- Cook on a griddle for 5–6 minutes until the beef is charred outside and pink inside.
- Serve with the lime wedges.

Beef kebabs with courgette
Wash and chop 2 medium-sized courgettes (zucchini) and thread along the skewers alternating with the beef.

Rice noodles with pork

PREPARATION TIME: **15 minutes**
COOKING TIME: **10 minutes**
SERVES: **4**

4 nests dried rice noodles
2 tbsp groundnut oil
2 cloves garlic, finely sliced
1 red onion, chopped
1 cm piece ginger, finely sliced
1 red chilli, deseeded and finely chopped
2 stalks lemongrass, inner stalks only, finely chopped
300 g / 10 oz / pork fillet, sliced
100 g pak choi, stalks removed
800 ml / 1 ½ pints hot water
2 tbsp brown miso paste
chopped chives, to garnish
1 tbsp soy sauce

- Cook the noodles according to packet instructions. Drain.
- Heat the oil in a wok and sauté the garlic, onion, ginger and chilli for a few minutes until golden.
- Add the pork and colour over a high heat, then add the soy sauce and allow to caramelize.
- Combine the hot water with the miso paste to make the broth. Stir well until the miso has completely dissolved. Add the noodles, miso broth and pak choi and cook for 5 minutes.
- Garnish with the chopped chives.

Noodles with pork and Thai basil
Add a handful of Thai basil leaves to the wok 2 minutes before the end of cooking time.

Cod, butterbean and tomato stew

PREPARATION TIME: 15 minutes
COOKING TIME: 20 minutes
SERVES: 4

2 tbsp olive oil
1 onion, peeled and diced
2 cloves garlic, crushed
2 tbsp tomato purée
2 large floury potatoes, peeled and cut into chunks
250 ml / 9 fl. oz / 1 cup dry white wine
400 g chopped tomatoes
400 g cooked butterbeans, drained and rinsed
500 g / 1 lb / 2 cups cod steak, cut into large chunks
1 tsp paprika
1 lemon, juiced
2 tbsp flat-leaf parsley, freshly chopped

- Heat the oil in a casserole and sweat the onion and garlic until softened.
- Add the tomato purée and cook out for 2 minutes.
- Add the potatoes, then pour over the wine, chopped tomatoes and stock. Add the paprika, lemon juice and fish and bring to a simmer.
- Cook gently for about 20 minutes until the potatoes are tender and the fish is just cooked.
- Season and serve scattered with parsley.

Cod, cannellini and chorizo stew
Replace the butter beans with cannellini beans and add some chopped chorizo with the cod.

Pork chops and sautéed potatoes

PREPARATION TIME: **15 minutes**
COOKING TIME: **30 minutes**
SERVES: **4**

2 tbsp goose fat or olive oil
500 g / 1 lb / 2 cups potatoes, peeled and diced
150 g / 5 oz pancetta, sliced
1 clove garlic
4 pork chops
2 tbsp butter
fresh chives, chopped

- Heat the fat in a large frying pan and add the potato, pancetta and garlic.
- Season and cook over a low heat until golden and crusty.
- Heat the butter in a frying pan and season the pork chops. When foaming add the pork and cook for 4 minutes per side, basting with the butter.
- Set aside to rest.
- Increase the heat under the potato. Cook until golden and tender then throw in the chives.
- Serve the pork chops with the pancetta, potatoes and season to taste.

Steak with sautéed potatoes
Replace the pork chops with 4 beefsteaks and follow the method as above. Cook for longer for a well done steak.

Chicken, bacon and avocado salad

PREPARATION TIME: 15 minutes
COOKING TIME: 20-25 minutes
SERVES: 4

4 chicken breasts, skinned and sliced into strips
8 rashers smoked streaky bacon, sliced
extra virgin olive oil
4 gem lettuces, leaves torn off and washed
4 hardboiled eggs, halved
2 hass avocados, skin and stone removed and sliced
fresh chives, chopped
1 tbsp mixed dried herbs

- Preheat the oven to 200°C (180°C fan) / 400F / gas 6.
- Place the sliced chicken and bacon in a roasting tin.
- Drizzle with oil, season and bake for 20–25 minutes until cooked through.
- In the meantime, prepare the salad. Combine the lettuce, eggs and avocado in the 4 serving bowls.
- Once the chicken and bacon is ready, divide between the 4 bowls of salad.
- Top with the chives, dried herbs and season to taste before serving.

Chicken and bacon salad with olives
Add a handful of pitted black olives before garnishing with the herbs.

Traditional cottage pie

PREPARATION TIME: **25 minutes**
COOKING TIME: **35 minutes**
SERVES: **4-6**

2 tbsp vegetable oil
450 g / 1 lb / 2 cups minced lamb
1 onion, peeled and finely chopped
2 carrots, peeled and finely chopped
2 sticks celery, finely chopped
1 leek, finely chopped
1 tbsp mixed dried herbs
100 g / 3 ½ oz / ½ cup flat field mushrooms, finely
chopped
1 tbsp tomato purée
1 bay leaf
350 ml / 12 fl oz / 1 ½ cups beef stock
900 g / 2 lb / 3 ½ cups floury potatoes, peeled and
cut into chunks
100 g / 3 ½ oz / ½ cup butter
fresh sprigs thyme, to garnish

- Preheat the oven to 180°C (160°C fan) / 350F
  / gas 4.
- Heat the oil in a large pan and briskly fry the
  lamb mince. Add the vegetables and sweat
  until soft.
- Stir in the tomato purée and cook out for 2
  minutes, before adding the herbs and pouring
  over the stock. Simmer until the stock has
  reduced and there is just a little liquid left in
  the bottom of the pan.
- Meanwhile cook the potatoes in boiling salted
  water until tender to the point of a knife.
- Drain thoroughly, then mash until completely
  smooth with the butter and season well.
- Pour the lamb base into a baking dish, then
  spoon over the mashed potato. Run a fork
  down the length of the potato to create edges
  that will crisp in the oven.
- Bake for 30 minutes until bubbling and
  golden.
- Garnish with some fresh thyme before
  serving.

Sweet potato-topped cottage pie
Replace the above potatoes with the same
amount of sweet potatoes for a delicious
alternative.

Three-cheese cannelloni

PREPARATION TIME: 40 minutes
COOKING TIME: 15 minutes
SERVES: 4

12 cannelloni tubes or 12 lasagne sheets

FOR THE FILLING
2 tbsp butter
1 tbsp olive oil
2 cloves garlic, chopped
1 kg / 2 lb / 4 ½ cups spinach leaves
¼ nutmeg, grated
400 g / 13 ½ oz / 1 ½ cups ricotta
2 tbsp Parmesan, grated

FOR THE TOMATO SAUCE
2 tbsp olive oil
1 clove garlic, chopped
2 x 400 g can chopped tomatoes
1 tsp paprika
1 tsp cayenne pepper
1 tbsp mixed dried herbs

TO GARNISH
grated mozzarella
fresh basil leaves

- Preheat the oven to 180°C / 350F / gas 5.
- Make the filling: heat the butter in a large pan with a little oil and cook the garlic for 2 minutes. Add the spinach and nutmeg and stir until wilted.
- Spoon into a sieve and press down firmly with a wooden spoon to extract as much liquid as possible. Once done, finely chop the spinach and leave to cool in a bowl.
- Stir in the ricotta, Parmesan and seasoning.
- Spoon into the tubes or onto the lasagne sheets and roll up to make 12 cylinders, then lay in a greased baking dish.
- Make the tomato sauce: heat the oil in a pan and add the garlic, spices and tomatoes. Leave to simmer, topped up with ½ a can of water, for 10 minutes, then add the dried herbs.
- Spoon the sauce around the cannelloni and add the torn mozzarella. Bake for around 15 minutes until bubbling.
- Garnish with the fresh basil leaves, then serve.

Rice noodles with carrot and ginger

PREPARATION TIME: **5 minutes**
COOKING TIME: **15 minutes**
SERVES: **6**

250 g / 9 oz / 1 cup rice noodles

½ cucumber, sliced into thin ribbons using a vegetable peeler

2 carrots, sliced into thin ribbons using a vegetable peeler

1 tbsp groundnut oil

2 cloves garlic, crushed

1 tbsp grated ginger

1 lemon, grated zest

1 tsp sesame oil

4 tbsp soy sauce

- Bring a saucepan to boil and cook the noodles according to packet instructions.
- Add the cucumber and carrots, 5 minutes before the end of cooking time.
- Heat the oil in a pan and cook the garlic gently for a few seconds.
- Tip into a food processor, add the parsley, lemon zest, sesame oil and soy sauce and blitz until nearly smooth.
- Drain the noodles and toss with the sauce.

Rice noodles with peanuts
Add 1 tbsp ground peanuts to the noodles before serving, for a nutty crunch.

Maple pork with vegetables

PREPARATION TIME: **10-15 minutes**
COOKING TIME: **20 minutes**
SERVES: **4**

4 pork fillets
olive oil
4 tbsp maple syrup
2 tbsp butter
2 courgettes (zucchinis), sliced
1 yellow pepper, deseeded and diced
1 red pepper, deseeded and diced
1 green pepper, deseeded and diced
1 tsp dried chilli (chili) flakes
fresh chives, finely chopped

- Preheat the oven to 200°C (180°C fan) / 400F / gas 6. Place the pork fillets in a roasting tin and season well. Drizzle with oil and maple syrup and roast for 20 minutes until just cooked through.
- Meanwhile heat the butter in a pan and add the vegetables. Pour in a glass of water, cover with a lid and stew gently for 10–15 minutes until all is tender. Season and add the chives and chilli flakes. Rest the pork for 5 minutes before carving and serving with the vegetables. Season with some rocket leaves, if desired.

Maple salmon with vegetables
Replace the pork with 4 boneless salmon fillets and follow the method as above. Wrap in tin foil before cooking in the oven. Reduce cooking time to 15 minutes.

Curried pork meatballs

PREPARATION TIME: **15 minutes**
COOKING TIME: **20 minutes**
SERVES: **4**

2 slices stale bread, crusts removed
1 kg / 2 ¼ lbs / 4 ¼ cups minced pork
1 onion, peeled and grated
1 clove garlic, crushed
10 curry leaves, finely sliced
400 g chopped tomatoes
1 tsp dried chilli (chili) flakes
1 tsp ground cumin
1 tbsp garam masala
fresh parsley, to serve

- Soak the bread in warm water then squeeze it out. Mix thoroughly with the meat, onions, herbs, spices and mustard and season.
- Form into small balls around 6 cm in diameter.
- Bring the chopped tomatoes to boil in a pan, then reduce the heat and add the meatballs and poach for around 20 minutes, in batches if necessary.
- Garnish with the fresh parsley before serving.

Pork meatballs with spaghetti
Serve the meatballs with some cooked spaghetti for a hearty Italian-inspired meal.

Deep-fried squid

PREPARATION TIME: **30 minutes**
COOKING TIME: **10 minutes**
SERVES: **4-6**

1 egg
200 ml / 7 fl. oz / ¾ cup ice cold water
225 g / 8 oz / 1 cup plain (all-purpose) flour
1 tsp mixed dried herbs
1 kg / 2 ¼ lb squid, cleaned and cut into rings
1 lemon, cut into wedges

- To make the batter for the squid: stir the egg into the cold water, then whisk in the flour and dried herbs to form a lumpy tempura-style batter.
- Season well then dip the squid rings in and coat thoroughly.
- Heat the oil to 180°C / 350 F and cook the squid in batches, removing to drain on kitchen paper when golden brown.
- Serve with the lemon wedges, parsley and a dip of choice.

Deep-fried mushrooms
Replace the squid with 400g button mushrooms. Dip each raw mushroom into the batter and cook as above.

Spaghetti bolognese with chilli

PREPARATION TIME: **5 minutes**
COOKING TIME: **25-30 minutes**
SERVES: **4**

3 tbsp olive oil
2 onions, peeled and finely chopped
2 cloves garlic, chopped
500 g / 1 lb / 2 cups minced beef
1 glass dry white wine
2 x 400 g can chopped tomatoes
1 tsp paprika
1 tsp cayenne pepper
1 tsp dried chilli (chili) flakes
fresh basil, chopped
500 g / 1 lb / 2 cups spaghetti

- Heat the oil in a pan and sweat the onion and garlic without browning. Add the mince and break it up with a wooden spoon, stirring frequently until browned.
- Season, then add the wine, bubble up, then add the tomatoes and spices. Partially cover and simmer for 20 minutes.
- Meanwhile cook the pasta in boiling salted water according to packet instructions. Drain and toss with a little oil. Toss the pasta in the sauce and garnish with the basil.

Veggie bolognese
Replace the minced beef with the same amount of vegetarian mince. Sprinkle over some vegetarian Parmesan (optional).

Chicken Kiev with parsley and lime

PREPARATION TIME: **10 minutes**
COOKING TIME: **20 minutes**
SERVES: **4**

4 chicken breasts, skinned
75 g / 2 ½ oz / ⅓ cup plain (all-purpose) flour
3 eggs, beaten
250 g / 9 oz / 1 cup breadcrumbs
4 tbsp vegetable oil
1 lime, cut into wedges

FOR THE STUFFING
225 g / 8 oz / 1 cup butter, softened
2-3 cloves garlic, crushed
½ bunch parsley, finely chopped
1 lime, juiced

- Using a sharp knife, cut a pocket in the side of each chicken breast.
- Mix together the stuffing ingredients until well combined.
- Use a teaspoon to stuff the pocket with the herb butter, then press the edges firmly together.
- Place the flour, eggs and breadcrumbs on separate plates. Season the flour.
- Dip each chicken breast into the flour, eggs then polenta, coating thoroughly each time.
- Heat the oil then add the chicken breasts and cook, turning regularly for about 20 minutes until cooked through.
- Serve with the lime wedges and enjoy.

Chicken Kiev with mozzarella
Add 150g mozzarella for a cheesy centre. Simply chop the mozzarella and stuff each pocket with the cheese and herb butter for extra decadence.

Spicy beef with quinoa and chickpeas

PREPARATION TIME: **2 hours**
COOKING TIME: **20 minutes**
SERVES: **4**

2 large rump steaks
4 tbsp tomato purée
splash of water
1 tsp ground cumin
1 tbsp paprika
½ tsp cayenne pepper
1 tsp dried oregano
3 tbsp olive oil
1 lemon juiced

FOR THE QUINOA

1 x 400 g can chickpeas (garbanzo beans), washed and drained
400 g / 14 oz cooked quinoa
200 ml / 7 fl oz / ¾ cup vegetable stock
1 clove garlic, peeled
fresh parsley, chopped

- Mix all of the sauce ingredients until it is a thick tomato paste.
- Rub the steaks all over with the paste and set aside in the refrigerator for at least 2 hours.
- Simmer the chickpeas in the vegetables stock with the garlic and thyme for 15 minutes.
- Add the quinoa and cook according to the packet instructions.
- Heat a griddle until very hot and cook the steaks for 2–3 minutes per side for rare.
- Wrap in foil and rest for 8 minutes, then season and serve with the quinoa and the resting juices poured over (optional).
- Garnish with some fresh parsley before serving.

Vegan spicy quinoa with raisins
Omit the steak and make the sauce as above. Add a handful of raisins to the quinoa and stock 5 minutes before the end of cooking time. Stir in the sauce and serve.

Tuna steak with egg

PREPARATION TIME: 5 minutes
COOKING TIME: 10 minutes
SERVES: 4

4 tbsp olive oil
4 tuna steaks, 2 cm thick
6 pitted green olives, sliced
1 tbsp capers
1 tsp mixed dried herbs
a handful of rocket (arugula) leaves
½ lemon, juiced
4 eggs
crusty bread, to serve (optional)

- Heat the pan with the oil, season the tuna on both sides and cook over a high heat for 30–60 seconds per side, depending on how rare you like your tuna.
- Add the herbs, lemon juice and season well.
- In the meantime, bring a saucepan to the boil and add the 4 eggs. Reduce to a simmer and for a runny centre, cook the eggs for 5 minutes.
- Divide the eggs and rocket between the 4 serving plates. Add the steak on top and spoon over the olives and capers.
- Once the eggs are ready, carefully remove the shell and cut open to reveal the runny yolk.
- Serve alongside some crusty bread and enjoy.

Gammon with herbed potatoes

PREPARATION TIME: **10 minutes**
COOKING TIME: **2 hours, 30 minutes**
SERVES: **4**

2 kg / 4 ½ lb gammon (ham), soaked to get rid of
excess salt

1 l / 2 ¼ pints / 4 ¼ cups dry cider

fresh thyme, to garnish

2 tbsp olive oil

4 tbsp honey

4 tbsp grain mustard

4 Maris Piper potatoes, halved

2 tbsp butter

1 tbsp honey

1 red onion, peeled and sliced

- Bring the gammon to room temperature and
  place in a large pot with the cider, thyme and
  some seasoning. Add enough cold water to
  cover and bring to a boil.

- Lower the heat to a 'blip' for 30 minutes,
  plus 30 minutes per 500 g / 1 lb.

- When the ham is cooked, remove from the
  pan and leave to rest for

- 10 minutes. Preheat the oven to 200°C (180°C
  fan) / 400F / Gas 7.

- Mix together the oil, honey and mustard.
  Cover the ham with the mixture and roast
  in the oven with the potatoes for about
  20–30 minutes until golden and caramelized.

- Heat the butter in a pan and when foaming,
  add the onions. Caramelize for a few minutes
  before drizzling over the honey.

- Once the gammon is ready, carve into
  portions and serve with the potatoes and
  caramelized onions.

Gammon with leeks
Add 2 washed and finely sliced leeks to the
pan with the onions and butter. Sauté for
5–8 minutes or until caramelized. Season
well and serve with the gammon.

Chilli beef stir-fry with sesame

PREPARATION TIME: **10 minutes**
COOKING TIME: **6 minutes**
SERVES: **4**

2 eggs, beaten
½ tsp salt
1 ½ tbsp cornflour (cornstarch)
vegetable oil for deep frying
150 g / 5 oz / ⅔ cup rump steak, sliced
1 head broccoli, roughly chopped
4 carrots, julienned or spiralized
1 red chilli (chili), deseeded chopped
2 tbsp rice vinegar
2 tbsp sweet chilli (chili) sauce
1 tbsp soy sauce
1 tbsp white sesame seeds
1 spring onion, ends chopped
fresh coriander (cilantro), roughly chopped
egg noodles, to accompany (optional)

- Whisk together the eggs, salt and cornflour and coat the beef strips.
- Heat the oil to 180°C / 350F and deep-fry the beef in small batches. Cook for about 5 minutes until brown and crisp. Remove and drain on kitchen paper. Transfer to a bowl with the sesame seeds and mix well to coat.
- Heat a little oil in a wok and stir-fry the carrots, broccoli, spring onion and chilli. Add the remaining ingredients and toss together, adding the beef at the last minute.
- Cook the noodles according to packet instructions and serve topped with the chilli beef and vegetable stir-fry.
- Garnish with fresh coriander before serving.

Veggie stir-fry with tofu
Omit the beef and cornflour and replace with 250 g firm tofu. Drain the tofu and pat with kitchen roll to dry. Cut into cubes and toss with the remaining ingredients.

Prawn, tomato and rice stew

PREPARATION TIME: **20 minutes**
COOKING TIME: **30 minutes**
SERVES: **4**

20 prawns (shrimp), tails removed
1 tbsp oil
50 g / 1 ¾ oz / ¼ cup butter
30 g / 1 oz shallots, finely chopped
30 g / 1 oz carrots, peeled and diced
200 g / 7 oz cooked white rice
1 tomato, chopped
1 tbsp tomato purée
1 sprig thyme
400 g tin chopped tomatoes
crusty white bread, to serve

- Heat the oil in a large pan and fry the prawns for 5 minutes. Add the butter and vegetables. Increase the heat slightly to turn the vegetables golden. Stir in the chopped tomatoes, tomato puree, thyme and cook over a high heat until the liquid has nearly evaporated.
- Add the fish stock and simmer for 30 minutes until reduced by half. Add the rice 10 minutes before the end of cooking time. Season to taste and serve with some crusty white bread.

Creamy tomato and prawn stew
Stir in 4 tbsp double (heavy) cream once cooked and ready to serve. Add the juice of ½ lemon for a subtle tangy flavour.

Basmati with spring onions and peas

PREPARATION TIME: **30 minutes**
COOKING TIME: **15 minutes**
SERVES: **4**

500 g / 1lb / 2 cups brown basmati rice
1 tbsp sesame oil
2 cloves crushed garlic
1 spring onion, finely chopped
100 g / 3 ½ oz / ½ cup fresh or frozen peas
500 ml / 1 pint / 2 cups vegetable stock
1 tsp freshly grated ginger
½ lemon, juiced

- Wash the rice in a sieve under cold running water, then leave to soak for 30 minutes.
- Heat the oil in a pan and lightly sauté the garlic. Add the spring onions, ginger and lemon juice, then tip in the rice and peas and stir well to coat in the oil.
- Pour over the stock and a little salt, bring to the boil and cover with a lid. Turn the heat down and leave to cook for 9–10 minutes.
- Turn off the heat and leave to stand for 5 minutes. Remove the lid and stir with a fork to separate the grains.

Asian rice bowl with tofu
Replace the basmati rice with the same amount of short grain brown rice. Add 250 g cubed firm tofu to the pan with the garlic and sauté before adding the other ingredients.

Red mullet with sweet peppers

PREPARATION TIME: **5 minutes**
COOKING TIME: **6-8 minutes**
SERVES: **6**

6 red mullet fillets, pin boned
150 g / 5 oz cherry tomatoes, halved
3 sweet red peppers, deseeded and sliced
extra virgin olive oil
1 lemon, juiced
lamb's lettuce, to serve

- Lay the fillets in a roasting tin skin side up. Add the tomatoes and peppers and drizzle with oil, lemon juice and seasoning.
- Grill under a hot grill until the skin becomes crisp – about 3–4 minutes.
- Working quickly, flip the fillets over, stir the tomatoes, peppers and return to the grill for a few more minutes.
- Remove from the grill, season to taste and serve with salad.

Red mullet with capers
Add 2 tbsp capers to the roasting tin and mix well with the tomatoes and peppers. Cook as above.

Toad in the hole casserole

PREPARATION TIME: **35 minutes**
COOKING TIME: **20 minutes**
SERVES: **4**

4 eggs
300 ml / 10 fl oz / 1 ¼ cups milk
250 g / 9 oz / 1 cup plain (all-purpose) flour
4 tbsp vegetable oil or beef dripping
8 chipolata sausages
1 tbsp grain mustard
1 tsp grated nutmeg

- Preheat oven to 220°C (200°C fan) / 425F / gas 7
- To make the batter, whisk together the eggs and milk and leave to stand for 15 minutes.
- Heat the oil in a roasting tin and brown the sausages on all sides to stop them looking anaemic.
- Whisk the flour into the milk and eggs then the mustard and nutmeg, then pour into the hot casserole dish around the sausages. Season well.
- Cook in the oven for 20 minutes until golden and billowing. Serve with roasted potatoes (optional).

Veggie toad in the hole
Replace the chipolata sausages with a vegetarian version and follow the method as above.

Guinea fowl with brown lentils

PREPARATION TIME: **10 minutes**
COOKING TIME: **40 minutes**
SERVES: **4**

1 Guinea fowl, jointed
olive oil
200 g / 7 oz / ¾ cup brown lentils
1 onion, peeled and chopped
1 carrot, peeled and diced
1 clove garlic, finely chopped
1 large glass dry white wine
200–300 ml / 7–10 ½ fl. oz / ¾–1 ¼ cups
chicken stock
2 bay leaves
2 tbsp red wine vinegar
fresh parsley, to garnish

- Preheat the oven to 200°C (180°C fan) / 400F / gas 6.
- Lay the guinea fowl joints in a roasting tin, drizzle with oil, season and roast for about 30–40 minutes until cooked through.
- Meanwhile, place the lentils in a pan with the vegetables, wine and enough stock to cover. Bring to a simmer and cook for about 25 minutes until the lentils are tender.
- If there is any liquid remaining, drain it off, then spoon into a serving dish and season the lentils with salt, pepper and vinegar.
- Lay the guinea fowl on top of the bed of lentils and serve.

Chicken with brown lentils
Replace the guinea fowl with 1 whole chicken. Season the cavity of the chicken with salt and pepper and stuff with 4 lemon halves and a sprig of fresh thyme before cooking as above.

Beef, carrot and butternut stew

PREPARATION TIME: **10 minutes**
COOKING TIME: **3 hours, 30 minutes**
SERVES: **6**

3 tbsp vegetable oil
600 g / 1 ⅓ lb / 2 ½ cups stewing beef, cubed
1 tbsp seasoned flour
½ butternut squash, peeled and diced
2 carrots, peeled and cut into short lengths
2 onions, peeled and sliced
100 g / 3 ½ oz / ½ cup fresh or frozen peas
1 tbsp tomato purée
2 bay leaves
300 ml / 10 fl. oz / 1 ¼ cups red wine
500 ml / 1 pint / 2 cups beef stock
fresh flat-leaf parsley, chopped

- Heat the oil in a casserole dish. Dust the beef with flour and sear in the oil on all sides, in batches, removing as you go with a slotted spoon.
- Cook the butternut squash, carrots and onions until softened, then stir in the tomato purée.
- Add the beef back to the pan with any resting juices and the bay leaves, then pour in the red wine and stock and bring to a simmer.
- Reduce the heat, season, partially cover with a lid and cook very gently for 2–3 hours until the meat is tender.
- Add the peas 10 minutes before the end of cooking time.
- Once cooked, remove from heat and garnish with the fresh parsley and serve.

Beef stew with aduki beans
Add 400 g cooked, washed and drained aduki beans to the stew with the peas, for a heartier meal.

Roast partridge with plum sauce

PREPARATION TIME: **10 minutes**
COOKING TIME: **30 minutes**
SERVES: **4**

4 sprigs thyme
4 partridges, cleaned
4 tbsp butter, softened
1 tsp pink peppercorns
1 sprig thyme

FOR THE PLUM SAUCE
1 tbsp butter
250 g / 9 oz / 1 cup ripe plums, stoned and quartered
3–4 tbsp light brown sugar
100 ml / 3 ½ fl. oz / ½ cup port
pinch Chinese 5 spice

- Preheat the oven to 200C (180 fan) / 400F / gas 6.
- Push the thyme sprigs into the cavity of the partridges, then rub the breasts all over with softened butter and season. Place in a roasting tin and roast for 25–30 minutes until just cooked.
- Meanwhile heat the butter in a pan, add the plums and cook until starting to soften.
- Add the sugar and caramelize for 4 minutes.
- Pour in the port and 5 spice and simmer until thickened.
- Leave the partridge to rest for 10 minutes before serving with the sauce.
- Garnish with the peppercorns and thyme before serving.

Roast chicken with plum sauce
Replace the partridge with 4 small roast chickens and increase the cooking time to 45–50 minutes.

Turmeric, pepper and mushroom risotto

PREPARATION TIME: 15 minutes
COOKING TIME: 25 minutes
SERVES: 4

2 tbsp olive oil
40 g / 1 oz butter
1 onion, peeled and finely chopped
2 cloves garlic, finely chopped
100 g / 3 ½ oz / ½ cup button mushrooms, sliced
1 red pepper, deseeded and finely chopped
320 g / 11 oz / 1 ⅔ cups risotto rice
100 ml / 3 ½ fl. oz / ½ cup dry white wine
1 l / 2 ¼ pints / 4 ¼ cups vegetable stock
3 tbsp butter
1 tsp turmeric
120 g / 4 oz / ½ cup Parmesan, grated
fresh parsley, chopped

- Heat the oil and butter in a large pan and add the onion and garlic. Cook until soft and translucent.
- Add the mushrooms and cook until lightly golden then add the pepper and cook for a few minutes.
- Add the rice and stir to coat in the butter. Pour in the wine and turmeric and stir the rice while the wine is absorbed.
- Once the wine has cooked in, reduce the heat a little and add the hot stock, a ladleful at a time, stirring fairly continuously. This will give the risotto its creamy texture.
- Keep stirring in the stock and tasting the rice. After about 15–20 minutes the rice should be so but with a slight bite. If you've run out of stock before the rice is cooked, simply use water.
- Season and remove from the heat. Add the butter and Parmesan and leave to melt into the risotto.
- Sprinkle the parsley over the top and serve immediately.

Coq au vin

PREPARATION TIME: **10 minutes**
COOKING TIME: **1 hour**
SERVES: **4**

50 g / 1 ¾ oz / ¼ cup butter
6 rashers smoked streaky bacon or pancetta, diced
2 onions, peeled and diced
3 cloves garlic, finely sliced
2 carrots, peeled and chopped
2 tbsp seasoned flour
2 stalks celery, sliced
2 sprigs thyme
1 chicken, jointed
600 ml / 1 pint / 2 cups medium white wine, such as Riesling
2 tbsp parsley, chopped
a squeeze of lemon juice

- Heat the butter in a casserole dish and fry the bacon until starting to colour.
- Add the onion and garlic and cook until lightly golden. Add the thyme.
- Using a slotted spoon, remove the bacon and onions from the pan to a bowl.
- Add a little oil. Lightly dust the chicken joints with flour, shake off any excess and brown on all sides in the pan.
- Add the carrots and celery. Pour over the wine, bubble up and cook gently for about 30 minutes until the chicken is cooked through.
- Add the parsley, season and add a little lemon juice. Heat until the stock starts to thicken, then serve.

Coq au vin with cream
Stir in some double (heavy) cream at the end for a creamy variation to this classic French dish.

Classic beef bourguignon

PREPARATION TIME: **15 minutes**
COOKING TIME: **3 hours**
SERVES: **6**

1 kg / 2 ¼ lb / 4 ¼ cups stewing beef, cubed
3 tbsp vegetable oil
225 g / 7 ½ oz / 1 ½ cups baby carrots, washed and scrubbed
1 onion, peeled and sliced
1 tbsp flour
400 ml / 14 fl oz / 1 ½ cups red wine, preferably Burgundy
2 cloves garlic, sliced
1 sprig thyme
1 bay leaf
12 pearl or button onions, peeled
1 apple, roughly sliced
200 g / 7 oz / ¾ cup chestnut mushrooms
1 spring onion, chopped

- Preheat the oven to 140°C / 275F / gas 1.
- Sear the beef in 1 tbsp oil in a casserole dish until brown all over. Remove with a slotted spoon.
- Add the onion and cook until beginning to brown, then return the meat to the pan.
- Stir in the flour and soak up the juices, then pour in the wine. Add the garlic and herbs, season, cover with a lid and cook for 2 hours.
- Meanwhile fry the onions and apple in a little oil, then add, with the mushrooms and carrots to the casserole and cook for 1 more hour.
- Adjust the seasoning and garnish with the chopped spring onion.

Bean and veg stew
Omit the beef, apple, flour and wine. Replace with 400 g mixed beans (cannellini, chickpeas, butter beans) and 400 g chopped tomatoes.

Oysters with herbed breadcrumbs

PREPARATION TIME: **5 minutes**
SERVES: **4**

16 oysters, opened
1 bunch parsley, chopped
1 clove garlic, chopped
75 ml / 2 ½ fl. oz / ⅓ cup olive oil
1 lemon, grated zest
1 tbsp mixed dried herbs
4 tbsp toasted breadcrumbs

- Place the opened oysters on a platter of crushed ice.
- Whiz the parsley, garlic, herbs, oil and zest in a food processor until
- the consistency of pesto. Loosen with more oil if necessary.
- Stir in the toasted breadcrumbs.
- Taste – it may need lemon juice as well as seasoning.
- Spoon a little of the herbed breadcrumbs on top of each oyster.

Roast chicken with lemon and sage

PREPARATION TIME: **15 minutes**
COOKING TIME: **1 hour, 30 minutes**
SERVES: **4-6**

1 chicken
olive oil
2 tbsp mixed dried herbs

FOR THE BUTTER
150 g / 5 oz / ⅔ cup butter, softened
6 sage leaves, finely chopped
4 lemons, thickly sliced

- Preheat the oven to 200C (180 fan) / 400F / gas 6.
- Place the chicken in a roasting tin. Using the handle of a teaspoon, gently loosen the skin from the meat, using the spoon to create pockets.
- Mix the butter with ½ the sage and seasoning.
- Push the butter into the pockets under the skin, using your fingers to massage it out and cover the breast.
- Drizzle the skin with oil, dried herbs and season, then roast in the oven with the lemons for 20 minutes, plus 20 minutes per 500 g/ 1 lb. The chicken is cooked when the juices run clear at the thickest part.
- Leave to rest for 10 minutes before carving and serving with the lemon pieces and juices.
- Garnish with the remaining sage leaves.

Roast chicken with orange and sage
Replace the lemons with 2 large oranges. Simply thickly slice the oranges before following the method as above.

Herbed rump steak with mushrooms

PREPARATION TIME: **15 minutes**
COOKING TIME: **20 minutes**
SERVES: **6**

3 rump steaks, about 3cm (1 in) thick
olive oil
50 g / 1 ¾ oz / ¼ cup butter
400 g / 14 oz / 1 ½ cups mixed wild mushrooms
2 sprigs thyme
1 tbsp mixed dried herbs
1 clove garlic, finely sliced
squeeze of lemon juice

- Rub the steaks all over with olive oil and season. Preheat a griddle pan or the barbecue until searingly hot.
- Place the steaks in the pan, placing them away from you and leave for 2 minutes until char marks form.
- Turn the steaks over and leave for 3 minutes.
- At this point, for rare steak, you can remove them from the heat. If you prefer your beef more well-cooked, turn the steaks once more and leave for another minute.
- Wrap the steaks securely in a large piece of foil and leave to rest for at least 5 minutes, but no longer than 8 minutes.
- Meanwhile heat the butter in the same pan and when foaming add the mushrooms, thyme and garlic. Cook until the liquid has evaporated from the mushrooms then season well.
- Toss with the thyme, dried herbs and lemon juice.
- Just before serving, season the steaks again and pour the juices back over the steaks on the plate. Serve with the mushrooms.

Steak with creamy mushrooms
Add 100 ml double (heavy) cream to the pan with the mushrooms to create a creamy gravy consistency. Cook for a few minutes before serving with the steak.

Tortellini in tomato sauce

PREPARATION TIME: **5 minutes**
COOKING TIME: **15 minutes**
SERVES: **2**

1 x pack fresh-made tortelloni, such as ham and cheese or spinach and ricotta

FOR THE SAUCE
2 tbsp olive oil
1 onion, finely chopped
1 clove garlic, finely chopped
1 x 400 g can chopped tomatoes
1 tsp mixed dried herbs
a handful of mint leaves
100 ml / 3 ½ oz / ½ cup mascarpone
1 lemon, juiced

- Heat the oil in a pan and sweat the onion and garlic without colouring.
- Add the tomatoes and a splash of water and simmer for 10 minutes, then stir in the dried herbs, lemon juice and mascarpone and season.
- Cook the pasta in boiling salted water according to packet instructions. Drain.
- Toss the pasta with the sauce and serve with the mint leaves.

Spicy tortellini with Parmesan
Add 1 tsp dried chilli flakes to the tomato sauce and sprinkle some vegetarian parmesan on top before serving.

Peppered loin of pork

PREPARATION TIME: **20 minutes**
COOKING TIME: **2 hours**
SERVES: **6**

5 shallots, peeled and halved
2 kg / 4 ½ lb pork loin, boned, derinded and rolled
olive oil
3 bay leaves
1 glass dry white wine
cracked black pepper

- Preheat the oven to 200°C (180°C fan) / 400F / gas 6.
- Lay the shallots in a roasting tin and place the pork on top, seasoning and tucking the bay leaves underneath. Drizzle with oil and roast for 1 hour, 40 minutes.
- Remove the pork from the oven and remove from the tin. Place the tin on the hob and pour in equal quantities wine and water, scraping at the bottom to deglaze. Bubble up and reduce until syrupy.
- Add a generous amount of cracked black pepper on the pork and serve the pork in thick slices with the shallots.
- Garnish with the bay leaves before serving.

Peppered loin of pork with baby potatoes
Replace the shallots with 10 halved baby potatoes and follow the method as above. Serve with a wedge of lemon on the side.

Tandoori chicken kebabs

PREPARATION TIME: 1 hour, 30 minutes
COOKING TIME: 30 minutes
SERVES: 4 (2 kebabs per serving)

4 skinless chicken breasts, diced
400 ml / 14 fl. oz / 1 ½ cups boiling water
pinch ground cinnamon
sprigs of coriander (cilantro)
1 lemon, halved and sliced
8 wooden skewers, soaked in water
natural yogurt, to serve

FOR THE MARINADE
300 ml / 10 fl. oz / 1 ¼ cups natural yogurt
1 tsp ground cumin
1 tsp ground coriander
1 tsp garam masala
1 tsp ground cinnamon
1 ½ tsp tandoori chilli powder
1 tsp caster (superfine) sugar
1 clove garlic, minced

- Prepare the tandoori marinade by mixing
  together all the ingredients for the marinade
  in a mixing bowl. Add the chicken, mix well,
  then cover and chill for at least 1 hour.
- Pre-heat the grill to hot. Remove the chicken
  from the marinade, shaking off any excess,
  and thread onto the wooden skewers.
- Grill for 8–10 minutes, turning occasionally
  until lightly charred and cooked through.
- Place the tandoori chicken skewers on the
  serving plates and garnish with the coriander
  and lemon wedges before serving with the
  natural yogurt.

Roast pork with apples and thyme

PREPARATION TIME: 20 minutes
COOKING TIME: 1 hour, 40 minutes
SERVES: 6

1 onion, peeled and thickly sliced
2 bay leaves
3 carrots, peeled and diced
2 apples, cored and diced
2 kg / 4 ½ lb pork loin, boned, derinded and rolled
olive oil
2 sprigs thyme
50 g / 1 ¾ oz / ¼ cup butter
1 kg / 2 ¼ lb / 4 ¼ cups onions, peeled and finely sliced
100 g / 3 ½ oz / ½ cup soft dark brown sugar
3 tbsp red wine vinegar or sherry vinegar
1 tsp pink peppercorns, to garnish

- Preheat the oven to 200°C (180°C fan) / 400F / gas 6.
- Lay the onion slices, carrots and apples in a small roasting tin and place the pork on top, seasoning and tucking the bay leaves underneath.
- Add the thyme sprigs, drizzle with oil and roast for about 1 hour, 40 minutes.
- Meanwhile melt the butter in a pan and add the onions. Cook very slowly for about 20 minutes until golden.
- Add the sugar, vinegar and a little salt and simmer gently for about 30 minutes until dark and sticky, stirring occasionally.
- Remove the pork and vegetables from the oven and rest for 10 minutes before carving.
- Garnish with the pink peppercorns before serving.

Roast pork with pears and thyme
Replace the apples with the same amount of cored and diced conference pears.

Bacon fondue

PREPARATION TIME: 5 minutes
COOKING TIME: 25 minutes
SERVES: 4

3 cloves garlic
1 onion
50 g / 2 oz butter
2 tsp cornflour
300 g / 10 oz grated Gruyère cheese
300 g / 10 oz chopped Camembert
300 ml / 10 fl. oz white wine
grated nutmeg
6 thin slices of cooked streaky bacon, to serve
crusty bread, cut into large chunks

- Peel the garlic cloves and onion. Finely chop the onion.
- Heat the butter in a large casserole dish.
- Add the onion. Fry for 5 minutes over a medium heat, stirring. Add the garlic, season and stir.
- Add the cheese and wine and raise heat to boiling point.
- Once the cheese had melted, reduce the heat to simmer and add the cornflour.
- Cover and cook on a very low heat for 20 minutes stirring from time to time. Add the nutmeg and season to taste.
- Serve immediately with the cooked bacon and some chunks of crusty bread.

Vegetable fondue
Replace the bacon with your choice of chopped raw vegetables, such as broccoli, cauliflower and courgette.

Lamb sesame burger

PREPARATION TIME: 45 minutes
COOKING TIME: 8-10 minutes
SERVES: 4

1 onion, peeled and chopped
2 cloves garlic, chopped
½ tbsp dried oregano
½ tbsp dried mint
500 g / 1 lb / 2 cups minced lamb
1 egg, beaten
4 tbsp feta, crumbled
1 red onion, sliced
1 beefsteak tomato, sliced
½ cucumber, sliced
rocket (arugula) leaves, to garnish
4 tbsp mayonnaise, to garnish
4 sesame-topped burger buns, toasted
mixed olives, to serve

- Whiz the onion, garlic and dried herbs in a food processor until combined.
- Place the lamb mince in a bowl and stir in the herb mixture with some of the egg and knead thoroughly to combine. Season the mix and form into 4 large lamb burgers. Refrigerate for 30 minutes.
- Heat a griddle pan to nearly smoking and cook the burgers for 3–4 minutes on each side, leaving the middle slightly pink.
- Rest the burgers covered in foil.
- Place the burgers in the buns with the remaining ingredients. Serve with a side of mixed olives.

Beanburgers
Replace the lamb with 400 g tin mixed beans. Simply drain and rinse the beans before adding to the blender with the herb mix. Add a little flour if necessary, before rolling into patties.

Chicken, mushroom and sweetcorn pie

PREPARATION TIME: **50 minutes**
COOKING TIME: **30 minutes**
SERVES: **6**

2 tbsp butter
3–4 chicken thighs, deboned and skinned, cut into chunks
100 g / 3 oz tinned sweetcorn, drained and rinsed
1 shallot, finely chopped
100 g / 3 ½ oz / ½ cup button mushrooms, quartered
3 sprigs thyme
2 sprigs tarragon leaves
1 ½ tbsp plain (all-purpose) flour
300 ml / 10 fl. oz / 1 ¼ cups milk
1 egg, beaten

FOR THE PASTRY
120 g / 4 oz / ½ cup plain (all-purpose) flour
60 g / 2 oz / ¼ cup butter

- Sieve the flour and salt into a bowl, then cut the lard and butter into cubes and work into the flour until the mixture resembles breadcrumbs.

- Work in 2 tbsp water and bring the mixture together using enough water to make a smooth ball of dough. Wrap in cling film and chill for 30 minutes.

- Preheat the oven to 200°C (180°C fan) / 400F / gas 6.

- Heat the butter in a pan and fry the chicken until golden.

- Remove the chicken then sweat the shallot and mushrooms with the herbs. Stir in the flour, then whisk in the milk to make a smooth sauce. Return the chicken to the pan, season and simmer for 10 minutes.

- Add the sweetcorn then tip the chicken into a pie dish. Roll the pastry out on a floured surface to slightly larger than the pie dish and sit on top of the filling.

- Brush with beaten egg, make a hole in the pastry to let the steam escape and bake for 30 minutes. Serve with a side salad (optional).

Turkey, mushroom and sweetcorn pie
Replace the chicken with the same amount of lean turkey breasts for a lighter variation. Follow the method as above.

Glazed pork chops with thyme

PREPARATION TIME: **10 minutes**
COOKING TIME: **12 minutes**
SERVES: **4**

4 pork chops

FOR THE GLAZE
230 g / 8 oz / 1 cup redcurrant jelly
100 ml / 3 ½ fl. oz / ½ cup port or cassis
2 sprigs thyme

- Preheat the oven to 180C / 350F / gas 5.
- Warm the jelly, port and 1 sprig of thyme in a small pan and reduce until thickened and syrupy.
- Using the rosemary, brush the glaze onto the pork chops in a roasting tin and season.
- Cook for about 12 minutes, glazing once again half way through, then remove from the oven and rest for 5 minutes before serving.
- Serve with the remaining sauce and sprig of thyme.

Lamb cutlets with thyme
Replace the pork chops with 4 lamb cutlets and follow the method as above. Serve with a wedge of lemon.

Red snapper with lime

PREPARATION TIME: **10 minutes**
COOKING TIME: **10 minutes**
SERVES: **4**

2 tbsp olive oil
4 red snapper fillets, boned
2 limes, cut into wedges
vegetable oil for deep-frying
fresh parsley, chopped

- Heat the oil in a pan and when very hot add the fish fillets skin side down.
- Cook for 2–3 minutes, depending on thickness, then carefully turn over and cook the other side for about 1 minute.
- Add the juice of 1 lime and season well. Sprinkle the parsley over the top before serving.
- Serve with the remaining lime wedges and enjoy.

Wild salmon with lime
Replace the red snapper fillets with 4 wild salmon fillets and follow the method as above, cooking until the outside skin is crisp.

Beef chilli with cheese

PREPARATION TIME: **5 minutes**
COOKING TIME: **2 hours**
SERVES: **4**

2 tbsp vegetable oil
500 g / 1 lb / 2 full cups minced beef
1 onion, peeled and chopped
2 cloves garlic, finely chopped
1 tsp paprika
1 tsp ground cumin
1 tsp cinnamon
1 tsp cayenne pepper
½ tsp dried chilli (chili) flakes
1 x 400 g can kidney beans, drained and rinsed
1 x 400 g can chopped tomatoes, drained and rinsed
300 ml / 10 fl. oz / 1 ¼ cups beef stock
a handful of red Leicester cheese, grated
fresh parsley, to garnish

- Heat the oil in a large casserole and cook the mince until browned. Remove with a slotted spoon.
- Add the onion and garlic and fry for a further 5 minutes until golden.
- Add the spices and mix well, then pour over the kidney beans, tomatoes and stock, add the beef back in and bring to the boil.
- Simmer over a low heat for at least 2 hours, stirring occasionally, until the chilli has thickened and reduced.
- When the meat is falling apart, season to taste.
- Garnish with the grated cheese and parsley.

Veggie chilli
Replace the minced beef with the same amount of vegetarian mince and omit the cheese for a vegan version. Use vegetable stock instead.

Lamb with pancetta and new potatoes

PREPARATION TIME: 20 minutes
COOKING TIME: 2 hours
SERVES: 4

1 leg of lamb, tunnel boned (ask your butcher)
120 ml / 4 fl. oz / ½ cup white wine
2 bay leaves
1 sprig rosemary
4 cloves garlic, whole
10 baby new potatoes, washed

FOR THE STUFFING

2 tbsp olive oil
4 slices pancetta, diced
1 onion, peeled and finely chopped
1 clove garlic, finely chopped
1 sprig rosemary, finely chopped
2 tbsp black olives, chopped
5 sage leaves, finely chopped

- Preheat the oven to 200C (180C fan) / 400F / gas 6.
- Make the stuffing: heat the oil in a pan and cook the pancetta till the fat runs and it starts to turn crisp.
- Add the onion and cook until soft and golden. Add the olives, sage and season carefully.
- Lay the lamb in a roasting tin and stuff the tunnelled-out section with the stuffing using a teaspoon. Seal the ends with toothpicks or skewers.
- Pour equal amounts wine and water into the roasting tin with the bay leaves, potatoes and garlic. Season the lamb, tent with foil and cook for about 1 ½–2 hours until meltingly tender.
- Leave for 15 minutes before carving and garnishing with the rosemary sprigs.

Apple cider pork chops

PREPARATION TIME: **10 minutes**
COOKING TIME: **30 minutes**
SERVES: **4**

2 tbsp butter
1 large onion, peeled and thinly sliced
2 apples, peeled, cored and sliced
2 sprigs thyme
1 clove garlic, finely sliced
4 pork chops
300 ml / 10 fl. oz / 1 ¼ cups dry apple cider
1 tbsp Dijon mustard
cooked white rice, to serve (optional)

- Heat the butter in a pan and cook the onions and apple with thyme and garlic for 15–20 minutes until all is golden and sweet.
- Remove from the pan with a slotted spoon and increase the heat.
- Sear the pork chops on both sides, seasoning as you go, then lower the heat slightly.
- Return the onions and apples to the pan, pour in the cider, bubble up and cook for 10 minutes.
- Stir in the mustard, adjust the seasoning and serve alongside the rice (optional).

Cider pork chops with pear
Replace the apples with the 2 pears and follow the method as above.

Egg noodles with peppers

PREPARATION TIME: **5 minutes**
COOKING TIME: **10 minutes**
SERVES: **2**

2 nests egg noodles
1 tbsp sesame oil
1 red pepper, deseeded and finely sliced
1 green pepper, deseeded and finely sliced
1 yellow pepper, deseeded and finely sliced
1 tsp dried chilli (chili) flakes
1 cm piece ginger, grated
2 cloves garlic, finely sliced
4 tbsp soy sauce

- Cook the noodles according to packet instructions and drain.
- Meanwhile heat the oil in a wok.
- Sauté the spring onions, peppers, ginger, chilli flakes and garlic over a high heat, then add the noodles and soy sauce.
- Toss well to heat through and serve.

Egg noodles with spring greens
Add 1 finely chopped head of broccoli and 1 leek. Simply sauté the greens with the spring onion, ginger and chilli flakes. Omit the peppers.

Lamb rogan josh

PREPARATION TIME: **5 minutes**
COOKING TIME: **50 minutes**
SERVES: **3-4**

4 cloves garlic
2 cm piece fresh ginger, sliced
4 tbsp vegetable oil
1 tbsp ground coriander
1 tbsp ground cumin
½ tsp cayenne pepper
2 tsp fennel seeds, crushed
2 tsp garam masala
1 onion, peeled and finely chopped
1 tbsp black peppercorns
6 cardamom pods
3 cloves
1 cinnamon stick
750 g / 1 ⅓ lb / 3 cups lamb leg, cubed
(preferably bone in)
400 g chopped tomatoes
fresh coriander (cilantro), to garnish

- Whiz the garlic and ginger to a paste in a food
  processor with a little water.
- Heat the oil in a large casserole and add the
  spices. Stir-fry for 2 minutes until fragrant.
- Add the onion and fry until golden brown,
  then add the lamb and sear on all sides.
- Stir in the garlic paste and cook out for a few
  minutes, then add the ground spices, a little
  salt and chopped tomatoes, reduce the heat
  and simmer for 15 minutes or until the sauce
  is nearly dry.
- Add enough water to come to nearly the top of
  the lamb and simmer for about 20 minutes or
  until the lamb is cooked through.
- Remove from the heat and garnish with fresh
  coriander before serving.

Beef rogan josh
Replace the lamb with the same amount of beef.
Simply cut the beef joint into large cubes and
follow the method as above.

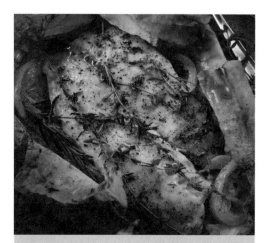

Sautéed lamb with caramelized shallots

PREPARATION TIME: 10 minutes
COOKING TIME: 40 minutes
SERVES: 4

3 tbsp olive oil
1 kg / 2 ¼ lbs / 4 ¼ cups cubed lamb fillet, cut into chunks
3 shallots, peeled and halved
2 carrots, peeled and julienned
2 cloves garlic, roughly chopped
1 tsp mixed dried herbs
fresh basil leaves, to garnish
200 ml / 7 fl. oz / ¾ cup chicken stock

- Heat the oil in a large pan and when smoking, sear the lamb chunks on all sides until golden. Remove with a slotted spoon.
- Add the shallots and carrots and cook gently until softened, then add the garlic and dried herbs. Pour in the stock, season and simmer over a medium-high heat until the liquid becomes syrupy and the shallots are tender.
- Add the lamb back to the pan toss well and season to taste. Garnish with the basil leaves.

Sautéed lamb with new potatoes
Add 6 washed and halved new potatoes to the pan with the lamb chunks, before adding the shallots and carrots.

Steamed halibut with rosemary and lemon

PREPARATION TIME: 10 minutes
COOKING TIME: 30 minutes
SERVES: 4

40 g / 1 ½ oz butter
4 shallots, peeled and sliced
4 thick slices halibut
1 lemon, halved and sliced
1 tbsp mixed dried herbs
1 sprig rosemary
1 sprig thyme
salt and freshly ground black pepper

- Heat the butter in a pan and cook the shallots over a very low heat for at least 20 minutes until golden and very sweet.
- Place the halibut on a plate in a steamer, add the herbs, lemon and season well.
- Cook for about 10 minutes or until the fish is just cooked through and a flake comes away easily.
- Serve the halibut on top of the golden shallots.

Steamed cod with herbs
Replace the halibut with 4 deboned cod steaks. Add 1 tsp fennel seeds to the steamer with the dried herbs and follow the method as above.

EVERYDAY COOKING | **COOK'S BIBLE**

Thai beef pepper curry

PREPARATION TIME: 15 minutes
COOKING TIME: 45 minutes
SERVES: 6

400 g chopped tomatoes
750 g / 1 ⅓ lb / 3 cups rump steak, sliced
2 red peppers, deseeded and sliced
1–2 tbsp caster (superfine) sugar
1–2 tbsp fish sauce
2 limes, juiced
fresh coriander (cilantro), chopped

FOR THE CURRY PASTE
1 tbsp coriander seeds
1 tbsp cumin seeds
2-4 green chillies
8 cloves garlic, peeled
2 stalks lemongrass
1 bunch coriander (cilantro)
2 tbsp fresh galangal or ginger
3 kaffir lime leaves
6 shallots, peeled
1 tbsp dried shrimp paste

- Pound the seeds in a pestle and mortar or in a freezer bag with a rolling pin until finely ground.
- Tip into a food processor and whiz with the rest of the ingredients until smooth. You will only need 4–5 tbsp for this recipe, so keep the rest in a sealed jar in the fridge.
- Heat a wok and add 4–5 tbsp curry paste and ½ the chopped tomatoes. Stir until sizzling.
- Add the beef and coat thoroughly in the paste, then pour in the remaining tomatoes.
- Add the peppers, sugar, fish sauce and juice of 1 lime and simmer gently for about 15–20 minutes or until the peppers are cooked and tender.
- Adjust the flavours with more sugar, fish sauce and lime juice, then serve with Thai sticky rice, sprinkled with coriander.

Pilau rice with chicken and turmeric

PREPARATION TIME: 45-50 minutes
COOKING TIME: 15 minutes
SERVES: 4

500 g / 1lb / 2 cups basmati rice

1 kg / 2 ¼ lbs / 4 ¼ cups boneless chicken, cut into chunks

30 g / 1 oz butter

1 onion, peeled and finely chopped

2 carrots, peeled and sliced

5 cardamom pods, lightly crushed

1 cinnamon stick

1 tsp fresh or ground turmeric

6 cloves

1 pinch saffron soaked in 500ml / 1 pint / 2 cups vegetable stock

- Wash the rice in a sieve under cold running water, then leave to soak for 30 minutes.
- Heat the butter in a pan and when foaming add the onion. Cook until golden and sweet.
- Add the spices and toast lightly, then tip in the rice and stir well to coat in the butter.
- Pour over the stock and a little salt, bring to the boil and cover with a lid.
- Meanwhile, for the chicken, heat some oil in a large pan and when smoking, sear the chicken chunks on all sides until golden. Remove with a slotted spoon.
- Add the chicken and carrots to the rice and stock and cook on a medium heat with the lid on for 45–50 minutes.
- Turn off the heat and leave to stand for 5 minutes. Remove the lid and stir with a fork to separate the grains.

Vegetarian pilau rice
Omit the chicken and replace with 2 deseeded and sliced red peppers. Add some garden peas 10 minutes before the end of cooking time.

Beef hot pot with root veg

PREPARATION TIME: 25 minutes
COOKING TIME: 2 hours, 45 minutes
SERVES: 4

2 tbsp vegetable oil or dripping
1 kg / 2 ¼ lb/ 4 ¼ beef shoulder joint
4 onions, peeled and chopped
1 tbsp butter
1 tbsp flour
500 ml / 1 pint / 2 cups beef stock
1 tbsp Worcestershire sauce
400 g chopped tomatoes
2 bay leaves
1 sprig rosemary
1 kg / 2 ¼ lb/ 4 ¼ cups Brussels sprouts, halved
10 cherry tomatoes, halved
2 medium carrots, peeled and roughly chopped
1 tbsp mixed dried herbs

- Preheat the oven to 170°C (150°C fan) / 325F / gas 3.
- Heat the fat in a large casserole and fry the meat until browned. Remove and set aside.
- Adding a little butter, cook the onions until translucent, then stir in the flour to make a paste.
- Whisk in the stock and Worcestershire sauce to make a smooth sauce and bring to a simmer. Add the chopped tomatoes.
- Add the sauce to a large casserole dish and place the beef joint on top.
- Add the vegetables followed by the herbs, seasoning the layers, arranging in an overlapping pattern.
- Cover with a lid and bake for 2 hours, then remove the lid and cook for a further 45 minutes to crisp up the sprouts.
- Season with black pepper before carving the joint and serving.

Beef hot pot with potatoes
Replace the Brussels sprouts with the same amount of Maris Piper potatoes, quartered. Follow the method as above.

Hot and spicy pork with rice

PREPARATION TIME: **40 minutes**
COOKING TIME: **3 hours, 30 minutes**
SERVES: **4**

1 piece pork belly, about 2 kg / 4 ½ lb
2 red peppers, deseeded and sliced
250 ml / 9 fl oz / 1 cup dry sherry or Shaoxing
rice wine
1 l / 2 ¼ pints / 4 ¼ cups chicken stock
8 tbsp soy sauce
100 g / 3 ½ oz / ½ cup sugar
3 cm piece fresh ginger, sliced
4 cloves garlic, sliced
1 tbsp Chinese 5 spice
2 star anise
1 stick cinnamon
1 red chilli (chili), pricked with a knife
cooked white rice, to serve

- Add the pork to a pan of boiling water, reduce
  the heat and simmer gently, skimming, for
  30 minutes to remove excess fat. Drain well.
- Combine the rest of the ingredients in a large
  stockpot and bring to a simmer.
- Add the blanched pork, return to a gentle
  simmer and cook for 3 hours, covered with a
  lid, skimming occasionally until the pork is
  very tender.
- Remove from the liquid and take off the skin.
  Cut the meat into bite size pieces.
- Skim as much fat as possible from the
  braising liquid and reduce over a high heat
  by half.
- Divide the cooked rice between the 4 serving
  bowls.
- Top with a generous amount of the pork with
  the braising liquid poured over the top.
- Garnish with some fresh coriander, if desired.

Hot and spicy chicken with rice
Replace the pork with 4 chicken breasts. Simply
cut the breast into large chunks and follow the
method as above.

Lamb chops with herb crust

PREPARATION TIME: **30 minutes**
COOKING TIME: **12 minutes**
SERVES: **4**

4 lamb chops
1 pomegranate, seeds removed
a handful of rocket (arugula) leaves, to serve
1 tbsp mustard

FOR THE CRUST
1 bunch parsley, finely chopped
3 sprigs thyme leaves
2 tbsp breadcrumbs
1 clove garlic, chopped
olive oil

- Preheat the oven to 180C / 350F / gas 5.
- Whiz the herbs, pine nuts and garlic in a food processor to a textured paste then add enough olive oil to loosen.
- Spread the herb paste on the chops with 1 tbsp mustard to act as glue. Press on the crust and season the lamb.
- Roast in the oven for 12 minutes for pink lamb.
- Rest the lamb for 5 minutes and transfer to the serving plates.
- Garnish with some rocket leaves and pomegranate seeds for decoration.

Lamb chops with pesto crust
Replace the thyme with a handful of basil leaves and add the juice of 1 lemon and 4 tbsp grated Parmesan to the food processor. Follow the method as above.

Moroccan lamb meatballs with couscous

PREPARATION TIME: **50 minutes**
COOKING TIME: **15 minutes**
SERVES: **4**

2 tbsp olive oil
500 g / 1 lb / 2 cups minced lamb
1 onion, very finely chopped
2 cloves garlic, finely chopped
6 tbsp breadcrumbs
1 tbsp tomato purée
1 tsp ground cinnamon
1 tsp ground cumin
½ lemon, juiced

FOR THE COUSCOUS

400 g / 14 oz cooked couscous, to serve
1 red onion, peeled and diced
½ cucumber, washed and diced
5 cherry tomatoes, quartered
fresh parsley, chopped

- Place the minced lamb in a large bowl and bring to room temperature.
- Add the rest of the ingredients and mix well with your hands to ensure even distribution.
- Roll the mixture into small walnut-sized balls with your hands and place on a baking sheet. Cover with cling film and refrigerate for 30 minutes.
- Heat the olive oil in a large pan.
- Add the meatballs in batches, cooking on all sides until golden and just cooked through – about 6–8 minutes.
- To make the couscous, combine the all the ingredients and season to taste.
- Serve the meatballs on a bed of couscous.

Lamb meatballs with quinoa
Replace the couscous with the same amount of cooked quinoa and follow the method as above. Serve with a wedge of lime on the side.

Glazed duck with orange

PREPARATION TIME: **5 minutes**
COOKING TIME: **1 hour, 45 minutes**
SERVES: **4**

4 duck legs, weighing about 2 ¾ kg / 6 lb

FOR THE SAUCE
100 g / 3 ½ oz / ½ cup caster (superfine) sugar
2 tbsp water
2 oranges, grated zest
250 ml / 9 fl. oz / 1 cup orange juice
1 tbsp marmalade
75 g / 2 ½ oz / ⅓ cup butter, chilled and cubed

TO SERVE
garden peas, cooked
roast potatoes

- Preheat the oven to 220C (200 fan) / 450F / gas 7.
- Prick the duck legs all over with a knife and place in a roasting tin. Season and roast for 20 minutes.
- Reduce the heat to 180C / 350F / gas 4 and cook for 1 hour. Remove from the pan, drain to remove excess fat and save the fat for the roast potatoes. Rest the duck on a plate.
- Make the sauce: set the sugar and water in a pan over a low heat and swirl until the sugar has melted. Do not stir. Allow to bubble up until golden.
- Once dark golden, remove from the heat and carefully, standing back, add any duck resting juices, orange zest and juice.
- Return to the heat and simmer gently for 10–15 minutes until thickened, stir in the marmalade then whisk in the butter a cube at a time until shiny.
- Season and serve the orange glaze with the duck. Serve with a side of cooked garden peas and roast potatoes.

Glazed roast chicken
Replace the duck legs with 4 chicken breasts. Follow the method as above and serve with the roast potatoes and peas.

Pancetta, Parmesan and asparagus risotto

PREPARATION TIME: **10 minutes**
COOKING TIME: **25 minutes**
SERVES: **4**

2 tbsp olive oil
40 g / 1 oz butter
1 onion, peeled and finely chopped
2 cloves garlic, finely chopped
150 g / 5 oz pancetta, sliced
320 g / 11 oz / 1 ⅓ cups risotto rice
8 asparagus spears, ends removed
100 ml / 3 ½ fl. oz / ½ cup dry white wine
1 l / 2 ¼ pints / 4 ¼ cups chicken or vegetable stock
3 tbsp butter
120 g / 4 oz / ½ cup Parmesan, sliced into slithers

- Heat the oil and butter in a large pan and add the onion and garlic. Cook until soft and translucent.
- Add the pancetta and cook until golden.
- Add the rice and stir to coat in the butter. Pour in the wine and stir the rice while the wine is absorbed.
- Once the wine has cooked in, reduce the heat a little and add the hot stock, a ladleful at a time, stirring fairly continuously. This will give the risotto its creamy texture.
- Add the asparagus spears and keep stirring in the stock and tasting the rice. After about 15–20 minutes the rice should be soft but with a slight bite. If you've run out of stock before the rice is cooked, simply use water.
- Season and remove from the heat. Add the butter and Parmesan (mantecatura) and leave to melt into the risotto.
- Garnish with the chopped parsley and serve immediately.

Pancetta, Parmesan and pea risotto
Replace the asparagus with 100g garden peas. Simply add the peas 10 minutes before the end of cooking time and serve with a wedge of lemon.

Sausages with red onion gravy

PREPARATION TIME: 10 minutes
COOKING TIME: 35 minutes
SERVES: 4

8 sausages
vegetable oil
2 tbsp butter
2 large red onions, peeled and thinly sliced
2 sprigs thyme
½ tbsp flour
150 ml / 5 fl oz / ⅔ cup Marsala or red wine
400 ml / 14 fl oz / 1 ½ cups beef stock
1 tbsp grain mustard

TO SERVE
mashed potato with spring onions

- Preheat the oven to 200°C (180°C fan) / 400F / gas 6.
- Prick the sausages all over with a fork.
- Drizzle the sausages with oil in a roasting tin and roast for 30 minutes until browned all over, turning occasionally.
- Meanwhile heat the butter in a pan and cook the onions with thyme for 15–20 minutes, until deep gold and sweet.
- Stir in the flour and cook out for 2 minutes, then stir in the wine and stock. Season and simmer for 20 minutes until thickened.
- Stir in the grain mustard, then serve with the cooked sausages and mashed potato.

Veggie sausages with red onion gravy
Replace the sausages with vegetarian sausages.
Use egg-free sausages for a vegan version.

Lamb and green bean casserole

PREPARATION TIME: **30 minutes**
COOKING TIME: **1 hour, 30 minutes**
SERVES: **4**

2 tbsp vegetable oil
500 g / 1 lb / 2 cups stewing lamb, cut into bite size pieces
1 carrot, roughly chopped
1 stick celery, chopped
1 onion, peeled and chopped
1 leek, white part only, chopped
1 tbsp flour
1 tbsp tomato purée
100 ml / 3 ½ fl. oz / ½ cup red wine
500 ml / 1 pint / 2 cups lamb stock
200 g / 7 oz chopped tomatoes
1 tsp paprika
1 tsp cayenne pepper
2 bay leaves
sprig thyme and rosemary
peas and green beans

- Preheat the oven to 180C / 350F / gas 4.
- Heat the oil in a casserole and cook the lamb in batches.
- Add the chopped vegetables and cook until soft.
- Stir in the flour to make a paste, then add the tomato purée and red wine and bubble up, scraping at the bottom to deglaze.
- Pour in the stock and add the herbs, bay leaves and spices. Season and cook in the oven for 1 ½ hours until the lamb is tender.
- Meanwhile heat a little butter in a pan and cook the vegetables individually in a little vegetable stock until tender. Keep warm in a low oven until needed, cooking the peas and beans at the end.
- When the lamb is ready, remove with a slotted spoon to a dish, strain the sauce, then pour back into the casserole and heat through. Add the lamb and vegetables back into the sauce and serve.

Desserts

Panna cotta with raspberry and mint

PREPARATION TIME: 2 hours, 15 minutes
COOKING TIME: 5 minutes
SERVES: 6

300 ml / 10 fl. oz / 1 ¼ cups double (heavy) cream
1 tbsp caster (superfine) sugar
1 tsp vanilla extract
1 leaf gelatine, soaked in cold water
200 g / 7 oz / ¾ cup raspberries
1 tbsp icing (confectioners') sugar
fresh mint leaves, to serve

- Pour the cream, sugar and vanilla into a pan and simmer. Remove from the heat and leave to infuse.
- Stir the softened gelatine into the hot cream and whisk until dissolved. Reheat if the cream has cooled too much.
- Blend half the raspberries to a purée with the icing sugar.
- Spoon the cream into individual serving glasses, then top with the raspberry purée.
- Refrigerate for 2 hours, then serve with fresh raspberries and mint leaves.

Polenta orange cake

PREPARATION TIME: 25 minutes
COOKING TIME: 45-50 minutes
SERVES: 6-8

250 g / 9 oz / 1 cup butter, softened
250 g / 9 oz / 1 cup caster (superfine) sugar
4 eggs, beaten
150 g / 5 oz / ⅔ cup fine polenta
200 g / 7 oz / ⅔ cup plain (all-purpose) flour
2 tsp baking powder
1 tsp ground cinnamon
2 oranges, grated zest and juice
½ lemon, grated zest
icing (confectioners') sugar, to dust

- Preheat the oven to 160°C (140°C fan) / 310F / gas 3. Grease and line a 23 cm cake tin.
- Cream the butter and sugar together until pale and creamy. Add the eggs a little at a time, beating thoroughly after each addition.
- Whisk in the polenta, flour, baking powder, ground cinnamon, orange and lemon zest until thoroughly incorporated then add the orange juice to make a smooth loose batter.
- Pour into the cake tin, spread evenly and bake for 45–50 minutes or until an inserted skewer comes out clean.
- Remove from the oven and transfer to a wire rack to cool.
- Cut into portions and dust with icing sugar before serving.

Spiced polenta and orange cake
Add 1 tsp ground ginger and 1 tsp ground cardamom for a subtle spicy flavour.

Raspberry and vanilla cupcakes

PREPARATION TIME: **20 minutes**
COOKING TIME: **20 minutes**
MAKES: **8-10**

120 g / 4 oz / ½ cup self-raising flour
120 g / 4 oz / ½ cup caster (superfine) sugar
120 g / 4 oz / ½ cup butter, softened
2 eggs, beaten
1 tsp vanilla extract
1 tsp vanilla powder
2 tbsp milk
200 g frozen raspberries

- Preheat the oven to 200°C (180°C fan) / 400F / gas 6. Line a muffin tins with cupcake cases.
- Place all the ingredients except the milk and raspberries in a food processor and blitz until smooth and combined.
- Add the milk, a little at a time, to make a dropping consistency.
- Divide the mixture evenly between the cases and push 3–4 raspberries down the middle of each cupcake. Bake for 20 minutes or until risen and golden.
- Remove the cakes from the tin to a wire rack to cool.

Blackberry and vanilla cupcakes
Replace the raspberries with the same amount of blackberries and follow the method as above.

Zabaglione with cherries

PREPARATION TIME: **3 hours**
COOKING TIME: **35 minutes**
SERVES: **6**

6 eggs
100 g / 3 ½ oz / ½ cup granulated sugar
1 lemon, grated zest
100 ml / 3 ½ fl. oz / ½ cup cherry brandy
500 g / 1 lb / 2 cups mascarpone
6 cherries, stalks left on

- Whisk the eggs, sugar and zest with an electric whisk until pale and tripled in volume.
- Tip into a bowl over a pan of simmering water.
- Very slowly, whisking constantly, pour in the cherry brandy, whisking until the eggs have doubled again in volume and the mixture is hot. Take your time and be careful not to let it curdle.
- Once combined and frothy, remove from the heat and whisk for a few more moments to cool.
- Spoon the mascarpone into a bowl and slowly whisk in half the zabaglione. Once combined, fold the remaining half in and spoon into glasses.
- Refrigerate for 3 hours. Decorate with the cherries before serving.

Zabaglione with strawberries
Replace the cherry brandy with the same amount of dessert or sweet wine and swap the cherries for slices of strawberries before serving.

Spiced Christmas loaf

PREPARATION TIME: **overnight,
plus 3 weeks to mature**
COOKING TIME: **3 hours**
SERVES: **6-8**

700 g / 1 ½ lb / 3 cups sultanas
225 g / 8 oz / 1 cup raisins
110 g / 4 oz / ½ cup currants
110 g / 4 oz / ½ cup mixed peel
120 ml / 4 fl. oz / ½ cup brandy, plus extra
225 g / 8 oz / 1 cup butter, softened
200 g / 7 oz / ¾ cup brown sugar
1 lemon, grated zest
1 orange, grated zest
4 eggs, beaten
1 tsp almond essence
350 g / 12 oz / 1 ½ cups plain (all-purpose) flour
1 tsp mixed spice
½ tsp ground cinnamon
a pinch of salt
200 g / 7 oz / ¾ cup apricot jam (jelly)
1 kg / 2 lb ready-to-roll icing (frosting) or icing
(confectioners') sugar

- Soak the sultanas, raisins and currants in the
  brandy in a bowl overnight.
- The next day preheat the oven to 150°C / 300F
  / gas 2. Grease and line a 23 cm springform
  cake tin.
- Cream the butter and sugar, then beat in the
  zest. Add the eggs a little at a time then add
  the almond essence.
- Fold in the flour, spices and the soaked fruit.
- Pour into the loaf tin and bake for about 3
  hours, until an inserted skewer comes out
  clean.
- Remove from the tin, wrap in foil and store
  in an airtight container for at least 3 weeks.
  You could feed the cake with a tablespoon of
  brandy every other day.
- Warm the jam in a small pan and paint over
  the cake. Roll out the icing and cover the cake
  with it, cutting away any excess. Decorate as
  desired. Alternatively, roll and dust heavily
  with icing sugar

Spiced marzipan loaf
Add 1 kg / 2 lb ready-to-roll marzipan on top of
the loaf before adding the icing.

Coconut and mango mousse

PREPARATION TIME: 1 hour
SERVES: 4

1 mango, peeled and diced
1 lemon, juiced
1 tbsp maple syrup
250 ml / 9 oz / 1 cup coconut yogurt
2 tbsp desiccated coconut

- Place the mango, reserving a few pieces for garnish, lemon juice and maple syrup in a pan with just enough water to cover and allow to simmer until the mango has a purée-like consistency.

- Remove from the heat, leave to cool and then chill for at least 30 minutes.

- Divide ½ the yogurt between 4 ramekins and spoon the mango purée on top.

- Add the remaining yogurt and top with the reserved mango pieces and desiccated coconut.

Chocolate and hazelnut torte

PREPARATION TIME: **30 minutes**
COOKING TIME: **1 hour**
SERVES: **6-8**

225 g / 8 oz / 1 cup plain (all-purpose) flour
2 tbsp cocoa powder
1 ½ tsp baking powder
300 g / 10 oz / 1 ¼ cup caster (superfine) sugar
3 eggs
250 ml / 9 fl. oz / 1 cup vegetable oil
1 tsp vanilla extract

TO DECORATE
200g / 7 oz / ¾ cup icing (confectioners') sugar
5 tbsp cocoa powder
150g / 5 oz / ⅔ cup cream cheese
a handful of chopped hazelnuts (cobnuts),
to garnish

- Preheat the oven to 190°C (170°C fan) / 375F / gas 5. Grease and line an 18cm springform cake tin.
- Sieve the flour, cocoa powder and baking powder into a large bowl. Stir in the sugar and set aside.
- Whisk the eggs, oil and vanilla extract together, then beat into the flour mixture until just combined.
- Pour into the cake tin and bake for about an hour or until an inserted skewer comes out clean. Set aside to cool, then remove from the tin.
- Make the frosting by beating the icing sugar and 3 tablespoons of the cocoa powder into the cream cheese with an electric whisk.
- Smooth over the cooled cake and decorate with the chopped hazelnuts and remaining cocoa powder.

Chocolate and orange torte
Add the juice and zest of 1 orange and 1 tsp orange essence to the cake batter and follow the method as above.

Banana, pecan and raisin loaf

PREPARATION TIME: 20 minutes
COOKING TIME: up to 1 hour, 30 minutes
SERVES: 4

350 g / 12 oz over ripe bananas
180 g / 6 oz / ¾ cup plain (all-purpose) flour
2 tsp baking powder
1 tsp ground cinnamon
¼ tsp mixed spice
a pinch of salt
150 g / 5 oz / ⅔ cup soft dark brown sugar
2 eggs, beaten
100 g / 3 ½ oz / ¼ cup butter, melted
120 g / 4 oz / ½ cup raisins
120 g / 4 oz / ½ cup pecans, chopped

- Preheat the oven to 170°C (150°C fan) / 325F / gas 3. Grease a medium loaf tin.
- Mash the bananas in a bowl until pulpy.
- Sieve the flour into a bowl with the baking powder, spices and salt.
- Whisk the sugar and eggs until pale and creamy and doubled in volume, then whisk in the butter. Fold in the bananas, raisins and flour until thoroughly combined.
- Pour into the loaf tin and sprinkle the pecans on top. Bake for 1–1 ½ hours or until an inserted skewer comes out clean.
- Turn onto a wire rack to cool.

Banana, walnut and ginger loaf
Add 1 tsp ground ginger to the ingredients and sprinkle over the chopped walnuts before baking as above.

Tiramisu pots

PREPARATION TIME: **3 hours, 25 minutes**
SERVES: **4**

600 ml / 1 pint / 2 cups double (heavy) cream
250 g / 9 oz / 1 cup mascarpone
3 tbsp Marsala dolce
5 tbsp caster (superfine) sugar
300 ml / 10 fl. oz / 1 ¼ cups strong coffee
2 tbsp coffee liqueur (optional)
175 g / 6 oz sponge fingers (ladyfingers)
25 g / 1 oz dark chocolate, grated
3 tsp cocoa powder
12 coffee beans, to garnish

- Place the cream, mascarpone, Marsala and sugar in a bowl and whisk until combined and thick.
- Pour the coffee (and liqueur) into a shallow dish and soak the sponge fingers in it, but be careful they don't disintegrate.
- Layer half the fingers into individual pots then spoon over half the mascarpone mixture and add half of the grated chocolate. Repeat until all the ingredients are used up.
- Chill in the refrigerator for 3 hours.
- Dust the pots with cocoa powder and the coffee beans to serve.

Ginger tiramisu pots
Add 1 tsp ground ginger to the dish with the coffee, liqueur and sponge fingers. Follow the method as above and garnish with the coffee beans and a sprinkling of ground ginger.

Chocolate cherry cake with buttercream

PREPARATION TIME: 30 minutes
COOKING TIME: 30 minutes
SERVES: 8-10

120 g / 4 oz / ½ cup self-raising flour
1 tsp baking powder
120 g / 4 oz / ½ cup butter, softened
120 g / 4 oz / ½ cup caster (superfine) sugar
2 eggs
1 ½ tbsp cocoa powder
100 g / 3 ½ oz fresh cherries, stalks left on

FOR THE WHITE BUTTERCREAM
100 g / 3 ½ oz / ½ cup butter, softened
150 g / 5 oz / ⅔ cup icing (confectioners') sugar
1 tsp vanilla extract

FOR THE CHOCOLATE BUTTERCREAM
100 g / 3 ½ oz / ½ cup butter, softened
150 g / 5 oz / ⅔ cup icing (confectioners') sugar
1 tsp vanilla extract
4 tbsp cocoa powder

- Preheat the oven to 170°C (150°C fan) / 325F / gas 3. Grease and line two 18cm (7 in) cake tins.
- Sieve the flour and baking powder into a large bowl, then add the other ingredients except for the cherries and whisk until completely combined.
- Divide the mixture equally between the two cake tins and bake for 30 minutes.
- Remove from the tins and cool on a wire rack.
- To make the white buttercream, cream the butter and sugar until pale and smooth, then stir in the vanilla. Set to one side.
- For the chocolate buttercream, cream the butter and sugar until pale and smooth, then stir in the vanilla and cocoa powder.
- Use the chocolate icing to sandwich the cakes together.
- Decorate with the white icing and cherries.

Carrot cake with buttercream

PREPARATION TIME: **20 minutes**
COOKING TIME: **1 hour, 30 minutes**
SERVES: **4**

300 g / 10 oz / 1 ¼ cups plain (all-purpose) flour
1 tsp ground cinnamon
1 tsp baking powder
½ tsp bicarbonate of soda
200 g / 7 oz / ¾ cup soft dark brown sugar
4 eggs
250 ml / 9 fl. oz / 1 cup vegetable oil
zest of 2 oranges
200 g / 7 oz / ¾ cup carrots, peeled and grated
125 g / 4 oz / ½ cup butter, softened
2 tbsp icing (confectioners') sugar
250 g/ 9 oz / 1 cup cream cheese
zest of ½ lemon
chopped pecans, to sprinkle

- Preheat the oven to 150°C (130°C fan) / 300F / gas 2. Grease and line a 20 cm cake tin.
- Sieve the flour into a bowl with cinnamon, baking powder and bicarbonate of soda, then stir in the sugar.
- Beat the eggs with the oil and fold into the flour with the carrots and orange zest.
- Spoon the batter into two shallow cake tins and bake for about 1 ½ hours until an inserted skewer comes out clean. Leave to cool.
- Beat the butter and sugar together until pale, then beat in the cream cheese and lemon zest.
- Chill until spreadable, then spread a thick layer on one side of one the cakes, using a palette knife to smooth.
- Place the other cake half on top and sandwich together. Spread the remaining buttercream on top of the cake and sprinkle the chopped pecans.

Carrot cake with lemon buttercream
Add 1 tsp lemon extract and the zest and juice of 1 lemon to the buttercream ingredients and whisk well. Follow rest of the method as above.

Chocolate fondant raspberry tart

PREPARATION TIME: **20 minutes**
COOKING TIME: **30 minutes**
SERVES: **8**

3 eggs
300 g / 10 oz / 1 ¼ cups muscovado sugar
175 g / 6 oz / ¾ cup butter, melted
1 tsp raspberry essence
1 tsp vanilla powder
2 tbsp plain (all purpose) flour
2 tbsp cocoa powder
50 g / 1 ¾ oz / ¼ cup dark chocolate, chopped
1 pastry case
16 fresh raspberries

- Preheat the oven to 180°C (160°C fan) / 350F / gas 4.
- Beat the eggs and sugar until pale and tripled in volume. Stir in the butter, raspberry essence and vanilla powder, then fold in the flour and cocoa. Scatter the chopped chocolate into the pastry base and pour over the filling.
- Bake for 30 minutes or until just firm.
- Top with some fresh raspberries before serving.

Chocolate fondant orange tart
Replace the raspberry essence with orange essence and add the juice of 1 orange. Garnish with the zest of 2 freshly grated oranges.

Vanilla and raspberry custard pots

PREPARATION TIME: **45 minutes**
COOKING TIME: **10 minutes**
SERVES: **4**

300 ml / 10 fl. oz / 1 ¼ cups single cream
3 egg yolks
1 tsp cornflour
1 tbsp caster (superfine) sugar
1 tsp raspberry essence
½ tsp vanilla extract
8 fresh raspberries, to garnish
1 tsp ground cinnamon, to garnish

- Heat the cream in a pan until nearly boiling.
- Whisk the egg yolks, cornflour, sugar, raspberry essence and vanilla extract. Pour the hot cream into the bowl, whisking all the time, then return to the pan. Whisk over a low heat until the sauce has thickened.
- If the sauce does start to curdle, simply remove from the heat and whisk vigorously as it cools. It will become smooth again. Pour the custard into individual ramekins and transfer to the fridge for 30 minutes or until set.
- Dust over a little cinnamon and top with the fresh raspberries before serving.

Vanilla and coconut custard pots
Replace the single cream with coconut cream and follow the method as normal. Garnish with some flaked coconut before serving.

Apple, coconut and raisin crumble pie

PREPARATION TIME: 25 minutes
COOKING TIME: 25-35 minutes
SERVES: 4

750 g / 1 ⅓ lb / 3 cups apples, peeled, cored and diced
75 g / 2 ½ oz / ⅓ cup raisins, soaked in a little Calvados or brandy
2 tbsp ground cinnamon
2 tbsp desiccated coconut
1 ready-made deep pastry case

FOR THE CRUMBLE
120 g / 4 oz / ½ cup plain (all-purpose) flour
90 g / 3 oz / ½ cup chilled butter, diced
3 tbsp muscovado sugar
3 tbsp caster (superfine) sugar

- Preheat the oven to 190°C (170°C fan) / 370F / gas 5.
- Cook the apples with a little water until soft.
- Put the flour in a bowl with a pinch of salt.
- Add the cold cubes of butter and, using the tips of your fingers, work the butter into the flour until the mixture resembles porridge oats.
- Place the cooked apple, coconut and soaked raisins with the cinnamon in the bottom of a baking dish and cover loosely with the crumble mixture.
- Cook in the oven for 25–35 minutes until golden on top.

Pear, coconut and cranberry crumble pie
Omit the apples and peel, core and dice the same amount of pears. Replace the raisins with dried cranberries and follow the method as normal.

Chocolate peppermint Swiss roll

PREPARATION TIME: **30 minutes**
COOKING TIME: **10 minutes**
SERVES: **8**

3 eggs
75 g / 2 ½ oz / ⅓ cup caster (superfine) sugar
60 g / 2 oz / ¼ cup plain (all-purpose) flour
1 ½ tbsp cocoa powder
300 ml / 10 fl. oz / 1 ¼ cup double (heavy) cream
1 tsp peppermint extract
a sprig of mint, to garnish

- Preheat the oven to 180°C (160°C fan) / 350F / gas 5.
- Grease and line a 33 x 23 cm (13 x 9 inch) Swiss roll tin or baking tray.
- Whisk the eggs and sugar together until tripled in volume.
- Sieve the flour and cocoa powder into a bowl, then fold into the egg mixture a little at a time. Pour into the Swiss roll tin and bake for 10 minutes. Whisk the cream to soft peaks and stir in the peppermint extract.
- Place a large piece of baking parchment on a work surface and sprinkle with sugar. Turn the cake out onto the parchment at one end, removing the paper from the tin.
- Trim the edges of the sponge to neaten, then spread with a layer of cream. Roll up from the short end to make a fat sausage shape while still warm. Leave to cool completely.
- Slice the Swiss roll into portions and garnish with some mint sprigs before serving.

Chocolate vanilla Swiss roll
Replace the peppermint extract with vanilla essence and follow the method as above.

Ginger cake with pomegranate seeds

PREPARATION TIME: 20 minutes
COOKING TIME: 45 minutes
SERVES: 6

250 g / 9 oz / 1 cup self-raising flour
1 tsp baking powder
½ tsp bicarbonate of soda
½ tsp ground ginger
½ tsp mixed spice
75 g / 2 ½ oz / ⅓ cup caster (superfine) sugar
200 ml / 7 fl. oz / ¾ cup milk
1 egg
75 g / 2 ½ oz / ⅓ cup unsalted butter, melted
2–3 tbsp stem ginger, finely chopped
1 pomegranate, seeds removed

- Preheat the oven to 200°C (180°C fan) / 400F / gas 6. Grease and line a 23 cm (9 in) round tin.
- In one bowl, combine the dry ingredients.
- Pour the milk in to a measuring jug and crack in the egg and whisk with a fork to amalgamate.
- Pour the liquid ingredients into the dry ingredients, stirring with a wooden spoon. The batter should remain somewhat lumpy – do not whisk until smooth. Add the stem ginger to the batter and stir in.
- Pour into the round tin and bake in the oven for about 45 minutes or until an inserted skewer comes out clean.
- Remove to a wire rack and allow to cool before sprinkling over the pomegranate seeds and serving.

Ginger and pear cake
Peel, core and dice 2 conference pears and combine with the liquid and dry ingredients, stir well before pouring into the cake tin and baking as above.

Lemon and coconut soufflés

PREPARATION TIME: **15 minutes**
COOKING TIME: **15 minutes**
SERVES: **4**

butter, melted
100 ml / 3 ½ fl. oz / ½ cup double (heavy) cream
1 tbsp plain (all-purpose) flour
3 tsp cornflour
100 ml / 3 ½ fl. oz / ½ cup milk
2 lemons, juice and zest
2 egg yolks + 4 egg whites
6 heaped tbsp caster (superfine) sugar + 2 tbsp
for dusting
4 tbsp desiccated coconut, to sprinkle
1 lemon, halved and sliced

- Preheat oven to 180°C (160°C fan) / 350F /
  gas 5.
- Brush the insides of 4 ramekins with the
  melted butter then add a little sugar to each
  and turn them to coat the sides and bottom.
  Refrigerate.
- Place the cream, flour and cornflour in a bowl
  and whisk until smooth. Heat the milk in a
  pan, then whisk into the cream mixture. Pour
  back into the pan and place over a gentle heat.
  Whisk until thickened, then whisk in the
  lemon zest and juice.
- Whisk in the egg yolks and sugar. When it
  starts to look like custard, set aside to cool.
- Whisk the egg whites to soft peaks. Once the
  lemon mixture is cool, fold in the remaining
  egg whites.
- Spoon the soufflé mix into the ramekins.
- Place on a preheated baking tray for
  15 minutes or until risen. Sprinkle the
  desiccated coconut on top and garnish with
  the lemon slices, serve immediately.

Chai-spiced soufflés
Add 1 tsp ground cinnamon, 1 tsp ground ginger
and 1 tsp ground cardamom to the saucepan
with the milk. Follow the method as above and
garnish with some cinnamon sticks and cloves.

Victoria plum cake

PREPARATION TIME: **25 minutes**
COOKING TIME: **1 hour**
SERVES: **8**

200 g / 7 oz / ¾ cup Victoria plums, stoned and sliced
3-4 tbsp sugar
120 g / 4 oz / ½ cup self-raising flour
120 g / 4 oz / ½ cup caster (superfine) sugar
¼ tsp baking powder
2 eggs
1 tbsp milk
1 tsp vanilla extract
100 g / 3 ½ oz / ½ cup butter, softened
icing (confectioners') sugar, to dust

- Preheat the oven to 180°C (160°C fan / 350F / gas 4. Grease and line a 20 cm (8 inch) cake tin.
- Toss the stoned plums in the sugar to macerate.
- Sieve the flour into a bowl and add the sugar and baking powder. Whisk the eggs, milk and vanilla.
- Beat the butter and some of the egg mixture into the dry ingredients until combined, then whisk in the rest until completely incorporated.
- Spoon into the tin and decorate the top with the plums.
- Bake for about 1 hour or until an inserted skewer comes out clean. Leave to cool completely before removing from the tin.
- Dust with some icing sugar before serving.

Mirabelle plum cake
Replace the Victoria plums with the same amount of Mirabelle plums and follow the method as above.

Baked raspberry and mint Alaska

PREPARATION TIME: **20 minutes**
COOKING TIME: **5 minutes**
SERVES: **4**

6 egg whites
a pinch of salt
1 tsp cream of tartar
200 g / 7 oz / ¾ cup caster (superfine) sugar
1 tsp vanilla extract
1 ready-made rectangular sponge base
1 kg / 2 lb / 4 cups ice cream, slightly softened
5 tbsp ready-made raspberry sauce
100 g / 3 oz raspberries, to garnish
50 g / 2 oz monkey nuts or peanuts, to garnish
1 sprig fresh mint
icing (confectioners') sugar, to dust

- Preheat the oven to its hottest temperature and place a shelf very low down.
- Whisk the egg whites until foamy, then whisk in the salt and cream of tartar until it forms soft peaks. Gradually, whisk in the sugar a little at a time until thick and glossy, then fold in the vanilla extract.
- Place the sponge base on a lined baking sheet.
- Using an ice cream scoop, place balls of ice cream on the base, leaving a good edge around the outside.
- Pile the meringue on top, spreading with a palette knife and ensuring the ice cream is completely covered.
- Place under a grill for 2 minutes until golden.
- Spoon the raspberry sauce over the top and garnish with fresh raspberries and mint leaves. Dust a little icing sugar on top before serving. Serve immediately.

White chocolate berry Alaska
Top with the raspberry sauce and add a handful mixed summer berries on top. Add some slithers of white chocolate before serving.

Cherry bake

PREPARATION TIME: **10 minutes**
COOKING TIME: **35-40 minutes**
SERVES: **6-8**

500 g / 1 lb / 2 cups cherries, stoned
125 g / 4 oz / ½ cup plain (all-purpose) flour
a pinch of salt
50 g / 1 ¾ oz / ¼ cup caster (superfine) sugar, plus extra for dusting
3 eggs, beaten
300 ml / 10 fl. oz / 1 ¼ cups milk
3 tbsp cherry brandy or liqueur

- Preheat the oven to 180°C (160°C fan) / 350F / gas 5.
- Grease a 23 cm (9 in) round baking tin with butter or vegetable oil, then place the cherries in the bottom.
- In a bowl, whisk together the flour, salt and sugar and the beaten eggs until smooth, then whisk in the milk and cherry liqueur, then mix to form a smooth batter.
- Pour the mixture over the cherries and bake for 35–40 minutes.
- Allow to cool before dusting over some sugar and serving.

Raspberry and strawberry fools

PREPARATION TIME: **10 minutes**
SERVES: **4**

150 g / 5 oz / ¾ cup raspberries
150 g / 5 oz / ¾ cup cups strawberries, chopped
150 ml / 5 fl. oz / ⅔ cup double (heavy) cream
125 ml / 4 fl. oz / ½ cup Greek natural yogurt
1 tbsp icing (confectioners') sugar
fresh mint leaves, to garnish

- Tip the raspberries and strawberries, reserving a few for garnish, into a bowl and lightly crush with a fork to release some of the juices.
- Lightly whip the cream to soft peaks, then fold in the yogurt.
- Fold the crushed fruit through to make a ripple effect. Adjust the sweetness with the sugar to taste.
- Serve in dessert glasses or bowls and garnish with the remaining berries and mint leaves.

Summer fruit coconut fools
Use 300 g / 10 oz / 1 ¼ mixed summer berries to replace the strawberries and raspberries and follow the method as above. Garnish with some flaked coconut before serving.

Dark chocolate and mint mousse

PREPARATION TIME: **20 minutes**
SERVES: **4**

200 g / 7oz / ¾ cup dark chocolate
1–2 drops peppermint essence
4 eggs, separated
4 strawberries
4 tsp grated dark chocolate
mint sprigs, to garnish

- Melt the chocolate with a tablespoon of water in a small bowl over a pan of simmering water.
- Remove the melted chocolate from the heat, leave for 2 minutes, add the peppermint essence, then beat in the egg yolks. Leave to cool for around 10 minutes.
- Meanwhile, whisk the egg whites to soft peaks. Use a metal spoon to fold into the chocolate mixture.
- Spoon into individual glasses or a bowl, cover with cling film and chill for at least 6 hours.
- Decorate with mint sprigs, strawberries and grated dark chocolate.

White chocolate and mint mousse
Replace the dark chocolate for the same amount of white chocolate. Decorate with a fresh strawberry, mint and some shards of white chocolate.

Poached pears with flaked almonds

PREPARATION TIME: **10 minutes**
COOKING TIME: **45-50 minutes**
SERVES: **4**

500 ml / 1 pint / 2 cups white wine
2 tbsp runny honey
75 g / 2 ½ oz / ⅓ cup soft brown sugar
1 cinnamon stick
1 vanilla pod, split
2 star anise
4 pears, peeled and halved
whipped cream, to garnish
4 tbsp flaked almonds

- Place the wine, honey, sugar, spices and vanilla pod in a large pan and bring to the boil.
- Simmer for 10 minutes to infuse.
- Place the pears upright in the pan and poach gently for around 30 minutes or until completely tender.
- Remove the pears from the liquor and set aside to cool.
- Reduce the poaching liquor by half.
- Serve the pears, with the poaching liquor spooned over, some whipped cream and the flaked almonds.

Vanilla poached pears with hazelnuts
Add 1 tsp vanilla essence to the saucepan with the rest of the poaching ingredients. Swap the flaked almonds with chopped hazelnuts.

Almond fruit cake

PREPARATION TIME: 20-30 minutes
COOKING TIME: 1-2 hours
SERVES: 8

175 g / 6 oz / ¾ cup butter, softened
175 g / 6 oz / ¾ cup light brown sugar
3 tbsp marmalade
3 eggs, beaten
225 g / 8 oz / 1 cup self-raising flour
1 tbsp ground almonds
1 tsp mixed spice
½ tsp ground cinnamon
400g / 14 oz / 1 ½ cups raisins
2 tbsp whisky
100 g blanched almonds

- Preheat the oven to 150°C (130°C fan) / 300F / gas 2. Grease and line a 20 cm (8 in) springform cake tin.
- Cream the butter and sugar in a food processor until pale and creamy. Add the marmalade and pulse, then add the eggs a little at a time, beating thoroughly after each addition.
- Add the flour, almonds, spices and mix well until combined. Stir in the raisins with a metal spoon, then stir in the whisky.
- Spoon into the cake tin, level out the surface and arrange the almonds in concentric circles on top.
- Bake for 1 ½–2 hours or until firm and golden brown.
- Leave to cool for 10 minutes, then remove from the tin and cool on a wire rack.

Pecan fruit cake
Replace the blanched almonds with the same amount of pecans and follow the method as described above.

Black Forest cupcakes

PREPARATION TIME: 1 hour
COOKING TIME: 25 minutes
SERVES: 20

250 g / 9 oz / 1 cup butter, softened
250 g / 9 oz / 1 cup caster (superfine) sugar
150 g / 5 oz / ⅔ cup self raising flour
3 tbsp cocoa powder
1 tsp baking powder
350 g / 12 oz / 1 ½ cups morello cherry jam (jelly)
1 jar or can bottled cherries and their juice
3 tbsp cherry brandy or liqueur
4 eggs
50 g / 1 ¾ oz / ¼ cup dark chocolate, grated
5 tbsp grated milk chocolate
12 fresh cherries, stalks left on

FOR THE WHITE BUTTERCREAM
6 tbsp unsalted butter
2 tbsp double (heavy) cream
½ tsp vanilla extract
250 g / 9 oz / 1 cup (confectioners') sugar
a pinch of salt

- Preheat the oven to 190°C (170°C fan) / 375F / gas 5. Line a cupcake baking tray with cupcake cases.
- Mix the butter, sugar, flour, cocoa powder, baking powder, jam, bottled cherries, cherry brandy and eggs in a food processor until smooth.
- Divide equally between the individual cases and bake for 25 minutes until risen. Transfer onto a wire rack. Leave to cool completely.
- To make the buttercream, simply whisk the buttercream ingredients until thick and light.
- Smooth the buttercream over the cupcake tops with a palette knife. Finish with grated chocolate and a cherry.

Black Forest cake
Replace the cupcake cases with a large round cake tin. Grease the tin before pouring in the cake batter. Bake as above and smooth the buttercream on top.

Date, ginger and walnut cake

PREPARATION TIME: 30 minutes
COOKING TIME: 1 hour
SERVES: 4-6

250 g / 9 oz / 1 cup self-raising flour

½ tsp mixed spice

1 tsp ground ginger

175 g / 6 oz / ¾ cup butter, softened

100 g / 3 ½ oz / ½ cup muscovado sugar

2 eggs, beaten

100 g / 3 ½ oz / ½ cup Medjool dates, stoned
and chopped

60 g / 2 oz / ¼ cup walnuts, chopped

- Preheat the oven to 160°C (140°C fan) / 325F /
  gas 3. Grease and line a 2 lb loaf tin.
- Sieve the flour into a bowl with the spices,
  butter, sugar and eggs. Add the dates and
  walnuts and blend with a wooden spoon or
  electric whisk.
- Spoon into the loaf tin then bake for 1 hour.
- Leave to cool for 15 minutes, then remove
  from the tin and cool on a wire rack.
- Top with any remaining walnuts before
  serving.

Spiced baked apples

PREPARATION TIME: 10 minutes
COOKING TIME: 20 minutes
SERVES: 4

4 eating apples, cored
2 tbsp butter, softened
1 tsp ground cinnamon
1 orange, grated zest and juice
1 tbsp granulated sugar, to sprinkle
cinnamon sticks, to garnish (optional)

FOR THE SAUCE
1 vanilla pod, split
250 ml / 9 fl. oz / 1 cup double (heavy) cream
80 g / 2 ½ oz / ⅓ cup butter
80 g / 2 ½ oz / ⅓ cup dark brown sugar

- Preheat the oven to 200°C (180°C fan / 400F / gas 7.
- Score a line around the centre of each apple to help prevent bursting.
- Mix together the butter, cinnamon and orange zest and squeeze in the juice of ½ the orange. Push some of the butter into the centre of each apple.
- Place in a roasting tin, pour a little water into the bottom and dot with any remaining butter mixture. Cover with aluminium foil and bake for 20 minutes or until tender.
- Meanwhile, heat the sauce ingredients together in a pan, stirring until smooth and thickened.
- Pour over the baked apples and sprinkle some granulated sugar on top. Garnish with some cinnamon sticks (optional) before serving.

Rum and raisin baked apples
Mix 2 tbsp rum and a handful of raisins with the butter, cinnamon, orange zest and orange juice. Follow the method as above.

Pear cake with maple drizzle

PREPARATION TIME: 20 minutes
COOKING TIME: 1 hour
SERVES: 6-8

200 g / 7 oz / ¾ cup butter, softened
100 g / 3 ½ oz / ½ cup caster (superfine) sugar
100 g / 3 ½ oz / ½ cup soft dark brown sugar
2 eggs, beaten
1 tsp vanilla extract
½ tsp ground cinnamon
200 g / 7 oz / ¾ cup self raising flour
½ tsp baking powder
a pinch of salt
2–3 ripe pears, peeled cored and thinly sliced
4 tbsp maple syrup
1 lemon, juiced

- Preheat the oven to 160°C (140°C fan) / 310F / gas 3. Grease and line a large round cake tin.
- Beat the butter and both sugars together, then whisk in the eggs a little at a time, beating thoroughly after each addition. Stir in the vanilla extract and cinnamon.
- Using a metal spoon, fold in the flour, baking powder and salt. Stir in the pears, reserving some for the top of the cake.
- Pour the batter into the cake tin and place the remaining pear slices on top. Bake for 1 hr or until an inserted skewer comes out clean.
- Leave to cool in the tin before turning out onto a wire rack to cool completely.
- For the maple drizzle, simply combine the maple syrup and the lemon juice and pour over the cake.

Pear and almond cake
Add 100 g flaked almonds to the batter before pouring into the baking tin.

Chocolate orange and walnut brownies

PREPARATION TIME: **15 minutes**
COOKING TIME: **30 minutes**
MAKES: **16**

120 g / 4 oz / ½ cup butter
50 g / 2 oz / ¼ cup dark chocolate
2 eggs, beaten
1 tsp orange essence
225 g / 8 oz / 1 cup granulated sugar
50 g / 2 oz / ½ cup plain (all-purpose) flour
1 tsp baking powder
a pinch of salt
150 g / 5 oz / ⅔ cup walnuts, chopped

- Preheat the oven to 180°C (160°C fan) / 350F / gas 4.
- Melt the butter and chocolate in a bowl over a pan of simmering water.
- Once melted, stir in the other ingredients until smooth and combined.
- Pour into a tin and bake for 30 minutes until the centre feels springy to the touch.
- Leave to cool in the tin before dividing into 16 squares and cooling on a wire rack.

Chocolate orange and pecan brownies
Replace the walnuts for the same amount of chopped pecans and bake as above.

Lemon and mint sorbet

PREPARATION TIME: **10 minutes (+ churning time)**
MAKES: **1 litre**

500 g / 1 lb / 2 cups caster (superfine) sugar
250 ml / 9 fl. oz / 1 cup lemon juice
1 lemon, grated zest
1 tsp lemon essence
fresh mint sprigs, to garnish

- Heat the sugar in a pan with 750 ml / 1 ⅓ pints / 3 cups water and stir until dissolved.
- If the lemon is waxed, dip into boiling water briefly to remove it. Stir in the lemon essence, lemon juice and half of the zest, then leave to cool.
- Churn in an ice cream machine to a smooth sorbet. Freeze until required.
- Transfer to the refrigerator 1 hour before eating.
- Garnish with the remaining lemon zest and mint leaves.

Lemon and lime sorbet
Add the juice and zest of 5 limes and combine with the rest of the ingredients for added citrusy flavour.

Peach pie

PREPARATION TIME: 10 minutes
COOKING TIME: 20-25 minutes
SERVES: 4-6

500 g / 1 lb / 2 cups peaches, halved and stoned
1 vanilla pod, halved
4 tbsp sugar
300 g / 10 ½ oz ready-made chilled puff pastry
1 egg, beaten
75 g / 2 ½ oz / ⅓ cup peach or apricot jam (jelly)

- To make the filling, cook half the peaches in a pan with a splash of water, the vanilla pod and sugar over a very low heat until tender, stirring occasionally. Leave to cool.
- Roll out the chilled puff pastry and divide into two thirds and one third. Flatten into circles and leave for 30 minutes.
- Preheat oven to 180°C (160°C fan) / 350F / gas 5.
- Roll out the larger pastry circle to line a 20 cm (8 in) greased pie dish and press into the dish. Roll the other dough circle out on baking parchment and chill.
- Spoon the cooked peaches over the pastry base, then top with the uncooked peach halves.
- Arrange the smaller pastry circle on top of the tart and brush with egg.
- Bake on a preheated baking sheet for 1 hour until crisp.
- Leave to cool, brushing with a little warmed peach or apricot jam (jelly) for shine.

Apricot and cardamom pie
Replace the peaches with the same amount of halved and stoned apricots. Add 1 tsp ground cardamom to the pan with the apricots, vanilla pod and sugar. Cook as above.

Apple and cinnamon strudel

PREPARATION TIME: 30 minutes
COOKING TIME: 35 minutes
SERVES: 4

750 g / 1 ⅓ lb / 3 cups eating apples, peeled, cored and chopped
1 orange, zested and juiced
100 g / 3 ½ oz / ½ cup caster (superfine) sugar
¼ tsp ground cloves
2 tsp ground cinnamon
grated nutmeg
60 g / 2 oz / ¼ cup sultanas
6-8 sheets ready-made filo pastry
60 g / 2 oz / ¼ cup butter, melted
3 tbsp breadcrumbs
1 tbsp icing (confectioners') sugar, to sprinkle

- Preheat the oven to 190°C (170°C fan) / 375F / gas 5.
- Place the apples in a bowl and coat well with the orange juice to prevent browning. Add the zest, sugar, spices and sultanas. Mix well.
- Brush each sheet of filo with melted butter, keeping the rest under a damp tea towel while not using.
- Lay out a large piece of baking parchment and layer the sheets of filo on top of one another. Sprinkle the top sheet with breadcrumbs.
- Spoon the apple mixture down the middle of the sheet.
- Roll the pastry around the apple to make a long and wide strudel shape, using the parchment to help you roll.
- Sprinkle the top of the strudel with the granulated sugar.
- Lift onto a baking sheet, brush with more melted butter and bake for 35 minutes or until golden and crisp.

Pear and cinnamon strudel
Replace the apples with the same amount of peeled, cored and chopped pears. Follow the method as normal.

Blueberry tartlets

PREPARATION TIME: 45 minutes
COOKING TIME: 20 minutes
MAKES: 12

175 g / 6 oz / 1 ¼ cups plain (all-purpose) flour
100 g / 3 ½ oz / ½ cup unsalted butter, cold cut
into cubes
30 g / 1 oz / ¼ cup icing (confectioners') sugar
4 free-range eggs
150 g / 5 ¼ oz / ⅔ cup caster (superfine) sugar
300 ml / 10 ½ fl. oz / 1 ½ cups double (heavy) cream
1 vanilla pod
200 g / 7 oz / 1 ½ cup blueberries

- To make the pastry, pulse the flour, butter and
  icing sugar together in a food processor until
  it forms a breadcrumb like consistency.

- Add one egg to the mixture with a tablespoon
  of cold water. Continue to mix until a rough
  dough forms. Turn out onto a lightly floured
  surface and knead just enough to bring the
  dough together. Roll into a ball and wrap in
  cling film. Chill in the fridge for 15 minutes.

- Preheat the oven to 200°C (180°C fan) / 400F /
  gas 6 and grease and line twelve 7.5 cm
  (3 inch) fluted tart tins.

- Roll out the pastry to a thickness of about
  5 mm and use a 10 cm (4 inch) round cutter to
  cut out the tart bases. Place into the tins,
  add a layer of baking parchment and a few
  baking beans.

- Blind bake the cases for 7-8 minutes, remove
  the parchment and beans and bake for a
  further 3-4 minutes until lightly coloured.
  Remove from the oven to cool.

- In a large mixing bowl, whisk the remaining
  egg yolks and caster sugar until light and pale.

- Heat the cream in a pan over a medium heat,
  taking care to no let it boil. Cut the vanilla
  pod in half and scrape out the seeds. Add
  both seeds and pod to the cream. Turn off the
  heat and leave to infuse for 10 minutes.

- Remove the vanilla pod and pour the cream
  into the sugar and egg mixture whilst
  whisking. Return to the pan and place back
  onto the heat, whisking continuously until
  thickened.

- Spoon the vanilla custard into the bases and
  top with the fresh blueberries.

Marble cake with hot chocolate sauce

PREPARATION TIME: 30 minutes
COOKING TIME: 50-60 minutes
SERVES: 8

225 g / 9 oz / 1 cup butter, softened
225 g / 9 oz / 1 cup caster (superfine) sugar
4 eggs, beaten
225 g / 9 oz / 1 cup self-raising flour
3 tbsp milk
1 tsp vanilla extract
2 tbsp cocoa powder

FOR THE HOT CHOCOLATE SAUCE
2 tbsp coconut oil
1 tbsp cocoa powder
2 tbsp maple syrup

- Preheat the oven to 180°C (160°C fan) / 350F / gas 4. Grease and line a 20 cm loaf tin.
- Cream the butter and sugar together until pale and creamy. Add the eggs a little at a time, whisking to combine each addition thoroughly.
- Using a metal spoon fold in the flour gently, then add the milk and vanilla extract and combine well.
- Divide the mixture equally between 2 bowls and sieve the cocoa powder into one. Using 2 large spoons, place dollops of the mixtures alternately into the loaf tin, then swirl around with a skewer to marble the mixture.
- Bake in the oven for 50–60 minutes until a skewer comes out clean.
- Turn onto a cooling rack and leave to cool.
- Meanwhile, to make the hot chocolate sauce, simply place the ingredients in a saucepan on a low heat. Stir frequently. Once the coconut oil has melted, remove from the heat.
- Pour the chocolate sauce over the loaf before serving.

Marble cake with chocolate and ginger sauce
Add 1 tsp ground ginger to the sauce ingredients for a fiery kick. Follow the method as normal.

Toffee cream pie

PREPARATION TIME: 2 hours
COOKING TIME: 40 minutes
SERVES: 4

300 g / 10 oz / 1 ¼ cups chocolate digestive biscuits

75 g / 2 ½ oz / ⅓ cup butter, melted

150 g / 5 oz / ⅔ cup dark chocolate, broken up

150 g / 5 oz / ⅔ cup butter, cubed

3 eggs

1 tbsp soft brown sugar

150 ml / 5 fl. oz / ⅔ cup double (heavy) cream

1 tsp vanilla extract

25 g dark chocolate, broken up into shards, to decorate

4 tbsp ready-made toffee sauce, to drizzle

- Stir the crushed biscuits into the melted butter until thoroughly combined, then press into the base of a 23 cm (9 inch) pie dish. Chill for 30 minutes.
- Preheat the oven to 180°C (160°C fan) / 350F / gas 4.
- Place the chocolate and butter in a bowl over a pan of simmering water and stir until melted. Remove from the heat and leave to cool for 5 minutes.
- Spread the chocolate mixture evenly on top of the biscuit base.
- Whisk the eggs with the sugars until pale and tripled in volume. Whisk in the cream and vanilla.
- Pour on top of the chocolate layer and transfer to the fridge until just firm.
- Decorate with the pieces of dark chocolate and toffee sauce before serving.

Chocolate, ginger and cream pie
Add 1 tsp ground ginger to the crushed biscuits and mix well. Follow the method as normal and garnish with shards of some ginger-flavoured dark chocolate.

Mini chocolate orange puddings

PREPARATION TIME: 30 minutes
COOKING TIME: 8 minutes
SERVES: 4

90 g / 3 oz / ⅓ cup caster (superfine) sugar
150 g / 5 oz / ⅔ cup butter
150 g / 5 oz / ⅔ cup dark chocolate, chopped
3 eggs + 3 egg yolks
1 tbsp plain (all-purpose) flour
1 tsp orange extract
1 orange, zested

- Preheat the oven to 180°C (160°C fan) / 350F / gas 4. Grease 4 individual mini moulds.
- Place the sugar, butter and chocolate in a bowl set over a pan of simmering water and stir occasionally until melted. Remove from the heat and whisk to combine. Leave to cool for 5 minutes.
- Add the egg yolks and eggs and beat well to combine, then fold in the flour, orange extract and zest.
- Pour into the moulds and chill for 20 minutes.
- Place on a baking tray and cook for 8 minutes.
- Turn out onto plates and serve immediately.

Mini chocolate and peppermint puddings
Omit the orange zest and replace the orange extract with peppermint essence for a minty version. Once cooked, garnish the puddings with mint leaves.

Orange loaf cake

PREPARATION TIME: 20 minutes
COOKING TIME: 50-60 minutes
SERVES: 6-8

120 g / 4 oz / ½ cup butter, softened
250 g / 9 oz / 1 cup caster (superfine) sugar
3 eggs, beaten
zest and juice of 1 orange
250 g / 9 oz / 1 cup plain (all-purpose) flour
1 tsp baking powder
1 orange, juiced
3–4 tbsp honey
2 drops orange blossom water (optional)
1 orange, sliced into rounds
icing (confectioners') sugar, to dust

- Preheat the oven to 180°C (160°C fan) / 350F / gas 5. Grease and line a large loaf tin.
- Cream the butter and sugar together until pale and creamy, then add the beaten eggs a little at a time, beating thoroughly after each addition.
- Fold in the zest and juice, flour and baking powder. Pour into the loaf tin.
- Bake for 50–60 minutes or until an inserted skewer comes out clean.
- Turn out of the tin onto a wire rack.
- Meanwhile, heat the juice and honey, then add the orange blossom water if using. Pierce the cake with a skewer a few times and drizzle the syrup over and leave to soak in.
- Decorate with the dried orange slices and dust a little icing sugar on top.

Spiced orange loaf cake
Add 1 tsp ground cinnamon, 1 tsp ground cardamom and 1 tsp ground ginger to the dry cake ingredients and follow the method as above.

Triple chocolate cake

PREPARATION TIME: **40 minutes**
COOKING TIME: **30 minutes**
SERVES: **8-10**

120 g / 4 oz / ½ cup self-raising flour
1 tsp baking powder
120 g / 4 oz / ½ cup butter, softened
120 g / 4 oz / ½ cup caster (superfine) sugar
2 eggs
1 ½ tbsp cocoa powder

TO DECORATE
25 g / 1 oz white and milk chocolate, shaved
4 tbsp ready-made chocolate sauce

- Preheat the oven to 170°C (150°C fan) / 325F / gas 3. Grease and line 1 deep 18 cm (7 in) cake tin.
- Sieve the flour and baking powder into a large bowl, then add the other ingredients.
- Spoon the cake batter into the tin cook for 30 minutes.
- Remove from the tin and cool on a wire rack.
- To decorate, sprinkle the chocolate shavings on top and drizzle over the chocolate sauce.
- Serve the cake on its own or alongside some ice cream for extra indulgence.

Summer fruit jellies

PREPARATION TIME: **3 hours**
SERVES: **4**

570 ml / 1 pint / 2 cups rosé wine
2 tbsp caster (superfine) sugar
3–4 leaves gelatine, soaked in cold water
350 g / 12 oz / 1 ½ cups strawberries, hulled and halved
225 g / 8 oz / 1 cup raspberries
350 g / 12 oz / 1 ½ cups mixed berries, e.g.
blackcurrants, redcurrants, blueberries and
blackberries

- Heat half the wine in a pan, then whisk in the
  sugar and soaked, squeezed gelatine. Stir to
  dissolve, then add the remaining wine and pour
  into a pouring jug to cool.
- Scatter the fruit into the bottom of individual
  moulds, then pour over the jelly mixture,
  pushing any fruit down that floats to the surface.
  Cover the pots with cling film and refrigerate for
  at least 2 hours, until set.

Clementine fruit jellies
Replace the rose wine with the same amount
of bucks fizz and the berries with 4 peeled
and chopped clementines. Follow the method
as above.

Nutty raisin loaf

PREPARATION TIME: **20 minutes**
COOKING TIME: **1 hour, 30 minutes**
SERVES: **4**

175 g / 6 oz / ¾ cup butter, softened
175 g / 6 oz / ¾ cup soft light brown sugar
3 eggs, beaten
275 g / 10 oz / 1 heaped cup self-raising flour
2 tsp mixed spice
175 g / 6 oz / ¾ cup raisins, soaked in a little brandy
3 tbsp milk
4 tbsp chopped hazelnuts (cobnuts)
4 tbsp granulated sugar, to garnish

- Preheat the oven to 180°C (160°C fan) / 350F /
  gas 5.
- Cream the butter and sugar until pale and
  creamy. Add the eggs a little at a time, beating
  thoroughly after each addition, until well
  combined. Fold in the flour, spice and raisins.
  Add a little milk to loosen the batter.
- Spoon into a large loaf tin and sprinkle the
  hazelnuts on top.
- Bake for 1–1 ½ hours until risen and springy or
  until an inserted skewer comes out clean.
- Turn onto a wire rack and leave to cool.
- Sprinkle with the granulated sugar before
  serving.

Nutty date loaf
Replace the raisins with dates. Simply pit and
chop 5 Medjool dates and fold in with the rest of
the ingredients. Bake as above.

Battenberg lemon cake

PREPARATION TIME: 45 minutes
COOKING TIME: 30 minutes
SERVES: 8

175 g / 6 oz / ¾ cup butter, softened
175 g / 6 oz / ¾ cup caster (superfine) sugar
3 eggs
175 g / 6 oz / ¾ cup self-raising flour
1 lemon, zested
1 tsp vanilla extract
red food dye
6-8 tbsp apricot jam (jelly), warmed
icing (confectioners') sugar
500 g / 1 lb ready rolled marzipan

- Preheat the oven to 190°C (170°C fan) / 375F / gas 5. Grease and line a 20cm (8in) square cake tin.
- Cut a piece of baking parchment 30 x 20cm (12 x 8 inch) and make an 8 cm (3 inch) fold in the centre. Place in the tin with the fold in the centre.
- Mix the butter, sugar, eggs, flour, lemon zest and vanilla in a food processor. Weigh out half the batter and place the two amounts in separate bowls. Add red food dye to one.
- Spoon the batters into each half of the sponge tin. Bake for 30 minutes. Cool for 5 minutes, then place on a wire rack.
- Place one sponge on top of the other and trim off any overhanging edges so they are exactly the same size. Cut in half lengthways to make 4 long rectangles.
- Brush the long side of one of the plain sponges with jam and press against a pink sponge. Repeat with the other two sponges.
- Sandwich the two pairs of sponges to make a checker board pattern, then brush all over with apricot jam.
- Dust the surface with icing sugar and roll out the marzipan to 5mm thick and large enough to completely encase the sponges. Wrap the marzipan around the cake, pressing the edges together to make a firm join.
- Turn seam side down, trim a thin slice off each end and sprinkle with some icing sugar before serving.

Chai crème brûlée

PREPARATION TIME: 2 hours
COOKING TIME: 30 minutes
SERVES: 4-6

450 ml / 1 pint / 2 cups double (heavy) cream
100 ml / 3 ½ fl. oz / ½ cup milk
1 tsp ground cinnamon
1 tsp ground ginger
1 tsp ground cardamom
1 vanilla pod, halved
5 egg yolks
2 tbsp caster (superfine) sugar, plus enough
for the topping
1 lemon, zested

- Preheat the oven to 180°C (160°C fan) / 350F
  / gas 5.
- Tip the cream into a pan with the milk and
  spices. Add the seeds from the vanilla pod
  and the pod itself. Heat almost to boiling
  point.
- Whisk the egg yolks and sugar in a bowl
  until pale in colour. Pour the hot cream into
  the egg yolks, whisking constantly. Add the
  lemon juice and zest. Strain through a sieve
  and stir well.
- Sit 4 ramekins in a roasting tin and divide the
  mixture evenly between them. Pour in enough
  hot water to come half way up the sides of the
  ramekins.
- Bake for about 30 minutes, until set.
- Leave to cool on a wire rack, then refrigerate
  until ready to serve.
- Sprinkle over a thick layer of sugar and either
  grill or blowtorch until deep golden and
  melted. Leave to cool and firm then serve.

Crème brûlée with raisins
Add a handful of raisins to the saucepan with
the cream, milk and spices. Follow the method
as normal. If using the blowtorch, careful not to
burn the raisins.

Coconut berry cake

PREPARATION TIME: **30 minutes**
COOKING TIME: **40 minutes**
SERVES: **8**

200 g / 7 oz / ¾ cup plain (all-purpose) flour
a pinch of salt
2 tsp baking powder
75 g / 2 ½ oz / ⅓ cup butter, chilled and cubed
75 g / 2 ½ oz / ⅓ cup caster (superfine) sugar
50 g / 1 ¾ oz / ¼ cup desiccated coconut
1 egg
120 ml / 4 fl. oz / ½ cup milk
1 tsp vanilla extract

FOR THE ICING
100 g / 3 ½ oz / ½ cup butter, softened
150 g / 5 oz / ⅔ cup icing (confectioners') sugar
1 tsp vanilla extract
desiccated coconut, to decorate
redcurrants, to decorate
blackberries, to decorate

- Preheat the oven to 180°C (160°C fan) / 350F / gas 5. Grease and line a 23 cm (9 in)round cake tin. Sieve the flour, salt and baking powder into a bowl. Using the pads of your fingertips, rub the butter in until it resembles breadcrumbs. Stir in the sugar, and coconut.

- Whisk the egg and milk together with the vanilla. Make a well in the flour mixture, then add the liquid a little at a time to for a smooth batter.

- Spoon into the cake tin and bake for about 40 minutes, or until an inserted skewer comes out clean. Cool on a wire rack.

- To decorate, cream the butter and sugar together until pale and creamy, then whisk in the vanilla. Spread over the cake with a palette knife and decorate with desiccated coconut and berries.

Coconut and lime cake
Add the juice and zest of 3 limes to the cake batter and follow the method as normal. Garnish with some more lime zest and the desiccated coconut before serving.

Summer berry cheesecake

PREPARATION TIME: 30 minutes
COOKING TIME: 40 minutes
SERVES: 6

100 g / 3 ½ oz / ½ cup digestive biscuits, crushed to crumbs
50 g / 1 ¾ oz / ¼ cup butter, melted
600 g / 1lb / 2 cups cream cheese
2 tbsp plain (all-purpose) flour
125 g / 4 oz / ½ cup caster (superfine) sugar
1 ½ tsp vanilla extract
1 tsp vanilla powder
2 eggs + 1 egg yolk
150 ml / 5 oz / ⅔ cup sour cream
500 g / 1 lb / 2 cups mixed summer berries
fresh mint leaves, to garnish
icing (confectioners') sugar, to dust

- Preheat the oven to 180°C (160°C fan) / 350F / gas 5.
- Stir the biscuits into the melted butter. Press into the bottom of a large springform cake tin.
- Place on a baking sheet and bake for five minutes.
- Whisk together the cream cheese, flour and sugar, then beat in the vanilla extract, vanilla powder, eggs and sour cream until pale and smooth.
- Spoon on top of the biscuit base. Return to the oven and bake for about 40 minutes.
- Once the centre is set, remove from the oven and leave to cool. Decorate with berries and mint and dust over some icing sugar before serving.

Berry cheesecake with white chocolate
Grate some white chocolate over the top of the cheesecake before serving.

Spiced apple tart

PREPARATION TIME: 20 minutes
COOKING TIME: 45 minutes
SERVES: 8

200 g / 7 oz ready-made chilled pastry
3 apples, peeled, cored and sliced
125 g / 4 ½ oz / ½ cup caster (superfine) sugar
125 g / 4 ½ oz / ½ cup brown sugar
1 tsp cinnamon, ground
1 tsp star anise, ground
1 tbsp lemon juice
2 tbsp butter
icing (confectioners') sugar, to dust

- Preheat the oven to 200°C (180°C fan) / 400F /
  gas 6. Grease and line a 23 cm (9 inch) fluted
  tart tin.
- Press the pastry into the tin, line with
  parchment paper and fill with cooking beans.
  Cook in the oven for 10 minutes.
- In a bowl, cover the apple slices with the
  two sugars, spices and lemon juice. Add just
  enough water to cover and combine with all
  the ingredients to soak the apple.
- Remove the tart tin from the oven. Remove
  the paper and beans, then return the pastry
  base for another 5 minutes.
- Drain the apple slices through a sieve and
  collect the juice. Place the slices in the tart
  case and dot with the butter. Bake in the oven
  for 30 minutes or until golden.
- Meanwhile, heat the collected juice in a pan
  over a medium heat and allow to reduce by
  half into a syrup.
- Remove the tart from the oven and brush
  liberally with the syrup. Return to the oven
  and bake for a further 10 minutes until glazed.
- Place the tart on a wire rack and allow to
  cool. Dust with icing sugar and serve with the
  remaining syrup if desired.

Spiced pear tart
Replace the apples with 3 peeled, cored and
diced conference pears and follow the method
as normal.

Crème caramel with mint

PREPARATION TIME: 25 minutes
COOKING TIME: 1 hour
SERVES: 4

125 g / 4 oz / ½ cup caster (superfine) sugar
2 tbsp hot water
150 ml / 5 fl. oz / ⅔ cup milk
1 tsp peppermint essence
300 ml / 10 fl. oz / 1 cup single cream
4 eggs
40 g / 1 ½ oz soft dark brown sugar
2 drops vanilla extract
fresh mint leaves, to garnish

- Preheat the oven to 150°C / 300F / gas 2.
- Place the sugar in a stainless steel pan and heat. When the sugar begins to melt, leave to darken to a rich dark gold. Do not stir. Remove from the heat, carefully add the water and pour into a soufflé dish.
- Pour the milk, essence and cream into a pan and heat gently.
- Whisk the eggs, sugar and vanilla in a bowl. When the milk is very hot but not boiling, pour onto the egg mixture, whisking constantly until blended.
- Pour into the soufflé dish and place in a roasting tin. Pour in enough hot water to come two thirds of the way up the sides of the dish.
- Bake in the oven for 1 hour, until set.
- Remove from the refrigerator 1 hour before serving, then release carefully from the mould onto a plate.
- Garnish with the fresh mint leaves, before serving.

Lemon and mango meringue pie

PREPARATION TIME: 1 hour
COOKING TIME: 1 hour, 10 minutes
SERVES: 6

125 g / 4 oz / ½ cup plain (all-purpose) flour
60 g / 2 oz / ¼ cup butter
a pinch of salt

FOR THE FILLING
3 level tbsp cornflour
60 g / 2 oz / ¼ cup caster (superfine) sugar
300 ml / 10 fl. oz / 1 ¼ cups cold water
2–3 lemons, juice and grated zest
3 mangoes, peeled and sliced
2 egg yolks
40 g / 1 ½ oz butter

FOR THE MERINGUE
2 egg whites
120g / 4 oz / ½ cup caster (superfine) sugar

- Preheat the oven to 190°C (170°C fan) / 370F / gas 5.
- To make the pastry, sieve the flour and salt into a large bowl, then work the fat into the flour with the pads of your fingers until the mixture resembles breadcrumbs.
- Work in two tablespoons of water and bring the mixture together with a knife, cutting it through to mix, using enough water to just make a smooth ball of dough. Wrap the dough in cling film and refrigerate.
- Roll the pastry out to just larger than your pie dish. Cut a 8 mm strip all round, dampen the rim of the dish and press the pastry strip on to it. Line the tin with the pastry and press the edges onto the pastry rim.
- Prick the base with a fork and bake for 25 minutes.
- Place the cornflour and sugar in a bowl and add enough water to make a smooth paste. Pour the remaining water into a pan with the lemon zest. Bring to the boil, pour onto the cornflour paste and mix.
- Tip back into the pan and bring back to the boil for 1 minute. Remove from the heat and beat in the egg yolks, lemon juice and butter.
- Layer the mango pieces at the bottom of the pastry.
- Pour the lemon mixture into the pastry shell and spread evenly.
- Whisk the egg whites until stiff, then beat in sugar at a time until thick and glossy. Spread over the filling, sealing the top completely.
- Reduce the oven heat to 150°C / 300F / gas 2 and bake for 45 minutes until the meringue is pale gold.

Sticky toffee pudding

PREPARATION TIME: **20 minutes**
COOKING TIME: **50 minutes**
SERVES: **6**

FOR THE SPONGE

75 g / 2 ½ oz / ⅓ cup Medjool dates, stoned and finely chopped

1 tsp bicarbonate of soda

50 g / 1 ¾ oz / ¼ cup butter

a pinch of salt

150 g / 5 oz / ⅔ cup demerara sugar

2 eggs

175 g / 6 oz / ¾ cup self-raising flour

1 tsp vanilla extract

1 tsp ground ginger

butter, softened

FOR THE SAUCE

250 ml / 9 fl. oz / 1 cup double (heavy) cream

80 g / 2 ½ oz / ⅓ cup butter

80 g / 2 ½ oz / ⅓ cup dark brown sugar

1 lemon, juiced and zested

- Preheat the oven to 180°C (160°C fan) / 350F / gas 4.
- Pour 275 ml / 10 fl. oz / 1 cup boiling water into a bowl and add the Medjool dates to soak.
- When the water is lukewarm, add the remaining sponge ingredients, mixing well to combine.
- Pour into a buttered baking dish and bake in the oven for about 40 minutes, or until just firm.
- Heat the sauce ingredients in a pan, whisking regularly.
- When the sponge is cooked, pour over the sauce and flash briefly under a hot grill until bubbling.

Ginger sticky toffee pudding
Add 1 tsp ground ginger to the sauce and cook as normal. Garnish the pudding with some freshly grated ginger before serving.

Pecan and maple tart

PREPARATION TIME: **20 minutes**
COOKING TIME: **45 minutes**
SERVES: **4**

250 g / 12 oz ready-made shortcrust pastry, rolled out thinly
120 g / 4 oz / ½ cup butter
120 g / 4 oz / ½ cup maple syrup
1 tsp vanilla extract
225 g / 8 oz / 1 cup soft brown sugar
3 eggs, beaten
300 g / 10 oz / 1 ¼ cups pecans, halved
a handful of chopped hazelnuts (cobnuts)

- Preheat the oven to 180°C (160°C fan) / 350F / gas 4.
- Line a 23 cm (9 inch) pie tin with the pastry.
- Place the butter, syrup, vanilla extract and sugar in a pan over low heat and stir until the butter has melted. Remove from the heat and leave to cool.
- Add the eggs and mix well.
- Setting aside a few for decoration, tip the pecans into the pastry case then pour over the syrup mixture.
- Add the remaining pecans and top with the chopped hazelnuts.
- Bake for 45 minutes until the pastry is golden. Allow to cool before serving.

Walnut and maple tart
Replace the pecans with the same amount of chopped walnuts and follow the method as above.

Lemon drizzle loaf

PREPARATION TIME: **25 minutes**
COOKING TIME: **40-45 minutes**
SERVES: **6**

120 g / 4 oz / ½ cup butter, softened
175 g / 6 oz / ¾ cup caster (superfine) sugar
2 eggs
1 lemon, grated zest
175 g / 6 oz / ¾ cup self-raising flour
100 ml / 3 ½ fl. oz / ½ cup milk

FOR THE SYRUP
2 lemons, juiced
100 g / 3 ½ oz / ½ cup icing (confectioners') sugar

- Preheat the oven to 180°C (160°C) / 350F / gas 4. Grease and line a large loaf tin.
- Cream the butter and sugar until pale and creamy, then whisk in the eggs, a little at a time.
- Whisk in the zest, then, using a metal spoon, fold in the flour and then stir in the milk. Spoon into the loaf tin and bake for 40–45 minutes until a skewer comes out clean when poked into the centre. Set aside.
- Heat the lemon juice and sugar in a pan until the sugar dissolves. Puncture the surface of the cake with a skewer and pour over the hot syrup. Leave to cool completely then remove from the tin.

Iced lemon drizzle loaf
Whisk together the juice of ½ lemon and 150 g / 5 oz / ⅔ cup icing (confectioners') sugar to make the glaze, then smooth over the top of the loaf.

Pineapple and cardamom cake

PREPARATION TIME: 25 minutes
COOKING TIME: 20 minutes
SERVES: 8

½ ripe pineapple, peeled and sliced into thin rings
4 tbsp caster (superfine) sugar
180 g / 6 oz / ¾ cup self-raising flour
2 eggs
150 ml / 5 fl. oz / ⅔ cup milk
1 tsp vanilla extract
2 tbsp cardamom pods, seeds removed and ground
using a pestle and mortar
1 lemon, juiced and zested

- Preheat the oven to 220°C (200°C fan) / 425F
  / gas 7.
- Arrange the pineapple rings in the base of
  an oven proof frying pan and sprinkle over
  2 tablespoons of the sugar. Heat gently until
  the sugar has melted and the pineapple
  caramelizes.
- Whisk the flour, eggs and milk in a bowl, the
  rest of the sugar, vanilla extract, cardamom
  seeds, lemon juice and zest and whisk
  thickened, adding more milk if necessary. It
  should be the consistency of whipped cream.
- Pour the batter over the pineapple and bake
  in the oven for about 20 minutes until golden
  and risen.
- Remove the cake from the oven and invert
  onto a plate.

Pineapple, raisin and cardamom cake
Add a handful of raisins to the cake batter and
mix well before pouring over the pineapple rings.

Eton mess with rose syrup

PREPARATION TIME: **15 minutes (+ Cooling Time)**
COOKING TIME: **1 hour**
SERVES: **4**

3 egg whites
175 g / 6 oz / ¾ cup caster (superfine) sugar
500 g / 1 lb / 2 cups raspberries
1 tbsp icing (confectioners') sugar
1 tbsp rose syrup
500 ml / 1 pint / 2 cups double (heavy) cream
a few drops of rose essence
4 tbsp toasted flaked almonds

- Preheat the oven to 150°C (130°C fan) / 300F / gas 2.
- Whisk the egg whites to soft peaks, then whisk in the sugar a little at a time, beating each addition in thoroughly, until thick and glossy.
- Spoon onto lined baking trays and bake for 1 hour. Turn the oven off and leave until completely cold.
- Purée half the raspberries with the icing sugar and rose syrup until smooth.
- Whisk the cream to soft peaks, whisking in the rose essence as you go.
- Break up the meringues and layer into individual serving dishes, spooning over a little purée, then adding raspberries and cream, swirling the purée in as you go.
- Serve immediately with the flaked almonds.

Eton mess with orange
Replace the rose syrup for orange syrup and rose essence for orange essence or extract for a sweet, fruity flavour. Top with marmalade or orange zest if desired.

Vanilla ice cream

PREPARATION TIME: **2 hours**
MAKES: **1 Litre**

300 ml / 10 fl. oz / 1 ¼ cups double (heavy) cream
300 ml / 10 fl. oz / 1 ¼ cups single cream
½ tsp vanilla powder
1 vanilla pod, split
4 egg yolks
40 g / 1 ½ oz caster (superfine) sugar

- Heat the creams in a pan with the vanilla powder, vanilla pod and seeds and leave to infuse.
- Whisk together the egg yolks and sugar, then remove the vanilla pod and pour the hot cream onto the egg mixture, whisking constantly.
- Return to the pan and whisk over a low heat until thickened and smooth.
- Leave to cool slightly then churn in an ice cream machine until done.
- Freeze until required. Transfer to the refrigerator 1 hour before serving.

Chocolate and vanilla ice cream
Add 2 tbsp cocoa powder to the pan with the vanilla powder, pod and seeds. Follow the method as above.

Almond and ginger thins

PREPARATION TIME: **40 minutes**
COOKING TIME: **8 minutes**
MAKES: **30**

100 g / 3 ½ oz / ½ cup butter, softened
100 g / 3 ½ oz / ½ cup caster (superfine) sugar
100 g / 3 ½ oz / ½ cup plain (all-purpose) flour
1 tsp ground ginger
1 lemon, zested
2 tbsp flaked (slivered) almonds

- Preheat the oven to 170°C (150°C fan) / 325F / gas 3.
- Line 2 baking trays.
- Beat the butter and sugar until pale and creamy. Stir in the flour, ginger and lemon zest.
- Roll out the dough until it's very thin and cut into squares.
- Bake for 3 minutes, then scatter on the almonds and bake for a further 5–6 minutes until golden brown but not too dark
- Transfer to a wire rack to cool.

Chai-spiced thins
Add 1 tsp ground cardamom and 1 tsp ground cinnamon and add stir in with the dry ingredients. Bake as detailed above.

Bread and butter pudding with custard

PREPARATION TIME: 15 minutes
COOKING TIME: 30-40 minutes
SERVES: 4-6

8 thick slices white bread, thickly buttered
50 g / 1 ¾ oz / ¼ cup sultanas, soaked in a little brandy
300 ml / 10 fl. oz / 1 ¼ cups milk
60 ml / 3 fl. oz / ¼ cup double (heavy) cream
50 g / 1 ¾ oz / ¼ cup caster (superfine) sugar
3 eggs
freshly grated nutmeg
250 g fresh vanilla custard
chopped pecans, to sprinkle

- Preheat the oven to 180°C (160°C fan) / 350F / gas 5.
- Cut each slice of bread into two triangles and arrange a layer in the base of a round buttered baking dish.
- Sprinkle with the soaked sultanas.
- Add another layer of bread triangles over the top.
- Whisk together the milk, cream, sugar and eggs until well combined, then pour over the bread layers. Push the bread down into the custard to soak it thoroughly.
- The custard should just reach the top of the bread – if it doesn't, add a little more milk and/or cream. Grate over the nutmeg.
- Bake in the oven for 30–40 minutes until set and golden.
- To serve, gently heat the fresh vanilla custard and spoon it over each serving. Sprinkle over some chopped pecans then enjoy.

Bread and butter pudding with white chocolate
Add a handful of white chocolate chips to each layer of bread before baking as normal. Garnish with some grated white chocolate and the pecans.

Banoffee pie with espresso

PREPARATION TIME: **2-3 hours**
SERVES: **6-8**

400 g / 14 oz / 1 ½ cups digestive biscuits, crushed
200 g / 7 oz / ⅔ cup butter, melted
2 tins of condensed milk
2-3 ripe bananas
500 ml / 1 pint / 2 cups double cream
1 tbsp cocoa powder
1 tsp espresso powder

- Combine the biscuits and butter in a bowl then press into the bottom of a 23 cm (9 in) springform tin. Refrigerate while you prepare the filling.
- Cover the condensed milk tins completely in boiling water and boil for 2 hours. Make sure they are completely covered at all times, topping up if necessary otherwise they will explode.
- Remove from the water and leave to cool. Open the tins and scoop out the toffee.
- Whizz the bananas with the toffee in a food processor until smooth.
- Whisk the cream to a light and fluffy soft peak.
- Spread the banana and toffee over the biscuit base, using a palette knife to even it out. Spread the cream evenly over the top.
- Combine the cocoa and espresso powder in a bowl, then sieve over the top of the pie.
- Refrigerate for 30 minutes to set before serving.

Mini almond lemon cakes

PREPARATION TIME: 30 minutes
COOKING TIME: 45 minutes
MAKES: 4-6

5 eggs, separated
200 g / 7 oz / ¾ cup caster (superfine) sugar
1 tsp almond extract
1 lemon, grated zest
200 g / 7 oz / ¾ cup ground almonds
1 tbsp plain (all-purpose) flour
2 tbsp flaked (slivered) almonds, chopped
2 tbsp icing (confectioners') sugar, to dust
1 lemon, sliced

- Preheat the oven to 180°C (160°C fan) / 350F / gas 4. Grease and line a 23 cm (9 inch) spring form tin.
- Whisk the yolks with half the sugar until pale and creamy. Add the almond extract and zest and combine well.
- Beat the egg whites to stiff peaks, add the remaining sugar a little at a time and beat until thick and glossy.
- Fold a third of the egg whites into the yolks to loosen, then fold in the rest with the ground almonds and flour. Spoon into individual small round tins and bake for about 45 minutes until springy.
- Leave for 10 minutes to cool, then turn onto a wire rack. Decorate with the chopped flaked almonds and icing sugar.
- Serve alongside some lemon slices.

Gluten-free almond lemon cakes
Replace the all-purpose flour with gluten-free flour for a delicious alternative.

Apple and maple tart

PREPARATION TIME: **50 minutes**
COOKING TIME: **30-40 minutes**
SERVES: **4-6**

FOR THE PASTRY
75 g / 2 ½ oz / ⅔ cup plain (all-purpose) flour
a pinch of salt
20 g / ¾ oz lard
20 g / ¾ oz butter

FOR THE FILLING
700 g / 1 ⅓ lb / 3 cups Bramley apples, peeled, cored and quartered
4 tbsp maple syrup
¼ tsp ground cloves
1 tsp ground cinnamon
grated nutmeg
apricot jam (jelly), warmed

- Preheat the oven to 200°C (180°C fan) / 400F / gas 6.
- Sieve the flour and salt into a large bowl, then cut the lard and butter into cubes and work into the flour until the mixture resembles breadcrumbs.
- Work in 2 tablespoons of water and bring the mixture together with a knife, cutting it through to mix, using enough water to just make a smooth dough. Refrigerate while you prepare the filling.
- Slice the apples thinly and tip three quarters into a pan with the maple syrup, cloves, cinnamon and nutmeg. Add a tablespoon of water and cook very gently with a lid on until the apples collapse completely to make a purée.
- Roll out the pastry on a floured surface to line a 20 cm (8 in) greased pie dish. Spoon in the filling, then arrange the apple slices on top. Sprinkle over a little grated nutmeg and bake for 30–40 minutes, reducing the heat to 180°C / 350F after the first 10.
- Brush with warmed jam when out of the oven to give a shine to the apples.

Apple, raisin and maple tart
Add a handful of raisins to the pan with the apples, maple syrup and spices. Cook as above.

Coffee, walnut and cinnamon cake

PREPARATION TIME: 30 minutes
COOKING TIME: 30 minutes
SERVES: 8-10

120 g / 4 oz / ½ cup self raising flour
1 tsp baking powder
120 g / 4 oz / ½ cup butter, softened
120 g / 4 oz / ½ cup caster (superfine) sugar
90 g / 3 oz / ½ cup mixed nuts, chopped
2 eggs
1 tbsp coffee mixed with 1 tbsp hot water
1 tsp ground cinnamon
100 g chopped walnuts
¼ tsp ground cinnamon

FOR THE FILLING
100 g / 3 ½ oz / ½ cup butter, softened
225 g / 8 oz / 1 cup icing (confectioners') sugar
2 tbsp instant coffee dissolved in 2 tbsp water

- Preheat the oven to 170°C (150°C fan) / 325F / gas 3. Grease and line two 18 cm (7 in) cake tins.
- For the cake, sieve the flour and baking powder into a large bowl, then add the other ingredients and whisk until completely combined.
- Divide the mixture equally between the two cake tins and top with the walnuts, cooking for 30 minutes.
- Remove from the tins and cool on a wire rack.
- To make the filling, cream the butter and sugar together, then stir in the coffee. Refrigerate until needed.
- Use the cream filling to sandwich the cakes together. Dust with a little cinnamon and sprinkle over any remaining walnuts, before serving.

Coffee, pecan and cinnamon cake
Replace the walnuts with 100 g chopped pecans for a deeper maple flavour.

Hazelnut chocolate brownies

PREPARATION TIME: 15 minutes
COOKING TIME: 30 minutes
MAKES: 16

120 g / 4 oz / ½ cup butter
50 g / 2 oz / ¼ cup dark chocolate
2 eggs, beaten
225 g / 8 oz / 1 cup granulated sugar
50 g / 2 oz / ½ cup plain (all-purpose) flour
1 tsp baking powder
a pinch of salt
120 g / 4 oz / ½ cup hazelnuts (cobnuts), chopped
icing (confectioners') sugar, to serve

- Preheat the oven to 180°C (160°C fan) / 350F / gas 4.
- Melt the butter and chocolate in a bowl over a pan of simmering water.
- Once melted, stir in the other ingredients until smooth and combined.
- Pour into a 20 cm (8 in) square tin and bake for 30 minutes until the centre feels springy to the touch.
- Leave to cool in the tin before dividing into 16 squares and cooling on a wire rack.
- Dust with icing sugar before serving.

Pecan chocolate brownies
Replace the hazelnuts for the same amount of chopped pecans for a slightly richer flavour.

Madeira loaf cake

PREPARATION TIME: 20 minutes
COOKING TIME: 40 minutes
SERVES: 4

175 g / 6 oz / ¾ cup butter, at room temperature
175 g / 6 oz / ¾ cup caster (superfine) sugar
3 eggs, beaten
250 g / 9 oz / 1 cup self raising flour
3 tbsp milk
½ lemon, grated zest
½ orange, grated zest
1 tsp vanilla powder
icing (confectioners') sugar, to dust

- Preheat oven to 180°C (160°C fan) / 350F / gas 4.
- Grease and line a large loaf tin. Cream the butter and sugar until pale and creamy, then beat in the eggs, a little at a time.
- Sieve the flour into the bowl and fold in with a metal spoon along with the milk to make a loose batter. Fold in the citrus zest and vanilla powder.
- Spoon into the loaf tin and bake for 40 minutes or until golden brown and an inserted skewer comes out clean. Leave to cool for 5 minutes, then transfer to a wire rack and leave to cool completely. Dust over a little icing sugar.

Spiced loaf cake
Add 1 tsp ground cinnamon and 1 tsp ground ginger to the dry ingredients before combining with the wet ingredients. Follow the method as normal.

THE COOKERY COLLECTION

Lemon tart

PREPARATION TIME: **1 hour**
COOKING TIME: **25 minutes**
SERVES: **6**

125 g / 4 oz / ½ cup plain (all-purpose) flour
a pinch of salt
60 g / 2 oz / ¼ cup butter
400 g lemon curd
1 lemon, zested
icing (confectioners') sugar, to dust

- Preheat the oven to 190°C (170°C fan) / 375F / gas 5.
- To make the pastry, sieve the flour and salt into a large bowl, then cut butter into cubes and work into the flour with the pads of your fingers until the mixture resembles breadcrumbs.
- Work in 2 tablespoons of water and bring the mixture together with a knife, cutting it through to mix, using enough water to just make a smooth ball of dough that leaves the bowl clean. Wrap the dough in cling film and refrigerate for 20 minutes.
- Roll the pastry out on a floured surface to just larger than your pie dish. Cut an 8mm strip all round, dampen the rim of the dish and press the pastry strip on to it. Line the tin with the pastry and press the edges onto the pastry rim. Prick the base with a fork and bake for 25 minutes until pale gold and cooked through.
- Pour the lemon curd into the pastry shell and spread evenly.
- Allow to set at room temperature. Garnish with the lemon zest and a dust of icing sugar.

Traditional Christmas pudding

PREPARATION TIME: **make at least 1 week in advance**
COOKING: **6 hours**
SERVES: **6-8**

500g / 1 lb / 2 cups mixed dried fruit
1 tbsp mixed candied peel, finely chopped
1 apple, peeled, cored and finely chopped
zest and juice of 1 orange
zest and juice of 1 lemon
100ml / 3 ½ fl. oz / ½ cup brandy
60g / 2 oz / ¼ cup self-raising flour
1 ½ tsp mixed spice
2 tsp ground cinnamon
120g / 4 oz / ½ cup shredded suet
120g / 4 oz / ½ cup soft dark brown sugar
120g / 4 oz / ½ cup fine breadcrumbs
2 eggs, beaten
butter, softened

- Lightly grease a 1 ½ l / 2 ½ pint pudding basin. Tip the fruits and citrus juice into a bowl, then add most of the brandy. Leave to macerate for at least 2 hours.

- Sieve the flour into a bowl with the spices, add the suet, zest, sugar and breadcrumbs, stirring to combine well. Add the marinated fruit and stir through.

- Beat the eggs into the bowl. Spoon into the pudding basin. Cover with a pleated layer of baking parchment (to allow it to rise), then a pleated layer of foil, securing it tightly with string. Tear off a piece of foil and fold three times to make a long strip. Sit the pudding on top and use as a cradle to carry to the steamer.

- Place on an upturned saucer in a large pan and pour in enough boiling water to come two thirds of the way up the sides of the bowl. Cover and steam for about 6 hours, checking it doesn't boil dry.

- Remove from the steamer. Check it is cooked by inserting a skewer – it should come out clean.

- Prick the top of the pudding and pour in a few tablespoons of extra brandy, then recover with fresh paper and store in a cool dry place until Christmas Day.

- To reheat, steam for 1 hour.

Vegetarian Christmas pudding
Simply replace the suet for the same amount of vegetarian suet and cook as normal.

Victoria sponge with strawberries

PREPARATION TIME: **40 minutes**
COOKING TIME: **25 minutes**
SERVES: **6-8**

120 g / 4 oz / ½ cup butter, at room temperature
120 g / 4 oz / ½ cup caster (superfine) sugar
2 eggs
1 tsp vanilla extract
120 g / 4 oz / ½ cup self-raising flour
600 ml / 1 pint / 2 fl oz double (heavy) cream, whipped
8 strawberries, sliced
icing (confectioners') sugar, to dust

- Preheat the oven to 170°C / 325F / gas 3. Grease and line 2 x 18 cm (7 in) sponge tins.

- Cream the butter and sugar together until pale and creamy.

- Whisk the eggs thoroughly, then beat into the butter mixture a little at a time until fully incorporated.

- Stir in the vanilla extract, then sieve the flour a little at a time into the bowl and fold in with a metal spoon. If the batter is a little thick, add a little hot water to loosen.

- Spoon into the tins, then bake for 25 minutes or until springy and golden.

- Leave to cool for 10 minutes. Remove from the tins and cool on a wire rack.

- Sandwich with the whipped cream and slices of strawberries. Dust with a little icing sugar to serve.

Classic Victoria sponge
Spread a generous layer of strawberry jam before adding the whipped cream for a more classic sponge.

Choux buns
with custard

PREPARATION TIME: **15 minutes**
COOKING TIME: **25 minutes**
MAKES: **28-30 Buns**

60 g / 2 oz / ¼ cup strong plain (bread) flour
1 tsp caster (superfine) sugar
150 ml / 5 fl. oz / ⅔ cup cold water
50 g / 1 ¾ oz / ¼ cup butter, cubed
2 eggs, beaten
200 g ready-made vanilla custard

- Preheat oven to 200°C (180°C fan) / 400F / gas 6.
- Crease a piece of baking parchment in half across the diagonal and open out again. Sift the flour onto the paper, add the sugar and fold into the crease to hold it.
- Pour the water into the pan with the butter and heat gently until the butter melts, stirring occasionally. As it comes to the boil, remove from the heat and tip the flour in quickly.
- Beat vigorously with a wooden spoon or electric whisk until the mixture forms a smooth ball. Beat in the eggs a little at a time.
- Grease a baking sheet and place teaspoons of the mixture at 1 inch intervals.
- Bake in the oven for 10 minutes then increase to 220°C (200 fan) / 450F/Gas 7 and bake for a further 15 minutes.
- Allow to cool on a wire rack. Gently warm the vanilla custard in a small saucepan over a medium heat.
- When the buns are completely cool, cut the top third off the choux buns and pipe the custard inside. Place the tops on and serve.

Index

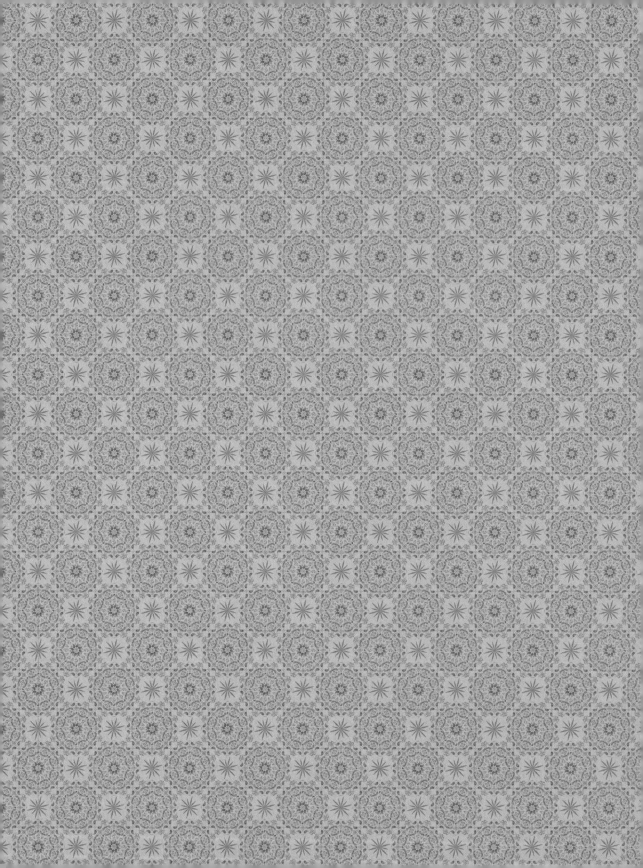